BACK TO BECKETT

BACK TO BECKETT

Ruby Cohn

PRINCETON UNIVERSITY PRESS

PRINCETON, NEW JERSEY

Publication of this book has been
aided by a grant from the
Whitney Darrow Publication
Reserve Fund of
Princeton University Press.

This book has been composed in
Linotype Caledonia

Printed in the United States of
America by Princeton University
Press, Princeton, New Jersey

Library of Congress Cataloguing
in Publication data will be found
on the last printed page
of this book.

TO

    Nan Del Monte
    Barbara Howard
    Bruce Langford
    and especially Jim Eigo
    who accompanied me back to Beckett

and with gratitude for the scrupulous reading of
                          Herbert Blau
                          Lawrence Harvey
                          Marilynn Meeker
                          Jerry Sherwood,
                          exemplary editor

1906   April 13 (Good Friday), Samuel Barclay Beckett was born in Foxrock, near Dublin, Ireland. "I have a clear memory of my own fetal existence. It was an existence where no voice, no possible movement could free me from the agony and darkness I was subjected to." (Gruen) He was the second and last son of Mary and William Beckett.

1910   Earliest extant photograph of Beckett was the result of the photographer's need of a subject for a title, "Bedtime." Beckett was posed praying at his mother's knee. "[I was brought up] almost a Quaker. But I soon lost faith. I don't think I ever had it after leaving Trinity." (Hobson)

1911   He attended kindergarten named Miss Ida Elsner's Academy. "You might say I had a happy childhood . . . although I had little talent for happiness. My parents did everything that could make a child happy. But I was often lonely." (Harvey)

1912   He attended Earlsfort House School in Dublin, where he began to study French and piano.

1920   He attended Portora Royal School in Northern Enniskillen, where his brother Frank had preceded him. The school emphasized sports, and Samuel Beckett was on the cricket and rugby teams. He excelled also at tennis, swimming, and boxing. He began to write poems and stories, some of which were published in the school newspaper.

1923   He attended Trinity College, Dublin, living at home in Foxrock. His school sports were limited to cricket and golf, as he became more absorbed in the academic curriculum.

1925   He studied Dante.

1926   He spent his summer vacation bicycling through the Loire Valley.

1927   He spent his summer vacation in Florence.

In December he took his B.A. degree.

1928   He spent the spring term as French tutor in Campbell College, Belfast.

In October, he took up a two-year fellowship at l'Ecole Normale Supérieure in Paris. There he was befriended by Joyce. He did research on the life and works of Descartes.

1929   He published fiction and criticism in *transition*. He participated in the twenty-fifth Bloomsday celebration, but he had to be "ingloriously abandoned . . . in one of those temporary palaces which are inseparably associated with the memory of the Emperor Vespasian." (Ellmann)

1930   He won first prize for a poem on Time, in a contest sponsored by Nancy Cunard, who later wrote of *Whoroscope*: "This long poem, mysterious, obscure in parts, centered around Descartes, was clearly by someone intellectual and highly educated."

With Alfred Péron, he translated into French the "Anna Livia Plurabelle" section of Joyce's *Work in Progress*. He spent the summer vacation writing a study of Proust, with the intention of pursuing his academic career. In September, he returned to Trinity as Assistant in French. "Sam would stand for minutes staring through the window and then throw a perfectly constructed sentence to his crumb-picking avid audience." (Leventhal) Beckett read the *Ethics* of Arnold Geulincx.

1931   In February, with Georges Pelorson, he wrote *Le Kid*, a parody of Corneille's *Cid*, and he played Don Diègue. The Trinity College newspaper lampooned him: "An exhausted aesthete who all life's strange poisonous wines has sipped, and found them rather tedious." Also: "I wish he would explain his explanations." He made friends with Jack Yeats.

In December he took his M.A. degree.

1932   Fleeing to the Continent, Beckett celebrated the new year by resigning from Trinity. "He could not bear the absurdity of teaching to others what he did not know himself." (Coe) "The College wits murmured that he wrote his resignation on a scroll of bumph but those in authority wailed because with him went the College master key." (Leventhal) He traveled in Germany and returned to Paris in March, beginning work on *Dream of Fair to Middling Women.* He translated Surrealist poems into English. Lucia Joyce was infatuated with him. After the assassination of French President Paul Doumer, he returned to Foxrock because his papers were not in order.

1933   In June William Beckett died of a heart attack. "What am I to do now but follow his trace over the fields and hedges." (Harvey) Beckett's brother Frank succeeded their father in the surveying firm of Beckett and Metcalfe. Beckett received an annuity of two hundred pounds a year, and he exiled himself to London, where he spent nearly three years—"bad in every way, financially, psychologically." (Fletcher) Later, Beckett noted: "They always know you're an Irishman. The porter in the hotel. His tone changes. The taxi-man says, 'Another sixpence, Pat.' They call you Pat." (Sigal)

1934   He published *More Pricks Than Kicks* and began *Murphy.*

1936–37 He visited museums in Germany, uneasy at Nazi oppression of Jewish intellectuals.

1937   In the fall he returned to Paris and renewed his friendship with Joyce, also making friends among painters. He wrote his first poems in French. In November, he returned to Dublin as a witness in an anti-Semitic defamation trial against Oliver St. John Gogarty: "It is soon established that the witness himself is author of a banned book (the title was enough; no censor would risk his immortal soul by reading it) called *More Pricks Than Kicks.* Counsel dare not speak its name. The Dublin evening papers carried banner headlines: THE ATHEIST FROM PARIS." (Leventhal) Living at Foxrock during the trial and afterward, Beckett wrote a friend: "I have done little work, that little on the Great Cham, in the hopes of making a play of his relations with Mrs. Thrale."

1938   On January 7, walking along a Paris street, Beckett was stabbed by a stranger. Joyce described the injury in a letter to his son: "The stab was above the heart; that is uninjured, and the lungs also, but there is a perforation of the pleura, the layer of tissue surrounding the lungs. My house on the day after your departure was like the stock exchange, telephone calls from everywhere. . . . Beckett has had a lucky escape." In the hospital, Beckett was visited by pianist Suzanne Dumesnil, who later became his wife. Once well, Beckett asked his imprisoned assailant why he had attacked him. "Je ne sais pas, monsieur," was the answer. In fall, Beckett found a small apartment at 6, rue des Favorites, near the slaughter-houses and the Impasse de l'Enfant-Jésus, which was his home until 1961. With the help of Alfred Péron, he began to translate *Murphy* into French. Beckett has described 1938-39 as "a period of apathy and lethargy."

1939   In September, war broke out while he was visiting his mother in Ireland. He returned at once to Paris. "I preferred France in war to Ireland in peace." (Shenker)

1940   In June, Beckett fled Paris. In Vichy, he saw Joyce, who arranged for Valéry Larbaud to cash his Irish check, enabling Beckett to go as far South as Toulouse. In October, he returned to occupied Paris. Through Alfred Péron, he joined a Resistance network: "I couldn't stand with my arms folded." (Reid) Thirty of the eighty members of his network survived World War II.

1942   Beckett escaped hours before the Nazis searched his apartment, having been warned by a wire from Madame Péron: "Alfred arrêté par Gestapo. Prière faire nécessaire pour corriger l'erreur." The "nécessaire" was to obtain false papers and flee to Free France, stopping at Roussillon in the Vaucluse. For two years Beckett spent his days doing agricultural work and his nights writing *Watt*.

1945   On May 8, Armistice. Beckett went to Ireland to visit his mother and brother. Finding it difficult to return to France, he joined an Irish Red Cross unit that left for war-ravaged Saint-Lô in August. There he served as interpreter and storekeeper for a field hospital. By winter he was back in his Paris apartment.

1946   He began five years of writing in French—his most fertile period. "I wrote all my work very fast—between 1946 and 1950. Since then I haven't written anything. Or at least nothing that has seemed to me valid." (Shenker)

1950   He returned to Ireland in time to see his mother die.

1953   On January 5, première of *En attendant Godot* at Théâtre de Babylone, Paris.

1954   He returned to Ireland in time to see his brother die.

1958   In February, the English Lord Chancellor refused to allow production of *Endgame* in London, since the Deity was called a bastard. The ban was lifted in November.

    In February, the Dublin Drama Festival Committee dropped O'Casey's *Drums of Father Ned*, whereupon Beckett refused permission for any of his works to be produced in Ireland. Permission was re-granted as of May, 1960.

1959   He received an honorary doctorate from his Alma Mater, Trinity College.

1961   He shared the International Publishers' Prize with Jorge Luis Borges.

1964   He visited New York City to take part in the filming of his *Film*.

1966   He directed the first French production of *Va et Vient*, his first independent direction. He then directed a German television version of his *Eh Joe*.

1967   He directed a German stage version of his *Endgame*.

1969   He directed a German stage version of his *Krapp's Last Tape*.

1970   While vacationing in Tunisia, he was awarded the

Nobel Prize in Literature. Earlier, he directed French stage versions of *Krapp's Last Tape* and *Acts Without Words 1* and *2*.

1971   He directed a German stage version of his *Happy Days*.

Sources of Quotations

Richard N. Coe, *Samuel Beckett* (New York, 1964)

Nancy Cunard, *These Were the Hours* (Carbondale, 1969)

Richard Ellmann, *James Joyce* (New York, 1959)

John Fletcher, *The Novels of Samuel Beckett* (London, 1964)

John Gruen, "Samuel Beckett Talks About Beckett," *Vogue* (December, 1969)

Lawrence Harvey, *Samuel Beckett, Poet and Critic* (Princeton, 1970)

Harold Hobson, "Samuel Beckett, Dramatist of the Year," *International Theatre Annual* (London, 1956)

A. J. Leventhal in *Beckett at Sixty* (London, 1967)

Alec Reid, *All I Can Manage, More Than I Could* (Dublin, 1968)

Israel Shenker, "Moody Man of Letters," *New York Times* (May 6, 1956)

Clancy Sigal, "Is This the Person to Murder Me?" *Sunday Times* (March 1, 1964)

CHRONOLOGY OF BECKETT'S WORK

YEAR*	POETRY	FICTION	DRAMA	CRITICISM
1929		Assumption Che Sciagura		Dante . . . Bruno . Vico . . Joyce
1930	Whoroscope From the only Poet . . . For Future Reference			
1931	Return to the Vestry Yoke of Liberty Enueg I, II, Alba Casket of Pralinen . . .		Le Kid	Proust The Possessed
1932	Dortmunder Home Olga	Dream of Fair to Middling Women Dante and the Lobster		
1934	Gnome Malacoda	More Pricks Than Kicks A Case in a Thousand		Leishman Review MacGreevy Review
1935	Echo's Bones Cascando			
1936		Murphy		Jack Yeats Review Denis Devlin Review
1938	Ooftish			
1939	Poèmes			

* Dates are those of completion, up to the end of 1972.
Titles are given in language originally written. Beckett's translations are noted in parentheses, collections are underlined.

YEAR	POETRY	FICTION	DRAMA	CRITICISM
1944		Watt		
1945	Saint-Lô			
1946	Mort d'A.D.	La Fin (The End-1954)		Review of MacGreevy book on Jack Yeats
		Le Voyage de Mercier et Camier autour du Pot dans les Bosquets de Bondy		
		Premier Amour (First Love-1972)		La Peinture des van Velde
		Le Calmant (The Calmative-1967)		
		L'Expulsé (The Expelled-1962)		
1947		Molloy (English 1951)	Eleuthéria	
1948	Six Poèmes	Malone meurt (Malone Dies-1956)		Peintres de l'empêchement
	(Four translated-1961)		En attendant Godot (Waiting for Godot-1954)	
1949		L'Innommable (The Unnamable-1958)		
1950		Textes pour rien (Texts for Nothing-1967)		
1954				Hommage à Jack Yeats
1955				Henri Hayden
1956		From an Abandoned Work	Fin de partie (Endgame-1958)	
			Acte sans paroles 1 (Act Without Words 1-1958)	
			All That Fall	

YEAR	POETRY	FICTION	DRAMA	CRITICISM
1958			Krapp's Last Tape	
1959			Embers	
			Acte sans paroles II (Act Without Words II-1959)	
1960		Comment c'est (How It Is-1964)		
1961			Happy Days	
1962			Play	
			Words and Music	
1963			Cascando	
1964			Film	
1965		Imagination morte imaginez (Imagination Dead Imagine-1967)	Come and Go	
1966		Assez (Enough-1967)	Eh Joe	
		Le Dépeupleur (The Lost Ones-1972)	Breath	
		Bing (Ping-1967)		
1969		Sans (Lessness-1970)		
		Work in Regress		
1971		Foirades	Not I	
1972				

Though unpublished works are included, this listing is not complete. Beckett is only now (summer, 1973) re-viewing his many unpublished pieces that date mainly from the 1950s and 1960s.

LIST OF ILLUSTRATIONS

TABLE OF CONTENTS

CONTENTS

BACK TO BECKETT

PERSONAL FOREWORD

I FELL in love with *Godot* at its first production in the now defunct Théâtre de Babylone. The small familiar theater could not contain the chilling warming searing reach of *Godot*. Moved beyond words, I went out into the damp winter night, as millions of others have gone out into various weathers, similarly moved.

I published my first Beckett article in 1959, after it had been rejected by a discriminating editor: "We like your criticism, but we don't feel your author merits publishing space." I went on writing about my author until there was a book. A little over a decade since I wrote that book, I can count on my Beckett shelf thirty-seven books devoted entirely to his work. Federman and Fletcher have compiled some two hundred pages of items of Beckett criticism, as of 1966.

When Beckett's publisher telephoned him in Tunisia to tell him about winning the Nobel Prize, his wife exclaimed: "C'est une catastrophe." And it has been catastrophic, in part. Since the award, writing has grown more painful for Beckett. Eager young readers may be alienated by establishment recognition, but the prize may introduce Beckett's books to readers deprived of better guidance.

Every Beckett reader is a student, and I have been Beckett's enthusiastic student for two decades. I am grateful for what I have learned from other Beckett students, who have been generous in sharing their learning and documents. In spite of them, however, I am impelled to write another book. Beckett has become a domain for scholarly research, which learns more and more about less and less. I have produced such scholarship, and I am dependent on such scholarship, but I want in this book to get

3

back to Beckett, to the words of the works, which penetrate the width and depth of human experience.

Beckett cannot help being one of the best-educated men of our time, but his education has been a tool with which to seek basic human truth—a tool that serves him less and less as he continues to write. Since Beckett's erudition is copiously footnoted in other volumes, I am going to dispense with footnotes. All the more reason to pay a few debts now. Not unfittingly, the first book on Beckett was written in German by Hungarian Niklaus Gessner, as a doctoral thesis in French literature at a Swiss university. This book impressed me with its analysis of how Beckett fractured the French language in *Godot*, so as to convey existential chaos. A few years later, in 1961, Hugh Kenner sent me his *Samuel Beckett* in typescript, along with several unpublished Beckett manuscripts. Kenner illuminates Beckett as an academic clown, but I have come to think that Beckett's finest works are the least academic, and that the clown mask is shattered by anguish. Richard Coe's book summarized the philosophic sources of such anguish, but I focus more directly on the experience itself. Far from representing a drive toward silence, as described by Ihab Hassan, Beckett's words form a unique verbal melody. Far from being the willed failure appreciatively analyzed by Michael Robinson, Beckett's work strikes me as a matchless achievement. Though I partly share Ludovic Janvier's view of Beckett—"avant tout réussite d'un langage exceptionnel" —I balk at "avant tout," however formidable the "réussite."

Several Beckett critics have used Beckett's criticism to describe his own works. I think that in "Dante ... Bruno . Vico .. Joyce" Beckett elucidates *Finnegans Wake*. I find that Beckett's *Proust* penetrates *A la recherche du temps perdu*. *Three Dialogues* illuminates the painting of Bram Van Velde. It may be that Beckett chose to write about these artists (even though the essays were commissioned) because he felt their affinities with his own vision, particularly

4

in the well-known sentence from the *Dialogues*: "The expression that there is nothing to express, nothing with which to express, nothing from which to express, no power to express, no desire to express, together with the obligation to express." But I would insist that Beckett's interior obligation to express *has* expressed intense emotions, with words stemming from or reacting against our cultural tradition. Above all, Beckett has felt obligated to express his deepest experience, which is wide in resonance.

I cringe today at the systematized structure of my first book on Beckett, but I would still hold to one of its basic insights: "Our world, 'so various, so beautiful, so new,' so stingily admitted to Beckett's work, is nevertheless the essential background for appreciation of that work." Like us all, Beckett has lived in the world. Like most of us, Beckett has had to defend his privacy against the world. Unlike most of us, Beckett has transmuted life and defense into something rich and strange, but also poor and familiar. The tawdry real world is the prism that reveals Beckett's spectrum of genres—essay, poem, story, novel, lyric of fiction, play, radio play, mime play, tape play, film. Through them all sounds the cry of human mortality.

Beckett's work is steeped in mortality—the outrageous fact of death. Beckett knows that other men have been haunted by mortality, and we occasionally hear their echoes in his work, most pervasively Dante. Though mortality has been Beckett's familiar for over half a century, he dwells also with other idea-feelings. 1) Since man is mortal, he lives in time, and the tricks of time fill Beckett's fiction and drama. 2) Mortal man, as Descartes insisted, is split between body and mind. The mind alone is rich and graceful, adds Geulincx, but it is fastened to a dying animal. 3) The mind expresses itself in words, at once a compulsion and a curse. 4) The mind knows that it is limited to and by words, which falsify whatever they approach. Beckett told Lawrence Harvey: "At that level you break up words to

5

diminish shame. . . . Painting and music have so much better a chance." 5) In Beckett's later work, where being is betrayed by words, nonbeing is temptation.

Words have been mistaken as the only subject of Beckett's own words. Beckett writes so large and small about words, so brightly and darkly about words, that they seem to be reflexive. But Beckett is not a metalinguist (Smuda's word); he is a speleologist of human essence—call it being, self, identity. This essence defies verbalization, and Beckett defiantly tries to verbalize it. As human beings, most of us investigate ourselves and our world with words. As a writer, Beckett can dig only with words.

I am writing this book to clarify my enthusiasm for Beckett, and I hope that it will interest people who are moved by Beckett's words. I call the book *Back to Beckett* because I always come back to Beckett's works, having read much Beckett criticism, some Beckett sources, and several Beckett epigones. But the book is back to Beckett in another sense too—turning my back on what may be Beckett's own view of his writing. He would probably concur with those who pronounce his work a failure. "Something wrong with all of them," he answered when I asked which of his works he preferred. Disagreeing, I claim that his works are prodigiously right in the way that they penetrate basic human experience.

Beckett has told several critics that, were he unfortunate enough to be a critic commenting on Beckett's work, he would begin with two quotations:

> Nothing is more real than nothing. (Democritus)
> Where you are worth nothing, there you should want nothing. (Geulincx)

Four nothings add up to something, but there too I turn my back on Beckett. Nothing begins to lure Beckett only after he has suffered through many somethings. He does not start with Porgy's axiomatic zero:

> I got plenty o' nuthin'
> An' nuthin's plenty for me.

Rather, he conceives his works at once threatened and tempted by nothing. Like Shakespeare's dying Timon, Beckett comes to feel:

> My long sickness
> Of health and living now begins to mend,
> And nothing brings me all things.

During the long sickness of his writing life, Beckett has shivered through many a fever to chart a being that is bounded by nothing. Under Beckett's spell, we too come to strain toward nothing—but through densities and immensities.

Finally a few technical points about this book. Though I hope it incorporates my scholarship, I have deliberately avoided the intimidating scholarly apparatus of footnotes and index. I have, however, had the usual scholarly dependence on libraries, and I acknowledge cooperation from Baker Memorial Library of Dartmouth College, the Humanities Research Center of the University of Texas, the Ohio State University Library, the Samuel Beckett Collection of the Washington University Libraries. For generous and genuine help, I warmly thank Betty Armstrong, Avigdor Arikha, Dorrit Cohn, Martin Esslin, Craig Fuller, Fred Gardner, Lawrence Harvey, Denise Helmer, Jules Irving, James Knowlson, John Kobler, Roger McHugh, Breon Mitchell, Leo Weinstein. For encouraging the Beckett issue of *Modern Drama* and *Perspective* I am grateful to Carroll Edwards and Jarvis Thurston. For revision and reprinting of my "Beckett Directs *Happy Days*," I thank the editors of *Performance*, Bill Coco and Erika Munk.

In the text of *Back to Beckett* I use the titles of Beckett's works in the language of original writing. Translations from Beckett's French (unless otherwise noted) are by Beckett, even when the translations have not been published. That is only one of his liberal gifts to me.

1.

THE BEGINNING WRITER

SAMUEL BECKETT was born in 1906 in Ireland. Samuel Beckett, the professional writer, was born in 1929 in Paris. Though he had earlier penned juvenilia, he did not attempt publication until he was twenty-three years old, and his first publications bear only the faintest promise of the masterworks to come. Without hindsight, the reader might fall easily into Malone's refrain: "What tedium!" And yet there is a certain variety amidst the tedium—an exegetical essay "Dante . . . Bruno . Vico . . Joyce," a short story "Assumption," and a satirical dialogue "Che Sciagura."

In order to publicize *Finnegans Wake*, then *Work in Progress*, James Joyce chose twelve disciples to pen laudatory essays—twelve cheers for Joyce. Beckett's piece was the first of the collection, obstreperously entitled *Our Exagmination Round his Factification for Incamination of Work in Progress*. Beckett's subject was suggested by Joyce, who knew that Beckett had studied Dante closely while he was a student at Trinity College, Dublin, and Joyce introduced Beckett to Vico and Bruno.

In Beckett's title "Dante . . . Bruno . Vico . . Joyce" each dot represents a century—three from Dante to Bruno, one from Bruno to Vico, and two from Vico to Joyce; the three Italians culminate in the Irishman. The title's erudition points to that of the essay, which a recent Joyce critic dismisses as a hodgepodge of phrases that Beckett heard from Joyce, setting them down without understanding them. But Beckett's phrases are quite comprehensible, and the essay, liberally sprinkled with quotations in Italian, seeks to be comprehensive.

8

Beckett begins with a warning against the systematization or abstraction of works of art—"Literary criticism is not book-keeping."—and then moves into Vico. Beckett belittles the originality of Vico's division of the development of human society into three ages: Theocratic, Heroic, Human with a corresponding classification of language: Hieroglyphic (sacred), Metaphoric (poetic), Philosophic (capable of abstraction and generalization). Beckett then proceeds to summarize Vico's *New Science*, indicating its debt to Bruno's theory of the fundamental identity of contraries. Only then does Beckett indicate how intimately Vico's three-part cycles are built into structure and texture of Joyce's *Work in Progress.*

Most interesting to the young Beckett was Vico's view of the primal spontaneity of language, poetry, and myth. Beckett sees Joyce's work as an effort to recapture a comparable spontaneity, now that language, poetry, and myth are diffused into separate realms: "[Joyce] is not writing about something: he is writing something." Beckett further claims that Joyce has "desophisticated" English after centuries of abstraction: "Here words are not the polite contorsions of 20th century printer's ink. They are alive. They elbow their way on to the page, and glow and blaze and face and disappear." And Beckett demonstrates how Joyce's words build concrete archetypes about which Vico had only theorized.

Moving on to Dante so as to justify his title, Beckett compares Joyce's linguistic achievement with that of Dante's Italian. Both authors shocked contemporary critics and provoked condemnation of the Catholic Church. Bending Dante to defend Joyce, Beckett concludes his essay by parallelling and contrasting their use of Purgatory as the only realm through which humanity can move, for there is stasis in Inferno and Paradise. In Beckett's last few sentences, describing "this earth that is Purgatory," it is not clear whether he presents Joyce's world or his own—an

9

amoral realm of energy, leading neither to "prize nor penalty."

At twenty-three Beckett was arrogant in his admiration of Joyce, but his essay elucidates *Work in Progress*, and it obliquely predicts certain of his own future intellectual attitudes: he will share Vico's view of the inextricable union of human history and language. Like Dante and Joyce, this young Irishman in Paris will assume the internationality of literature, but unlike them he will see internationality as the lowest common human denominator. However, neither Beckett nor anyone else could have foreseen this in 1929.

In the June, 1929, issue of *transition*, along with Beckett's Joyce piece, appeared his short story "Assumption." Recondite vocabulary and laborious syntax relate story to essay. An extremely condensed "Portrait of the Artist as a Young Man," Beckett's "Assumption" is structured on a conflict between sound and silence. The nameless artist-protagonist has an extraordinary voice, able to "whisper down" the surrounding noise. But he imposes silence upon himself until a woman enters his life, eroding both his resolution and his life. "Thus each night he died and was God, each night revived and was torn, torn and battered with increasing grievousness, so that he hungered to be irretrievably engulfed in the light of eternity, one with the birdless cloudless colourless skies, in infinite fulfilment." Irresistibly, he is delivered of "a great storm of sound" that finally "fused into the breath of the forest and the throbbing cry of the sea." His sound uttered, the artist dies. His "assumption" is at once the arrogance of the artist, the hypothesis of silence, and his cosmic climb after death.

The story reveals a young man's romantic yearning, and Beckett's next publication is comparably juvenile. In the same year that story and criticism appeared in the Paris avant-garde quarterly—1929—"Che Sciagura" was published in the Trinity College weekly. The Italian title is a quotation from Voltaire's *Candide*. Uttered by a eunuch when he finds himself before the nude loveliness of the heroine, the entire exclamation is "O che sciagura d'essere senza cogli-oni!" (What tough luck to be without balls.) Beckett drops the "O," uses the first two words as his title and the first letters of the last four words—D.E.S.C.—as his pseudonym for a dialogue about contraception in Ireland, so opaquely learned that no one thought to censor it from a student newspaper.

The following year, still a student, Beckett gained some small recognition as a poet. His *Whoroscope* won a contest sponsored by the Paris-based Hours Press. Though written within a few hours to meet the contest deadline, *Whoroscope* rested on Beckett's study of the works of Descartes, and of his life as recorded by Adrien Baillet in the seventeenth century. By the terms of the contest, the poem had to be under a hundred lines, and Beckett compressed several hundred pages of reading into ninety-eight lines. Time, the subject specified by the Hours Press, is present only in the punning title *Whoroscope* (containing Greek *horo*, hour) and the last line—"starless inscrutable hour." If the poem's subject is indeed Time, it is a human lifetime, the life of René Descartes, Seigneur du Perron, though one might not realize this on first reading the poem. At the suggestion of Richard Aldington, who, along with press-owner Nancy Cunard, judged the contest, Beckett added notes for publication, in the manner of T. S. Eliot's *Waste Land*. The notes puzzle as much as they enlighten, but they *do* make clear that the speaker of the poem is Descartes.

A dramatic monologue, the poem is characteristic of its genre in combining sympathy with judgment of the speaker —sympathy through use of the first person and judgment through limitation of the speaker's viewpoint. Beckett's dramatic monologue strays from its genre, however, in the difficulty (without notes) of identifying the speaker and in the ambiguity of authorial attitude toward the speaker. The poem is opaque with references to the biographic, scientific, and philosophic details of Descartes' life. At the same time, there is perhaps an implicit judgment against Descartes for being so absorbed in the recondite details of his life that he left small time for merely human experience.

In spite of its vexingly erudite allusions, the poem is worth reading aloud. Opening with a question—"What's that?"—Descartes calls five times for his breakfast omelette. Following each of those calls, he meanders by association through the events of his life. His speech is sharp and colloquial, rhythmed by questions, exclamations, imprecations. Even his name-dropping—the Boot brothers, Gillot, Galileo, Copernicus, Gassendi, Harvey, Hobbes, Bacon—rings musically. Read aloud, an un-Cartesian melody arises from puns, refrains, off-rhymes, and alliterations. But it takes determination to hear that melody through the barrage of learned references.

Whoroscope brought Beckett to the attention of Richard Aldington, who obtained for him a commission to write a monograph on Proust. Beckett therefore devoted the summer of 1930, the last months of his Paris fellowship, to rereading *A la recherche du temps perdu.* He has said that he disliked this second assignment in criticism, but he produced an analysis that is still a useful guide through Proust's novel.

Like most subsequent commentators, Beckett sees that Proust's implicit subject is Time, which he characterizes as "that double-headed monster of salvation and damnation." But salvation and damnation, like Purgatory in the Joyce essay, are secular. Damnation means the erosion of self through Habit; salvation means the re-collection of self through Involuntary Memory. "Memory and Habit are attributes of the Time cancer." Beckett calls Proust's long book "a monument to involuntary memory and the epic of its action."

In the Grove Press reprint, Beckett's *Proust* occupies nearly seventy-two pages. No Proust scholar has claimed that the monograph is a hodgepodge of imperfectly understood quotations, but today the small volume seems to attract Becketteers rather than Proustians. And this is understandable, for it is in *Proust* that Beckett first extensively bares his literary prejudices, obliquely predicting his own works to come. However, I would insist that *Proust* is primarily about Proust and not about Beckett. His study is anchored to references to the long text, with graceful translations of excerpts.

For all Beckett's learning, he does not lead us to the human familial heart of *Finnegans Wake* in his Joyce criticism. Since language is the most startling element of that work, that is what Beckett stresses. In *Proust*, by contrast, Beckett explains and illustrates Proust's vision as adumbrated in the book-long tension between Habit and Involuntary Memory. Though Beckett deals only summarily with Proust's style, Beckett's own style calls attention to itself here more surely than in the Joyce essay, with which it shares the same tone of disdainful superiority. Beckett's syntax has grown smoother in the year's interval, and his imagery more copious and functional. Learned references are far more plentiful than in the Joyce essay, and they are inter-European, if not international; at least passing mention is made of classical and biblical myth, Leopardi, Gide, Cocteau, Shadwell, Descartes, d'Annunzio, Shakespeare, Constant, Nietzsche, Racine, Calderón, Shelley, Stravinsky, Dostoievsky, Dante, Baudelaire, De Sanctis, Blake, Coppée, Hugo, Huysmans, Musset, Chateaubriand, Amiel, the Goncourt brothers, Curtius, Renan, Schopenhauer, Spenser, Keats, Giorgione, Leibniz, Montegna. But none of them usurps more than a sentence or two, and our eye is always on Proust.

Written in 1930, the beginning of a socially conscious decade, Beckett's *Proust* takes a firm stand against realism. Though there is no evidence of any mutual admiration between Proust and Joyce, and though Beckett does not mention either one in his essay on the other, he finds in them both a praiseworthy dedication to art, as opposed to a mere

13

ability to record surfaces. Art is essentially a matter of vision: "for the artist, the only possible hierarchy in the world of objective phenomena is represented by a table of their respective coefficients of penetration, that is to say, in terms of the subject." In the works of both Proust and Joyce, Beckett finds no divorce, indeed no difference, between form and content. In the works of both, the intuitive and involuntary are valued above the rational and intellectual—by this very intellectual young man.

Joyce became an ethical ideal for Beckett; in 1969 he said, "Joyce had a moral effect on me—he made me realize artistic integrity." But Proust became, if not an esthetic ideal, at least a guidepost. Like Proust, Beckett will be concerned with man as time's victim, and like Proust he will often depict life as a struggle between Habit and Involuntary Memory, between the boredom of living and the suffering of being. As pitilessly and compassionately as Proust, Beckett will investigate, through the lens of time, those primal human experiences, love and death.

Beckett finds Proust romantic in his belief that Art redeems Time, that "lost time" is found ever and again in the immortality of art. Beckett, in contrast, will find neither salvation nor redemption in art. Inhuman time is relentlessly infinite; human time is relentlessly finite. And neither is redeemed by words. Beckett closes his essay on the significance of Proustian music that reveals the meaning of the word "defunctus." Though Beckett analyzes redeemed time in Proust, his own final word is "defunctus"—discharged, deceased.

In a sardonic poem of 1932, "Casket of Pralinen for a Daughter of a Dissipated Mandarin," Beckett turns scatological humor against Proust's concept of redemption through time:

> Oh beauty!
> Oh thou predatory evacuation
> from the bowels of my regret—

14

readily affected
by the assimilation of a purging gobbet
from my memory's involuntary vomit—
violently projected,
oh beauty!

For Proust Involuntary Memory is the stimulus to artistic creation of beauty. For Beckett Involuntary Memory is purge, causing evacuation of regrets. The violence of Beckett's imagery may indicate how much he was tempted by the beauty of a time-stopping art.

Through the decade of the 1930's, as Beckett found no home in Ireland, Germany, France, or England, he wrote in several genres—reviews, fiction, poetry, embryonic drama. Early in that decade he renounced academic security, without any idea of what would take its place. He appeared to be a brilliant young man with his future behind him, so slowly did his artistic vision develop.

   Though several critics have insisted upon the influence of Joyce and Proust upon Beckett, the one work where their combined influence is apparent is largely unpublished. Beckett wrote *Dream of Fair to Middling Women* quite fast, in Paris in spring, 1932, after his resignation from Trinity College and travels through Germany. The only extant typescript contains 214 pages and is thus his first extended piece of fiction. The narrator of *Dream*, revealed as a "Mr. Beckett," calls the book a "virgin chronicle," and it certainly lacks the coherent structure of the traditional novel. The 214 pages are nevertheless unified by the detached irony of the narrator and the continuous presence of the protagonist, Belacqua—a name drawn from Dante's *Purgatorio* and found again in Beckett's *More Pricks Than Kicks, Murphy, Molloy, How It Is.*

   In Canto 4 of the *Purgatorio* Dante and Virgil have begun the difficult ascent of the Mountain of Purgatory. With typical pedantry Virgil explains the surroundings, and he assures Dante that the longer they climb, the easier the climbing will become, until finally it will seem like a boat descending a stream. Suddenly, as if out of the very rock, a sardonic voice remarks, "Before that you may want to sit down." And a moment later "Go on up, you valiant one." The voice belongs to Belacqua, a Florentine lute-maker who is "more indolent than if sloth were his sister." Amidst the purgatorial traffic he sits in fetal position, meditating. Belacqua had been too lazy to repent until his last living moment, and he therefore was condemned to spend the equivalent of his lifetime in Antepurgatory. Unlike the damned of the Inferno, however, whose sin becomes the fulcrum of their punishment, Belacqua's fault feeds his preference. Indolent in life, he is indolent after death, motionless in the shade of a rock. Dante condemns Belacqua's sloth, but Beckett implies approval of the attitude imputed to the historical Belacqua, who quoted Aristotle: "*Sedendo et quiescendo anima efficitur prudens*" (Sitting quietly, the soul acquires wisdom). The Belacqua of *Dream* even quotes *sedendo et quiescendo*, emphasizing the *et* but renouncing any ambition to wisdom. Only midway through *Dream* does Beckett clarify the significance of the sloth of his Belacqua. The narrator presents him as trine: "Centripetal, centrifugal and . . . not." After summarizing the adventures of Belacqua, the narrator continues:

> The third being was the dark gulf when the glare of the will and the hammer strokes of the brain doomed outside to take flight from its quarry were expunged, the Limbo and the wombtomb alive with the unanxious spirits of quiet cerebration, where there was no conflict of flight and flow and Eros was as null as Anteros and Night had no daughters. [Belacqua] was bogged in indolence, without identity, impervious alike to its pull and goading. The cities and forest and beings were also without identity, they were shadows, they exerted neither pull nor goad. His third being was without axis or contour, its centre

everywhere and periphery nowhere, an unsurveyed marsh of sloth.

Most of *Dream* deals with centripetal and centrifugal Belacqua, for whom the "unsurveyed marsh of sloth" is a dream juxtaposed against the all-too-fleshly reality of "fair to middling women." In Vienna Belacqua has a Proustian love affair with the Smeraldina-Rima, occasionally narrated in styles imitative of *Ulysses* or in the portmanteau words of *Finnegans Wake*. During two months in Paris, despite interruptions of men friends and the Syra-Cusa, Belacqua retires into a mental tunnel, which enables his mind to go "wombtomb." Returning to Vienna for Christmas with the Smeraldina and her family, he terminates his love affair to begin the new year. Back home in Dublin Belacqua embarks on an ambiguous relationship with the Alba, and the book closes after a party.

Dream shows Beckett feeling his way into sustained fiction. In spite of the ruse of a narrator named Mr. Beckett, Belacqua's adventures seem closely based on those of the young Beckett, and several sentences foreshadow his own future development. Belacqua's friend Lucien maintains that Racine and Malherbe write without style, and he concludes: "Perhaps only the French can do it. Perhaps only the French language can give you the thing you want." In Vienna the Smeraldina's father tells Belacqua: "The reality of the individual, you had the cheek to inform me once, is an incoherent reality and must be expressed incoherently." And Belacqua himself confesses: "I shall write a book. . . . The experience of my reader shall be between the phrases, in the silence, communicated by the intervals, not the terms, of the statement, between the flowers that cannot coexist, the antithetical (nothing so simple as antithetical) seasons of words, his experience shall be the menace, the miracle, the memory of an unspeakable trajectory." These scattered comments of *Dream* will be gathered into the coherent incoherence of Beckett's French fiction.

17

Of more marginal interest is a covert reference to *Whoroscope*, when Belacqua declares: "There is a long poem . . . waiting to be written about hens and eggs." And three times, in connection with narration as a melody, the narrator uses the nonword "ping" for a liŭ, apparently a Chinese note.

Shortly after completing *Dream*, Beckett had to leave France when foreigners were *personae non gratae* after the assassination of French President Paul Doumer. Less than a year after his resignation from Trinity College, Beckett returned to the family home in Foxrock near Dublin, and with him came his Belacqua. Almost at once, Beckett plunged that hero into a short story, "Dante and the Lobster." Back near Dublin, Beckett kept his hero in greater Dublin as he shaped other stories about him (salvaging from *Dream* only "A Wet Night" and "The Smeraldina's Billet-Doux"). By 1934 ten Belacqua stories formed a picaresque novel, published in London as *More Pricks Than Kicks*. The title plays upon the words of Jesus to Saul in *Acts* 9:5: "I am Jesus whom thou persecutest; it is hard for thee to kick against the pricks." Pricks are at once martyrdom and sexuality, and the combination was sufficient to cause the book to be banned in Ireland.

Indolent as Belacqua is, it *is* hard for him to kick against his pricks—largely sexual. Like his Florentine ancestor, the picaresque Belacqua is "sinfully indolent, bogged in indolence," "an indolent bourgeois poltroon." But Beckett eliminated the significance of indolence for the life of the mind, and the stories give an impression of considerable movement, particularly among women. Of the ten stories, six focus on Belacqua's relations with women—Winnie, Ruby, Lucy, Thelma, and, transplanted from *Dream*, the Smeraldina and the Alba. As in *Dream*, Belacqua cannot manage to keep his affairs "pewer and above-bawd." The story of his wedding—in a second marriage—is entitled "What a Misfortune," translating Voltaire's "Che Sciagura." Even in his death-story, "Yellow," Belacqua observes in the hospital: "What a number of women there seemed to be in this place!" Though women predominate, a large number of men *and* women populate *More Pricks*—perhaps a hundred in the ten stories—for Beckett creates a caricature society in larger Dublin.

More Pricks Than Kicks is divided into ten stories, and yet Belacqua gives the impression of continuous life. As a student, Belacqua Shuah has fixed and precise habits. He eats meticulously, drinks copiously, reads tenaciously, and takes his girl-friends for long walks in the country. One fine spring day he deserts his girl-friend Winnie. After "a wet night"—sodden with both rain and alcohol—he spends the first few hours of Christmas with Alba, his "current one and only." It is with another woman, Ruby Tough, that Belacqua makes a suicide pact, but instead "our two young felons" commit "the inevitable nuptial." Still another woman, his fiancée Lucy, is paralyzed by an accident, while Belacqua is beaten for the voyeurism that is his pleasure. After marrying and burying Lucy, Belacqua marries Thelma bboggs, with the Alba serving as one of the maids of honor. Having received a love letter from the Austrian Smeraldina, Belacqua is next seen in a hospital, where he is to undergo operations on his neck and toe, but where he dies of an overdose of anesthetic. Finally, Belacqua's corpse is visited by his third wife, the Smeraldina, and his best friend, Hairy Quinn. Prepared for burial, Belacqua serves to unite a new couple formed by his widow and his best friend, who cannot remember the inscription for Belacqua's headstone. *More Pricks* closes at Belacqua's grave, with the narrator commenting: "So it goes in the world."

But if it does go so in the world, Beckett leaves many worldly questions unanswered: What does Belacqua live on? How does Belacqua meet his various women? When did his afflictions on neck and toe appear? How serious were they? Such worldly questions are ignored by Beckett, who dwells instead upon trivialities, descriptions, or conversational repartee, and who dwells *in* the language of his narration, under firmer control than in *Dream*.

19

Except for "The Smeraldina's Billet-Doux," a facile parody of Germanic syntax and female sensuality, the stories are told by a self-conscious, omniscient narrator whose style had finally evolved by the end of *Dream*. A reader of traditional fiction might be disturbed by the opening sentence of *More Pricks*: "It was morning and Belacqua was stuck in the first of the canti in the moon." The sentence is incomprehensible without knowledge of Dante. But even with such knowledge, we are abruptly shifted, after noon strikes, to Belacqua's mundane preoccupations—the preparation of a lunch, the purchase of a lobster, and the absorption of a lesson on Dante. Lunch, lobster, and lesson converge in the evening when Belacqua delivers the lobster to his aunt. His desultory thoughts have wandered over McCabe, a condemned murderer, and Cain, the first murderer. In the evening Belacqua learns that the lobster is alive, and that "lobsters are always boiled alive. They must be. They feel nothing." Belacqua rationalizes: "Well, it's a quick death, God help us all." But the narrator ends the story with a sharp reversal of Belacqua's rationalization: "It is not."

Though these three monosyllables are the most forceful intrusion of the narrator, his customary elegance does not veil the substratum of suffering in *More Pricks Than Kicks*. In "Dante and the Lobster" a murderer is executed, and a lobster is boiled alive. In "Fingal" the insane are regimented, and Dean Swift has virtually imprisoned his Stella. In "Ding-Dong" whose title comes from Ariel's dirge in *The Tempest*, a little girl is run over, and a woman steals her loaf of bread. In "A Wet Night" Christ's passion is the subject of witticisms. In "Love and Lethe" Ruby Tough suffers from an incurable disorder that will kill her. In "Walking Out" Lucy is paralyzed in an accident. At the wedding of "What A Misfortune" Belacqua's only relatives are a cretin and a cripple. In her "Billet-Doux" the Smeraldina mentions "some dam thing on my leg so that I can bearly walk." In "Yellow" Belacqua dies on the operating table. In "Draff" Belacqua's maid butchers a fowl, whereupon the gardener rapes the

20

maid and sets fire to the house where Belacqua has brought three brides. *So* it goes in the world.

Beckett's first published book of fiction will be his last to deal so extensively with the world, and his last to maintain so caustically ironic a distance from his protagonist. Far from a dashing lover, Belacqua is described as fat and pasty-faced, with impetigo, spavined gait, ruined feet, and a heart in the Portrane Lunatic Asylum. But as with subsequent and older Beckett heroes, Belacqua's physical defects are accompanied by a fascinating mind. In spite of the narrator's ironic guard, we do occasionally follow Belacqua's thought processes, and the more we do, the more significant the story seems.

"Dante and the Lobster" traces Belacqua's difficulties in reconciling piety and pity, justice and compassion. Quite early in the story, as we watch Belacqua's meticulous preparations for lunch, we are suddenly immersed in the following paragraph:

> For the tiller of the field the thing was simple, he had it from his mother. The spots were Cain with his truss of thorns, dispossessed, cursed from the earth, fugitive and vagabond. The moon was that countenance fallen and branded, seared with the first stigma of God's pity, that an outcast might not die quickly. It was a mix-up in the mind of the tiller, but that did not matter. It had been good enough for his mother, it was good enough for him.

The paragraph is like a poem—associational and rhythmic, rather than logical. Cain is at once the tiller of the field and the countenance in the moon; at once a murderer and a victim who is not allowed to die quickly. As in medieval belief, the man in the moon is Cain crowned with thorns, like Christ. The "it" that Cain has from his mother, Eve, may be the knowledge of God's wrath, the expulsion from Eden, or the explanation of the spots on the moon. Leaving "it" vague, however, encompasses all suffering of all time— the *un*fortunate fall. Incantatory repetition in first and last

21

sentence, diffusion and dissolution of the Cain image, the triplets of suffering in the second and third sentences, alliteration and assonance: all these give us a rare insight into the poetic quality of Belacqua's mind.

"Yellow" reveals Belacqua's determined courage in the face of danger that proves to be fatal. Beckett stiffens his narrator's ironic attitude toward death, and Belacqua's death is narrated as the punch-line of a joke, toward which he decides to react with laughter.

> Here, as indeed at every crux of the enterprise, [Belacqua] sacrificed his sense of what was personal and proper to himself to the desirability of making a certain impression on other people, an impression almost of gallantry. He must efface himself altogether and do the little soldier. It was this paramount consideration that made him decide in favour of Bim and Bom, Grock, Democritus, whatever you are pleased to call it, and postpone its dark converse to a less public occasion. . . .
>
> So now his course was clear. He would arm his mind with laughter, laughter is not quite the word but it will have to serve, at every point, then he would admit the idea [of the operation] and blow it to pieces. Smears, as after a gorge of blackberries, of hilarity, which is not quite the word either, would be adhering to his lips as he stepped smartly, ohne Hast aber ohne Rast, into the torture-chamber.

The evocation of comedians in the first paragraph is eroded in the second paragraph by doubts about the words "laughter" and "hilarity." The Goethean German undercuts the torture-chamber, and yet Belacqua *does* emerge as a gallant soldier.

Nine Belacqua stories are larger than their protagonist. (I except "The Smeraldina's Billet-Doux.") Peopled with caricatures, they arouse a certain compassion through the lack of compassion of the characters. Belacqua is more disturbed by a lobster's death than a man's; he does not react to a little girl's accident, or indeed to that of his fiancée. With bravado, he instructs his nurse to give his amputated toe to the cat. But his very callousness demands our counter-compassion. And yet, it is unlikely that we would be sensitive to that demand, did we not know Beckett's later work. On first reading, *More Pricks Than Kicks* calls attention to its style rather than its compassion, and the first reviewers saw it as a display of style.

That style is the burden of Beckett's omniscient narrator, who is more consistently controlled in *More Pricks* than in *Dream*. The narrator is more learned than Belacqua, and he is responsible for most of the learned references. However, his ironic tone seems to mock the very learning he displays so ostentatiously. Moreover, he does not explain the origin of Belacqua's name, or the Alba's, or the nurse Miranda's. Above all, he does not explain the writing as writing, though he comments on it in four footnotes, and he makes cross-references from story to story. He even assigns Beckett's first novel *Dream of Fair to Middling Women* to Walter Draffin, the illegitimate father of Belacqua's second wife. Rarely does he intrude seriously, as at the end of "Dante and the Lobster," and he introduces himself only in the third story. After comparing his friendship for Belacqua with that of Pylades and Orestes, the narrator confesses: "I gave [Belacqua] up in the end because he was not *serious*." It is an incongruous charge, coming from a narrator who takes every opportunity to indulge in his comic techniques, and yet the charge foreshadows Beckett's own fictional path. Though all Beckett's narrators will ply their ironies, they will do so about more *serious* heroes, who will take their sloth more seriously. As erudite as Belacqua, they will scorn his learned witticisms and studied repartee. And the narrators, dealing with more serious protagonists, will renounce quotation quilts, grotesque particularizations, and fatuous conversations.

23

I have tried to give some sense of the anguish below the elegant surface of *More Pricks Than Kicks*, precisely because the elegance is all too polished. Belacqua was conceived when Beckett was rootless geographically and professionally. He came to an end after the death of Beckett's father in 1933, when Beckett exiled himself to London. During that period Beckett was also writing lyric poetry—traditionally a personal genre. In 1935, while living in London, Beckett submitted thirteen poems for publication by George Reavey's Europa Press in Paris. He gave the collection the title of the last poem, *Echo's Bones*.

Though neither Echo nor Narcissus is named in the poems, their spirits hover through them. Nine of the thirteen poems are spoken by a first-person persona as self-loving as Narcissus. Wasting and pining like Echo, the persona reveals himself in fragments—voice and bones moving through Dublin, London, and Paris.

Lawrence Harvey devotes some hundred pages to exegesis of the thirteen poems in *Echo's Bones*, which are hermetic in their ellipsis and erudition. Among major sources Harvey lists Ovid, Rimbaud, Schopenhauer, Habbakuk, Dante, Goethe, and the troubadour tradition. The collection begins and ends with short poems, spare of reference and strictly rhythmed. The opening poem, "The Vulture," is an invocation without a muse. Borrowed from Goethe's "Harzreise," the Vulture is the artist who feeds on corporal reality. A kind of reality is traced through nine allusive and elusive poems, to culminate in "Malacoda," a death poem. The collection then closes on two *post mortems*, "Da Tagte Es" and "Echo's Bones." The first of these, based on a medieval German dawn poem, turns dawn into death, where all voyages end. The last poem is crueller in its picture of the dead, "taken by the maggots for what they are." As the title suggests, after the flesh withers, Echo's bones endure.

Beckett's full title is *Echo's Bones and Other Precipitates*; all the poems are metaphoric deposits after life's fluids are gone, and they are carefully grouped from birth to *post mortem*. Following the birth-poem are two enuegs, two aubades, two disease poems, and three serenas. Enueg, aubade, and serena are traditional Provençal forms, and their modern equivalents surround the invented "Sanies" or poems of diseased blood.

Lawrence Harvey indicates how Beckett modifies the Provençal enueg, which is a discontinuous and witty catalogue of vexations. (The word will recur in *Mercier et Camier*.) In spirit, Beckett's enuegs resemble the melancholy Provençal planh or complaint. Nevertheless, Beckett kept the name enueg to justify his disjunctive lines, each line resting on an image. "Enueg I" is a sequential narrative; the persona, leaving his love in the hospital, strolls through Dublin, seeing sufferers—down-and-outs on a barge, an old man and a child, verminous hens, a malevolent goat, and sweaty heroes. Throughout his observations, the wind sounds in the speaker's skull, and the poem closes on a translation of the refrain from Rimbaud's "Barbare." "Enueg II" seems to equate the death of day, the death of Christ, and a general sense of the death of a sick world.

"Alba," the first of the two dawn poems, is distinctive in its continuous syntax and musical imagery, as may be seen in these lines that rhapsodize simultaneously about a Chinese lute and night rain:

> grave suave singing silk
> stoop to the black firmament of areca
> rain on the bamboos flower of smoke alley of willows.

"Dortmunder," the second dawn poem, casts the persona as Habbakuk the scribe, paying homage to a bawd who creates a night of music. Both these dawn poems follow tradition in regretting the passing of night, but the quality of dark love is exotic, illicit, and sadly tentative.

Day does break in *Echo's Bones*, and the two sanies catalogue a miscellaneous sequence of horrors, I in the country-

25

side near Dublin, II in a Paris brothel. Perhaps the two most irritatingly hermetic of these thirteen poems, the sanies couple relishes tainted details.

In the three serenas Beckett returns to a Provençal genre, in which the lover longs for the coming of evening. Beckett's persona wanders through the daytime cruelties of London, the Irish countryside, and the city of Dublin. In all three poems the tortures of day are emphasized more than the anticipated relief of night on "this clonic earth." "Serena I," joining persona to housefly, suggests that night brings the relief of death. "Serena II" closes on an ironic prayer "here at these knees of stone," and, recalling the title of the whole collection, "then to bye-bye on the bones." "Serena III" paints the life of a lover in puritanical Ireland; it ends, not with a longing for night, but with the injunction to "keep on the move." In *Echo's Bones* the move is toward death, described most vividly in "Malacoda." Inspired by the death of Beckett's father, this poem is named for Dante's trumpet-rumped devil, whose contemporary avatar is an undertaker's assistant. Lawrence Harvey's exegesis explains the poem's subtle details, but immediately evident is the persona's grief, with its variations on the refrain, from "hear she may see she need not" to "hear she must see she need not" to "hear she must see she must." The poem's entire final stanza is "nay"—a denial of mortal "must"s.

In its movement toward death *Echo's Bones* resembles the book that Beckett had published a year earlier. *More Pricks Than Kicks* follows Belacqua from student days to burial. Though birth and death are more general in *Echo's Bones*, a few poems are elucidated by the stories. Most obvious are poems named after characters—"Alba" and "Malacoda." In "Sanies I" we find a bicycle ride that recalls that of Belacqua in "Fingal"; like Belacqua, the persona wishes to be back in the caul, and, like him, the persona deserts his companion. "Sanies II" refers to Dante and Beatrice, recalling the Dantean origin of Belacqua himself.

Both Sanies poems are reflected in a sentence from "Yellow": "This dribble of time, like sanies into a bucket." The persona of "Enueg I," like Belacqua, has ruined feet; he sees Democritus, whom Belacqua calls to mind. The Irish countryside is similarly described in "Walking Out" and "Serena II." Thus, *Echo's Bones* and *More Pricks Than Kicks* are the earliest of Beckett's published works to reveal an interrelationship. On the other hand, Lawrence Harvey has shown that *Echo's Bones* is closer to the unpublished *Dream* than to *More Pricks*. At the time Beckett published the poems in book-form, he evidently wanted to weaken connecting links.

Difficulty of comprehension was of little concern to Beckett. In a poem written in 1931, but not included in *Echo's Bones*, "Casket of Pralinen for a Daughter of a Dissipated Mandarin" [the Smeraldina], we find the lines:

> Oh I am ashamed
> of all clumsy artistry
> I am ashamed of presuming
> to arrange words
> of everything but the ingenuous fibres
> that suffer honestly.

And yet these lines occur in a poem where the words are arranged with great artifice, where suffering is all but buried in obscure references to literature, painting, and personal experience. The lines would seem to indicate some conflict between one esthetic ambition of Beckett and his highly mannered production of this decade, which is seen in a sentence from a 1938 review: "The time is perhaps not altogether too green for the vile suggestion that art has nothing to do with clarity, does not dabble in the clear and does not make clear." Beckett defines artistic probity as "a minimum of rational interference." Extrapolating back to *Echo's Bones*, we might guess that Beckett allowed images to flow up from his unconscious, that he cast these images in various rhythms and forms, and that he gave no care to

27

the understanding of his readers. But a series of images, however arresting, is not a poem in which image, syntax, and rhythm are integrated into a whole that is more profound than the sum of its parts.

In *Echo's Bones* as in *More Pricks Than Kicks* Beckett's sophistication cloaks his metaphysical uneasiness and human compassion. In both genres he was striving for a distinctive style, which would cover an anguished response to human agony. Beckett has judged his poems harshly as "the work of a very young man with nothing to say and the itch to make." Yet Lawrence Harvey's exegesis reveals that the young poet, like the young fiction-writer, had almost too much to say but was afraid to say it without guidance from authors in several languages and several centuries. It was only when Beckett conceived of a character who was "a strict non-reader" that he produced his first work that can be read pleasurably without arcane knowledge—*Murphy*.

2.

WHAT MORPH?

IN FALL, 1933, a few months after the death of his father, Samuel Beckett left the family home at Foxrock, never to return to Ireland to live. He spent the next three years in London, highly conscious of being an exile, though the exile was self-imposed. His first occupation was to revise and collect the ten stories that were published in 1934 as *More Pricks Than Kicks*. He then turned to writing, revising, and arranging the thirteen poems that were published in 1935 as *Echo's Bones and Other Precipitates*. During this period he visited a doctor friend who worked at a mental institution located on the border of Kent and Surrey. Beckett's reaction to this experience was the seed of *Murphy*, written over the next year or so and published in 1938, when Beckett was no longer living in London.

MURPHY

Murphy is a funny book in which we laugh at and with the hero. *Murphy* has been analyzed as a Menippean satire by Robert Harrison, but, unlike most satire, it implies no norm of conduct. *Murphy* has been illuminated as a novel of ideas by Samuel Mintz and David Hesla, but we can enjoy it without knowledge of its philosophic influences. *Murphy* contains two deaths and a morgue scene, and yet it is irresistibly comic because the narrator has control of his irony. The narrator moves us methodically through space and time, while his hero approaches the stasis of death. The book moves us as well as amuses us, in spite of the narrator's irony.

Like Beckett in 1935, Murphy is an impecunious Irishman self-exiled in London. Not until we are halfway through the book does the narrator inform us: "All the puppets in this book whinge sooner or later, except Murphy, who is not a puppet." In E. M. Forster's terminology, Murphy is a round character, whereas the other characters are deliberately flat. It is the narrator who rounds Murphy out, while keeping him at some comic distance.

Unlike the narrator of *More Pricks Than Kicks*, who explains his narration by his friendship with Belacqua, *Murphy*'s narrator never intrudes in his own person. Rather, he poses as the traditionally omniscient narrator of nineteenth-century fiction, and his omniscience ranges not only over his characters but over many areas of knowledge, so that he sends us scurrying to atlases, biographies, dictionaries, encyclopedias, familiar and unfamiliar quotations. The more we learn, the funnier we find the book, and yet there is a basic level of humor that almost anyone can enjoy, as in our first view of Murphy: "He sat naked in his rocking-chair of undressed teak, guaranteed not to crack, warp, shrink, corrode, or creak at night." Who would not smile at the image of an undressed man on undressed teak, described by a series of insurances rising to an improbable climax?

Though the narrator is not a persona, his presence is felt throughout the novel. He comments continually on action—"So all things hobble together for the only possible"; on character—"Liberal to a fault, that was Murphy"; on dialogue—"Scratch an old man and find a Quintilian." He acknowledges that he expurgates, accelerates, improves, and reduces Celia's account of how she met Murphy, Neary's account of why he left Cork, and Cooper's account of how he found (and lost) Murphy in London. The narrator summarizes Ticklepenny's autobiographical revelations to Murphy, and he informs us when Miss Carridge is lying. The narrator tells us that certain phrases are chosen with an eye on the censor, and others with an eye on the depravable reader. He asks the compositor for a particular type-face. He prefaces two chapters with epigrams, one in Latin and one in French. He belittles the English language he uses so adroitly through pun, catalogue, sound play, cliché, paradox. Occasionally, he falters over a word—particularly "pleasure."

Once only, the narrator addresses the reader directly: "Oh, monster of humanity and enlightenment, despairing of a world in which the only natural allies are the fools and knaves, a mankind sterile with self-complicity, admire Bom feeling dimly for once what you feel acutely so often, Pilate's hands rustling in his mind." This extraordinary sentence groups us, monstrous and civilized readers, with sadistic Bom and Christ's murderer by complicity.

The narrator has at his disposal an impressive amount of information. Not only is he conversant with his characters' obsessions—Murphy's astrology and chess, Neary's pre-Socratic affinities, Mr. Kelly's kite-flying, Miss Rosie Dew's spiritualism, and the various syndromes of the inmates of the Magdalen Mental Mercyseat—but he refers to philosophers, poets, painters, and psychiatrists. More often than not, this display of learning functions contextually. At the very beginning of the book, for example, the narrator describes naked Murphy in his rocker, assimilating a cuckoo-clock with a street cry that sounds like Latin: *"Quid pro quo! Quid pro quo!"* But this is also a summary of the macrocosm from which Murphy wishes to retreat—a world made of timepieces, sexual betrayals, and mercantile exchange.

Or, in the first direct discourse of the book (which the narrator relates in flashback) Neary affirms: "Murphy, all life is figure and ground." And Murphy retorts: "But a wandering to find home." Throughout the book, there will be tension between this external view of life as a painting and the internal search for true being, the only human home.

Like omniscient narrators of the traditional novel, the narrator of *Murphy* situates the story in time and place, but he does so with such meticulous and unnecessary exactitude that his account becomes a parody of preoccupation with time and place. (Beckett himself insured the accuracy of his narration with close attention, as he wrote, to the calendar and to the London in which he was living. And in order to be sure that Neary could dash his head against the buttocks of the statue of Cuchulain in Dublin, Beckett wrote his friend A. J. Leventhal to "measure the height from the ground of Cuchulain's arse.") The narrator leads us a merry, Keystone-cops chase through Dublin and London, but sooner rather than later he moves us back to Murphy.

Murphy is one of the commonest Irish names, but Beckett's Murphy puns on Greek *morph*, form, and Beckett's Murphy suggests a basic form for subsequent Beckett heroes. Without Christian name, legitimate occupation, or fixed abode, Murphy is free to explore his inner being. We cannot follow his exploration, since the narrator controls our knowledge of Murphy, and the narrator spends most of the book outside Murphy's mind. Though the narrator tells us nothing of Murphy's origin, he affirms that Murphy's birth-cry was "off the note," and he prophesies: "His rattle will make amends." Though the narrator tells us little of Murphy's appearance (he has sallow skin and dull gull's eyes), he itemizes his belongings—a bag, a rocking-chair, and the worn clothes he wears when not in that chair or in bed with Celia. Birth-cry and belongings present a comic surface, but they offer us a subsurface understanding of Murphy.

Piecemeal, the narrator informs us of Murphy's appreciable education: one-time amateur theologian and Latinist; one-time traveler in Paris, Toulon, and Hanover; one-time owner of books, pictures, postcards, musical scores and instruments; one-time student at the feet of Pythagorean Neary in Cork; a connoisseur of cathedrals, painting, and music; an amateur of mathematics, philosophy, and neurology; a devotee of astrology; an accomplished chess player; a collector of jokes; a discriminating linguist, suiting his vocabulary to his audience, and correctly deriving "cretin" from "Christian," "gas" from "chaos." Though a "strict non-reader" in 1935, the unmentioned year of the events of *Murphy*, Murphy has done his share of reading in the past.

Alone in the world except for an uncle in Holland, Murphy cherishes his loneness. Unemployed, Murphy cherishes his indolence. Murphy has been deeply impressed by Dante's Belacqua and, like Beckett's Belacqua, Murphy finds that women are the main obstacle to his retreat into the pure life of the mind. But Belacqua's several women crystallize into Murphy's Celia Kelly, whose name is redundant of heaven: Latin *caelum*, sky. On the other hand, Celia's grandfather makes a French pun upon her name—Celia, *s'il y a*—if there is indeed celestial bliss to be found in her company.

Murphy's mind and body are in conflict over Celia, who has streetwalked her way into the affections of the latter. "The part of him that he hated craved for Celia, the part that he loved shrivelled up at the thought of her." Finding that she cannot accommodate both Murphy and her profession, Celia urges Murphy to seek a profession of his own. She does this through the power of her "serenade, nocturne, albada." Though Murphy attempts resistance, he bows to the pleas of the whore armed with a horoscope. Celia triumphs over Murphy's indolence and the resistance of his language—"each word obliterated, before it had time to make sense, by the word that came next; so that in the end she did not know what had been said." But Celia's is a Pyrrhic victory. On the very day that Murphy is offered a position at the Magdalen Mental Mercyseat—October 11, 1935—their neighbor slits his throat. The "old boy" dies, and Celia never recovers from his wound. When Murphy departs for work at the Mercyseat, Celia intuits that he is leaving her forever: the *Magdalen* Mercyseat will apparently replace the *whore* Celia. And yet, like Mary Magdalen, Celia undergoes a kind of conversion. On October 16, Celia moves into the "old boy's" room, and there behaves

33

in Murphyan mode, naked in his rocking chair, seeking to retreat into her mind. When the Irish posse moves in on Celia, she enunciates a view of Murphy that resembles his own. As the others speak, Celia allows involuntary memory to claim her. The narrator calls Celia "intact," but he apparently groups her with the "puppets." She is an appealing puppet who looks almost human in certain lights. Particularly moving is her last glimpse of Murphy alive. Having left Celia for his job, Murphy is ridiculed and imitated by some neighborhood boys. "[Celia] watched [Murphy] multiplied in their burlesque long after her own eyes could see him no more." Her eyes do not resemble those of a puppet as they watch the puppetization of Murphy.

The other puppets are all painted surface and mechanical gesture, whether in Dublin or in London. Neary, Wylie, and Miss Counihan are mobile and voluble in their Murphy-hunt, each caricatured by an obsession and by mannered dialogue. When the hunt becomes a collective safari, they fire disjunctive aphorisms at each other. Cooper, in contrast, who serves as their bloodhound, utters only twenty-nine words in the whole novel, but he moves through many miles, spurred by his deep-seated and long-standing acathisia.

Cooper, the consonants of whose name suggest Greek *copros*, dung, is the converse of Murphy. Not only do the Greek roots of their names diverge, but Murphy's mind is balanced by Cooper's body. Murphy loves to sit in his rocker, but Cooper never sits. Murphy avoids wearing a hat because it awakens poignant memories of the caul, but Cooper never removes his bowler. Murphy never touches alcohol, but Cooper thrives on it. Murphy speaks lavishly (in spite of Suk's attribution of silence to him); Cooper is monosyllabic and a gifted mime: "The skill is really extraordinary with which analphabetes, especially those of Irish education, circumvent their dread of verbal commitments." Murphy pens an elegant last testament, whereas Cooper is illiterate. As Murphy in his interiority is the ancestor of

34

Beckett's subsequent heroes, Cooper seems to be their physical progenitor.

Outside the safari, a paler group of puppets has direct contact with Murphy, but they are not affected by him. On Friday, October 11, 1935, Murphy approaches a chandler who advertised for a smart boy, and who derides Murphy, as does his "semi-private convenience" and his "eldest waste product." Murphy tries to revive his shaken morale with a combination of lunch and fraud, bending a waitress to his purpose. His success in this enterprise is mitigated by the attack of Austin Ticklepenny, "the merest pawn in the game between Murphy and his stars." Once a Dublin pot poet, Ticklepenny is now an attendant at the Magdalen Mental Mercyseat, where Murphy soon offers to replace him. After this day of head-on collisions in the macrocosm, Murphy seeks peace in the Cockpit of Hyde Park, but there puppet Miss Rosie Dew conscripts him to guard her dachshund Nelly, who promptly devours all but one of Murphy's ill-gotten lunch biscuits. This adventure-crammed day causes Murphy to enter the MMM with even more pleasure than he has anticipated.

That institution houses its own grotesque puppets—a Dr. Killiecrankie who literally cranks and kills, Bim and Bom Clinch named after the Stalinist clowns who, in Beckett's story "Yellow," inspired Belacqua's bravado in the face of death. From the lunatic background that seeded Beckett's novel, only one patient is singled out: the schizoid Mr. Endon, whose name is Greek for "within," and whose "psychosis [is] so limpid and imperturbable that Murphy felt drawn to it as Narcissus to his fountain." But though Neary had earlier called Murphy a "schizoidal spasmophile," the truly schizoid Mr. Endon remains as cool as the fountain to Murphy.

On Murphy's night of duty Mr. Endon defeats him in their final Fabian chess-game. Though Murphy plays white, it is Mr. Endon who succeeds in retreating. Conquered and on his knees, Murphy contemplates Mr. Endon, and comes to the realization that he can never attain the pure mentality of these "microcosmopolitans." Murphy leaves the wards "without reluctance and without relief." After dropping his clothes along the way, he lays his body down and tries to summon creatures to his mind, but he can manage only fragments. He retreats to the rocking chair in the warmth of his garret, intending to rock a little, then rejoin Celia for serenade, nocturne, albada. At this point the narrator describes Murphy in the same phrases as at the beginning of the book. We last see Murphy as we saw him first, naked in his rocking chair, trying to retire into his mind, and identical sentences create the distribution of light for that mind. The book life of the only non-puppet has a neat circularity.

Chapter eleven closes: "The gas went on in the w.c., excellent gas; superfine chaos. Soon his body was quiet." A sentence derived from Murphy's mind is followed by a sentence of apparent observation. Together, the two sentences imply that Murphy returns to the chaos from which all being emerges. Between chapters 11 and 12 of the book, the gas explodes in Murphy's heating apparatus, and he is burned to death—"A classical case of misadventure." The narrator avoids direct confrontation with death; both Murphy and the "old boy" die between scenes.

No one sees Murphy die, but the fictional puppets see him dead. The hunters trap their quarry as a charred corpse. No one sheds a tear for Murphy. Celia recognizes him by the birthmark on his right buttock, and the coroner remarks: "How beautiful in a way . . . birthmark, deathmark, I mean, rounding off the life, somehow, don't you think, full circle." The birthmark rounds off the Celia-Murphy relationship as well, since it is this same birthmark she notices when we first see them together. While the others go their ways, Celia returns to her grandfather and her trade. Only Cooper is noticeably changed by Murphy's death: he can remove his hat, and he can sit. He combines the two actions by sitting on his hat.

Murphy's testament—an incongruous document addressed to a nonexistent Mrs. Murphy—has specified that his remains be flushed down the toilet of the Abbey Theatre, Dublin, "if possible during the performance of a piece." The resonance is excremental; the life of the body is a turd to be flushed away.

Cooper is entrusted with Murphy's ashes. However, Cooper does not even reach London, much less Dublin. Lured by the nearest bar, he soon uses the package of Murphy's ashes as a missile, whereupon others seize upon it as a football. When the wrapping bursts open, "the body, mind and soul of Murphy were freely distributed over the floor of the saloon." In the final, thirteenth chapter of *Murphy*, Celia and her grandfather are back in Hyde Park, and Murphy's name does not cross their lips.

Sad end notwithstanding, *Murphy* is an indomitably funny novel. Its plot is improbably funny in the pointlessness of earnest purpose and careful choice of chance encounter. Its characters are variously funny, endowed with physical quirks and idiosyncratic modes of expression. Above all, the narrator of *Murphy*—the prodigiously omniscient narrator—is funny, through misquotation, incongruity, linguistic play, and ironic distance. But there are vital chinks in the narrator's irony—all the more vital because they are rare.

Murphy is such a funny book that its first reviewers overlooked its seriousness. An exception was Dylan Thomas, who wrote: "It is serious because it is, mainly, the study of a complex and oddly tragic character who cannot reconcile the unreality of the seen world with the reality of the unseen, and who, through scorn and neglect of 'normal' society, drifts into the society of the certified abnormal in his search for 'a little world.'"

Starting with Samuel Mintz, Beckett critics have located *Murphy*'s seriousness in chapter 6, which describes Murphy's mind, and which conceals considerable philosophic background. Chapter 6 begins with a distorted quotation from Spinoza, and it continues with a blend of Descartes and Geulincx, though none of the three philosophers is mentioned by name (in that chapter). Spinoza wrote in his *Ethics* of the intellectual love with which God loves himself, but the narrator replaces God with Murphy: "*Amor intellectualis quo Murphy se ipsum amat*"—the intellectual love with which Murphy loves himself. Murphy's intellectual love does not make him a philosophic idealist, like his fellow-countryman Berkeley. Murphy is willing to concede the existence of the material world. Similarly, Murphy's self-love does not tease him with the central problem of seventeenth-century philosophy—how mind and body communicate. Descartes located the communication mechanism in the pineal gland, Geulincx in an occasion for God's miracle. But Murphy simply finds the problem of little interest.

What does interest Murphy passionately is *his* mind, which he pictures as a hermetically sealed sphere divided into three different zones: 1) the light zone contains forms drawn from the material world, but these forms are entirely subject to his imaginative manipulation; 2) the half-light zone contains unparallelled forms for his pure contemplation—a state that the narrator designates as "Belacqua bliss"; 3) the dark zone contains a flux of forms, where "he was not free, but a mote in the dark of absolute freedom." In that dark alone, the mind approaches the will-lessness, differently dear to Geulincx and Proust. Only in that dark can consciousness approach being, the barest and therefore purest form of life. Murphy wills this will-lessness, but the very effort defies the narrator's powers of description.

Moreover, the effort to will-lessness is rarely, if ever, successful. The Magdalen Mental Mercyseat tempts Murphy precisely because he is unable to remain in the microcosm of his mind. That mind is explored in chapter 9 (as well as 6), where Murphy enters the Mercyseat, and this is the book's second chapter to be preceded by an epigram: "*Il est difficile à celui qui vit hors du monde de ne pas rechercher les siens.*" (It is difficult for one who lives outside of the world not to seek his own kind.) Malraux' sentence comments on a committed terrorist in a novel called *The Human Condition,* but Beckett applies the sentence to Murphy, committed to the microcosm of his mind, and terrorized by the macrocosm of the world. Because Murphy strives to live outside the world, he seeks his own kind among the "microcosmopolitans" of the Mercyseat. But the search ends in failure. Murphy escapes from *the* outer world in the Mercyseat, but the Mercyseat is still *an* outer world, in which Mr. Endon alone achieves within-inness.

Mr. Endon's retreating triumph in the chess-game signals Murphy's defeat in his commitment to the microcosm of his mind. Murphy lays down his king, and sinks his head in his arms. Gradually, all images fade from his mind, and he is vouchsafed a view of Nothing—"the Nothing, than which in the guffaw of the Abderite naught is more real." But humankind, as T. S. Eliot observed, cannot bear very much reality, and especially of the reality which is Nothing, as Beckett will imply again and again in later works.

Murphy's brief perception of Nothing becomes his swan song. He puts away the chess set, he tucks Mr. Endon into bed, and he looks long and searchingly into Mr. Endon's eyes. "Murphy heard words demanding so strongly to be spoken that he spoke them . . .

> 'the last at last seen of him
> himself unseen by him
> and of himself.' "

The fourteen words condense to three—last, see, him. The barely coherent words belong to a compulsive voice, which talks on into syntactical clarity. But we can hardly forget this fourteen-word hint of unmediated interiority—indefinite, unadorned, repetitive, musical, and anguished.

Through the good offices of Herbert Read, *Murphy* was published in London in 1938, at approximately the time that

39

Beckett decided to live permanently in Paris. The novel was not unfavorably reviewed, and James Joyce pleased Beckett by reciting the account of the disposal of Murphy's ashes. With the help of his French friend Alfred Péron, Beckett set about translating his novel into French.

In 1938 and 1939 Beckett wrote a dozen poems in French, his first creative work in that language. Quite short, with brief lines and few images, the poems do not form a whole but are a series of meditations. In contrast to the geographic and literary range of the English poems, the French verse is wholly original in form. As Lawrence Harvey has noted, the wandering of *Echo's Bones* is almost completely replaced by stasis in the French poems. And yet, form and atmosphere seem to follow from the short poems of *Echo's Bones*.

Though the group has no title, five of the poems have names, three after places. All but one of the poems are written in the free unpunctuated verse lines of *Echo's Bones*, but rhythm rather than image determines the verse line. Enjambement leads to ambiguity, since there is no guiding punctuation. Five of the poems have a first-person narrator, and almost all deal with impermanence, death, and love. Several poems imply a Murphyan conflict between macrocosm and microcosm. In the last poem (numbered XIII when published), as at the end of *Echo's Bones*, the persona broods about death. In the English volume death brings asylum, in the French cessation from suffering. But neither volume closes on a death wish, for life and love remain in tension with any such wish.

At about the time he wrote these poems—Beckett's first serious creative venture in French—he composed a still unpublished critical piece, "The Two Needs." Reminded of the essay (no longer in his possession) in 1971, Beckett still named these needs as 1) man's unfulfillable need for fulfillment and 2) man's need to continue to need. From this combination, the critical essay derives "a vain cry, a series

40

of pure questions, a work of art." The essay suggests that Beckett in the late 1930's desired to commit himself to a private art springing from his private need, and the arrogant tone of the essay indicates satisfaction with such élitist art. At the same time, his poems express a more direct and intuitive reaction to artistic need, and they betray the demands of the world upon the artist and upon the man. All Beckett's subsequent work posits "The Two Needs," not only for the artist but for every man.

After his 1933 departure from Ireland Beckett visited his widowed mother at least once a year, and the outbreak of World War II surprised him in Ireland. He managed to return at once to Paris, through a darkened Normandy. When the Nazis approached Paris in June, 1940, he joined the general exodus. In Vichy he saw Joyce for the last time. He traveled as far south as Arcachon, but by October, 1940, he was back in occupied Paris, where he entered a Resistance network, through his friend Alfred Péron. Beckett belittles his wartime activity—collating information about Nazi troop movements, for transmission to London—but he nevertheless risked his life in that activity. When Péron was captured (to die shortly after his return from a German concentration camp), Beckett and his wife went into hiding, moving stealthily south. Like other refugees, they came to rest in the mountain village of Roussillon in unoccupied France. During 1942-44, living in a single room, Beckett worked in the fields during the day. At night he wrote *Watt*. To preserve his sanity, Beckett traced Watt's path to insanity.

WATT

Watt reflects Beckett's living situation more obliquely than does either *More Pricks Than Kicks* or *Murphy*. *More Pricks* is specifically set in the Dublin area, where Beckett was living when he wrote many of the stories. *Murphy* is largely set in London, where Beckett was living when he

41

wrote that novel. These two books depict a recognizable surface reality. Belacqua and Murphy, idiosyncratic though they are, move through external reality. But as Beckett's French poems of 1938-39 turned inward from the earlier English poems, *Watt* turns inward from *Murphy*. While Beckett was exiled in the Vaucluse, he set *Watt* in an abstracted Ireland. The spareness of Watt's world may reflect the limitations of Beckett's world, far from family, friends, and books. *Watt*'s world quite certainly reflects Watt's mind, in the tradition of the Symbolist soul-landscape, mentioned in the Addenda to *Watt*.

Watt's soul, like that of Murphy, seems to be located in his mind. Rather than a place—Murphy's three zones—Watt's mind resembles a perpetual-motion machine, energized by the scantiest data of the senses. Empiricism and rationality are Watt's household gods, even without a house to hold them. Strict adherence to these gods alienates Watt from society, even before he undertakes his perilous journey to Mr. Knott's establishment. Once there Watt is estranged from Mr. Knott by his unshakable dedication to empiricism and rationality. As Jacqueline Hoefer first suggested, Watt is a logical positivist in a domain at once illogical and negative.

Watt is a novel about a rationalist who undertakes service in Mr. Knott's irrational establishment. All his life Watt has reduced meaning to language, and at Mr. Knott's establishment his mind-machine continues its momentum. Since language is both a tool and a product of his rational mind, the book runs rational language into the ground. Gone is the polished prose of *More Pricks* and *Murphy*, to be replaced by efforts at exhaustive and exhausting clarity. Instead of a recondite vocabulary, the same words are used and reused in a novel that is stuffed with repetition. Certain phrases recur like formulaic chants, and others din through paragraphs or even pages. The prose of *Watt* abounds in constructions more suitable to logic than to fiction—lists, series, alternations, hypotheses, permutations and combinations.

Phrases of explanation—"One of the reasons for that was this"—alternate with phrases of illustration—"To mention only" or "Add to this." The conjunctions "because" and "for" are qualified by "but" or contradicted by "not" and "never." But then the very names of protagonist and antagonist, Watt and Knott, are part of the repetitive play of language. WHAT always dissolves into KNOT or NOT.

Watt is a maddening book to read because of its pages of meticulous enumeration. We are impatient with the pedantic prose because there is more to the book, and we want to get on with its moreness. The novel opens on Mr. Hackett, who reminds Mr. Nixon of Watt. And with reason. Mr. Hackett, like Watt, depends for information on the evidence of his senses, from which his mind moves in logical steps, and since we follow the workings of those senses and of that slow mind, the book's beginning sparkles comically.

A comic introduction of Watt leads to questions and guesses on the part of his observers. Watt is not only a reasoner himself (though we do not know that yet), but a cause of reason in others. Without warning, the narrator leads us away from the observers to follow Watt through description, dialogue, permutations and combinations, song (with music), reasoning, and Arsene's twenty-three-page monologue, which we later learn Watt hears "by bits." After Part I of *Watt*, the body of the book intersperses the minutiae of reason with passages of lyricism or comedy. About one-third of the book is devoted to lists, sequences, alternations, logical possibilities, genealogies, and an academic investigation. On first reading, *Watt* seems to be an example of imitative form: madden the reader with reason in order to show the madness of reason.

At one level—probably the most obvious—this *is* Beckett's intention. Moreover, as John Mood has shown, the reasoning is imperfect. Watt seeks to encompass the world by reason, but his reason is faulty or incomplete, at least as transcribed by the narrator, Sam, who is himself incomplete in his enumerations. Sam as writer builds a symmetrical edifice to house Watt's mental quest. According to Sam, Watt divided his story into four parts, which he told in the order ii, i, iv, iii, but Sam has rearranged them in the chronological order we read: i—Watt's approach to and arrival at Mr. Knott's house; ii—Watt's service on the ground floor of Mr. Knott's house; iii—Watt's service on the first floor of Mr. Knott's house; iv—Watt's departure from Mr. Knott's house. Each of the first three parts contains a long digression from Watt's adventures, and each of these digressions is a narrative within the main narrative: Arsene's monologue in Part i, Watt's account of the Lynch clan in Part ii, Arthur's story of Mr. Louit's report in Part iii; Part iv is followed by Sam's Addenda that epigrammatically recapitulate various motifs of the book. Part i opens and Part iv closes on a lively surface of social satire. Part i opens at a tram stop, and Part iv closes at a railway station; a journey is an old metaphor for life, and Watt's significant life—his exposure to Mr. Knott—is bounded by these terminals. In Parts i and iv, not yet and no longer at Mr. Knott's house, Watt suffers physical injury at the hands of respectable members of society. In Parts i and iv, Watt is an offense to common sense, but in Parts ii and iii, on Mr. Knott's home ground, Watt is offended by uncommon non-sense.

Beneath these symmetries lies considerable variety. Though Sam imposes chronology on Watt's account, he himself violates chronology. Part iii opens and closes on Watt's relation to Sam, which postdates the main story. The opening pages of Part iii present the friendship of Sam and Watt, and we witness Watt's narration of the end of his service at Mr. Knott's house, which takes place in a fenced area between the separate gardens of Sam and Watt. Though it is never explicitly stated, the gardens are evidently on the grounds of a mental asylum: Sam wears a uniform, he and Watt live in mansions (Boswell's word for the cells of Bedlam), they have attendants, and they have "no truck with the other scum." The opening sentence of

44

Part III informs us that Watt has been transferred to a new pavilion, while Sam remains behind in the old one. The two meet by chance on a sunny windy day, and they approach one another through convenient holes in their respective fences. It is unclear how often they meet, Watt walking and talking backward, and Sam doing his best to follow steps and words. While they walk, with hands on one another's shoulders, Sam listens to Watt's account of his second or closing period at Mr. Knott's house, before hero and writer part forever. Part III not only violates chronology; it presents our last tragic view of a rational hero in an irrational world, and it provides the rationale for Sam's book.

Midway through the book, the narrator informs us: "For all that I know on the subject of Mr. Knott and of all that touched Mr. Knott, and on the subject of Watt, and of all that touched Watt, came from Watt, and from Watt alone." Earlier, the narrator's presence is betrayed through question marks, footnotes, and predictions of what "will be described please God at greater length, at another time." Some two-thirds of the way through the book, in Part III, the narrator reveals that he, Sam, is the writer. But Sam points out that, although he heard Watt's story from Watt himself, and took careful notes at the time (or times) of narration, there may be many a slip between Sam's book and Watt's lips. Watt may have added to or subtracted from events. Watt's memory was perhaps faulty, as his delivery surely was—rapid and low in utterance, careless in grammar and syntax. Watt's narration took place at increasingly long intervals, and his speech became increasingly inverted, so that Sam's comprehension may have been warped, as his hearing was certainly dimmed. Watt's possibilities of misstatement are many, as are those of Sam.

"So much depends on the accuracy of the record," exclaims Mr. Louit in Arthur's story as recalled by Watt and transcribed by Sam. And Sam's own record is of questionable accuracy. He claims to have all his information from Watt, but he presents scenes from which Watt is absent. The resemblance between Watt's style and his own is highly suspicious; both express themselves with inordinate formality, reducing things to their names, reasoning their way through hypotheses, to arrive at no conclusion—at Nothing. Narrator Watt and Scribe Sam are both in mental institutions when their communication takes place. All these factors erode "the accuracy of the record."

And yet, the novel is overpowering in its impression of authenticity. Questions, quotations, footnotes, disjunctions, hiatuses, and the Addenda foster our faith in Sam as Watt's scribe. On the other hand, Sam lures us into the book with an appearance of authorial detachment. Only at the end do we grasp the pattern: certain men leave the workaday world to seek service in the establishment of Mr. Knott. Theirs is a mysterious call, and they fulfill it variously. Arsene and Arthur are sociable and loquacious; Erskine and Micks are active and terse; Walter and Vincent are beyond recollection. Watt is dutiful, impersonal, and incurably nominalistic. Any logical construction of words will serve to answer the pun on his name—WHAT.

Sam does not often favor us with direct quotation of Watt's words, but he is generous with irrelevant circumstantial information about Watt. He quotes Mr. Nixon on Watt, who presents his debtor as red-nosed, homeless, truthful, and gentle. Watt is an experienced traveler, probably a university man, certainly impecunious, and rigidly a milk-drinker. Through the course of the novel, Watt's appearance takes form for us; his hair is reddish gray, his ears protrude, he has a vacant look. He rarely closes his eyes, but he sees fairly well when he focuses. His wounds heal slowly or not at all. He wears a once-yellow bowler and a once-green coat with nine buttons; on one foot is a brown boot that is too large for him, and on the other a brownish shoe that is too small; he attempts to compensate by wearing two socks with the boot. Watt has an eccentric way of walking and an extraordinary way of smiling—

actions to which he has applied his analytic powers. His past, habits, and education are imparted to us piecemeal: his father is dead, he has had at least two romances, he has been close to suicide. Watt affirms nothing of himself. He picks his nose but never uses a handkerchief; his virility is waning; and he smokes cigars. Watt hates earth and sky, sun and moon, but he is partial to rats, the wind, Mrs. Gorman, and venerable Saxon words. He is ignorant of painting and physics, but seems familiar with music. He knows his clouds and is a very fair linguist. However, these incongruous characteristics figure only obliquely in the plot, which hinges on Watt's unconquerable mind.

Watt is first introduced as "a solitary figure," and solitary he remains throughout the book. Slow to move, he swiftly dominates the narrative. Even before we know Watt, we see his effect on others: he inspires abuse from the conductor and the porter, conjectures from the Nixons and Mr. Hackett, courtesy from Mr. Evans, efforts at conversion from Mr. Spiro, and violence from Lady McCann. After Watt leaves Mr. Knott's house, he arouses a glance from an ass or goat, courtesy from Mr. Case, an accidental blow from the door kicked open by Mr. Nolan, a solicitous dousing from Mr. Gorman and Mr. Nolan, a series of questions from one and all, and the final thumbnail portrait by Mr. Gorman: "Is it the long wet dream with the hat and bags?" Except, perhaps for Mrs. Gorman (no noticeable relation to Mr. Gorman), Watt arouses confidence in no one, least of all Sam (no noticeable relation to the paralyzed progenitor of several Lynches). Sam's greeting to Watt may be taken as a comment on the entire quest: "Why, Watt, that is a nice state you have got yourself into, to be sure."

We see Watt through the words and actions of several characters, but only Sam introduces us into Watt's mind. Watt's very first words, as reported by Sam, reveal the logic of his language. Having seated himself in the train, back to the engine, Watt observes a porter wheeling a can from one end of the station platform to the other, and then another can in the opposite direction. "He is sorting cans," is Watt's instant deduction, without reference to the fact that this was the very porter who has just knocked him down. Then Watt amplifies the possibilities, "Or perhaps it is a punishment for disobedience, or some neglect of duty."

In his first encounter with Mr. Knott's premises, Watt behaves similarly. Having found the front door locked, he tries the back door; having found the back door locked, he tries the front door again. Finding the front door still locked, Watt tries the back door again, and inexplicably finds it open. But the word "inexplicably" is not in Watt's vocabulary, and two possible explanations immediately occur to him, which are meticulously detailed by Sam.

A few minutes later, in Mr. Knott's kitchen, Watt finds himself in the presence of Arsene, again inexplicably. This time, however, Watt ventures no explanation, but begins a rhythmic reverie that predicts the quality of his experience at Mr. Knott's house. Though Watt will try to name and explain phenomena at Mr. Knott's house, his efforts will come to nothing, as in the italicized section of the following dense sentence:

> But [Watt] found it strange to think, of these little changes of scene, the little gains, the little losses, the thing brought, the thing removed, the light given, the light taken, and all the vain offerings to the hour, strange to think of all these little things that cluster round the comings, and the stayings, and the goings, *that he would know nothing of them, nothing of what they had been, as long as he lived, nothing of when they came, of how they came, and how it was then, compared with before, nothing of how long they stayed, of how they stayed, and what difference that made, nothing of when they went, of how they went, and how it was then, compared with before, before they came, before they went.*

In short, Watt finds it strange to think of Nothing, but that is what confronts him at Mr. Knott's house.

48

Of traumatic impact upon Watt is the incidence of the Galls, which occurs early in his stay. When Watt answers a knock at the door, he sees two men arm in arm; the younger of the two says: "We are the Galls, father and son, and we are come, what is more, all the way from town, to choon the piano." Voluntarily, then, Mr. Gall, Jr. precludes a good many Whats; he announces his name, his residence, his function. There is no necessity for the operation of Watt's analytic powers, but the momentum of his mind is not arrested by mere lack of necessity, and he begins to hypothesize about the blindness of the elder man, the veracity of the younger man, and his own temerity in admitting them on their face value to the music-room. After a rhythmic duet, the two men leave, but their visit lingers on in Watt's mind. Its meaning dissolves into a purely plastic content, as though Watt has moved from the light zone to the half-light in Murphy's mind. "This fragility of the outer meaning had a bad effect on Watt, for it caused him to seek for another, for some meaning of *what* had passed, in the image of *how* it had passed" (my italics). Though Watt has always formulated questions, it is only now that Watt becomes his name. The Galls, too, are aptly named, bitter as gall to Watt, since they forecast the quality of all events at Mr. Knott's establishment—"of great formal brilliance and indeterminable purport." Doggedly, however, Watt ignores form to focus on the purport of things and events at Mr. Knott's establishment. "To explain had always been to exorcize, for Watt," and his explanations begin at the simplest level, with names and numbers. He seeks to apply words to his situation—to call a pot a pot, to call himself a man, but he is no longer able to find "semantic succour."

In partial retreat, Watt takes refuge from namelessness in sense data and logic. He concentrates on Mr. Knott's habits upon retiring and rising. Every Saturday night he prepares Mr. Knott's meals for the week, and he projects twelve possibilities of responsibility for this arrangement. Somehow Watt is instructed to feed Mr. Knott's leftovers to the hungry dog. He considers four solutions to this instruction, and fourteen objections to these solutions. He then constructs an elaborate plan to insure that a hungry dog is always on hand to eat Mr. Knott's remains. From a simple instruction is born the genealogy of the ailing Lynch clan, whose twin dwarfs, Art and Con, lead a hungry dog every evening to Mr. Knott's door. Watt's mechanical mind has enabled him to turn "a disturbance into words, he has made a pillow of old words, for a head."

In the matter of the bell in Erskine's room, however, Watt is not so fortunate. Hypotheses do not beget hypotheses with the fertility of the Lynch clan, and Watt is obliged to answer his questions empirically, entering Erskine's room without a key but "Ruse a by." Ruses, skirting reason, cause Watt to blush, and they are not worthy of Sam's narration, for Sam confines our knowledge of events to ruse-free reason, progressively more difficult as this becomes. When Watt enters Erskine's room to inspect the bell, he sees a picture of a circle and a dot. After prolonged meditation, Watt concludes that the picture is "a term in a series, like the series of Mr. Knott's dogs, or the series of Mr. Knott's men, or like the centuries that fall, from the pod of eternity." Watt decides illogically and without apparent reason that Erskine's picture belongs to a series and is therefore subject to time.

Toward the end of Watt's service on the ground floor, he is so fatigued that he allows himself two human relationships upon which he erects no rational edifices—with Mrs. Gorman and with Mr. Graves. The meaning of these names —gore man and grave—suggests their ultimate lack of solace for Watt, who reserves his waning suppositions for Mr. Knott.

When Arthur arrives, Erskine leaves, and Watt begins his service on the first floor. So tired is Watt by that time that his mind grinds out only two hypotheses about Mr. Knott: "And Mr. Knott, needing nothing if not, one, not to need, and, two, a witness to his not needing, of himself knew nothing. And so he needed to be witnessed. Not that he might know, no, but that he might not cease." Whereupon Watt, with his imperfect senses, becomes that witness of a being who has come to resemble him, in Sam's description. Watt determinedly lists his empirical evidence about Mr. Knott, whose attributes may be finitely variable, but who is at once infinity and nothing. As infinity and zero require a new mathematics, Watt requires a new mind to encompass Mr. Knott, but all he has is the old one, with its compulsion to convert sense data into the language of logic. Almost predictably, Watt hears Arsene's cautionary monologue only "by bits," whereas he has total recall of Arthur's monologue, which focuses on rational numbers—perfect cubes. (Significantly, the forms of the monologues reflect their contents: Arthur's account alternates dialogue with description, but Arsene's speech is disjunctive and associational—a foretaste of Beckett's French monologues.) Watt is brave enough to face Mr. Knott, but he cannot contemplate the void indefinitely. When Micks arrives, Watt knows that it is time to depart. Watt's facial expression is one of such vacancy that Micks recoils in horror, but Watt's mind, in contrast, is full of the old permutations and combinations. Once at the train station, Watt sees a figure on the highway, and his invincible mind goes to work on it—to no effect. Watt cannot affirm anything about the figure, by either observation or deduction. The figure grows fainter and finally disappears. In the waiting room where Watt spends the night, he is skeptical about the evidence of his ears, eyes, and nose. But dawn restores his faith; he sees a chair, a horse in a painting, flies on the windowpane—each one a member of a temporal series. Semiconscious after a blow, Watt lies on the floor and recalls phrases from a verse of Hölderlin (in German), comparing human beings in time to water over crags. It is a new insight into Watt's mind, replacing logic with poetic image.

By that time, however, we know the nature of Watt's failure. It is the failure of Western man. *Homo sapiens* ponders the imponderable.

Watt has undertaken his quest with some reluctance: he may have intended to turn back when first we see him at the facultative tram stop; in the train he turns his back on his destination; he once passed the station by being unready to descend; this time he procrastinates by lying down at the side of the road. Finally, he *does* arrive at Mr. Knott's house. He never knows how he enters it, but he *does* enter, like a knight into the Chapel Perilous, where he attacks an irrational domain with his rational mind "whatever that might mean" and with his senses "his most noble faculties." Against all reason, Watt persists in reason, learning nothing about Mr. Knott. In spite of Mr. Knott's various clothes and monotonous meals, his displacement of self and furniture, his changing appearance and incomprehensible songs, his sneering dactyls and mocking gestures—in spite of all this evidence, "Of the nature of Mr. Knott himself Watt remained in particular ignorance."

Instead of accepting the inadequacy of names, explanations, and observations at Mr. Knott's house, Watt apparently concludes that he went about it backward. At the railroad station he merely inverts distances and numbers, but in the garden of his pavilion he inverts his language, with systematic thoroughness. In Sam's last recording of Watt's speech, the pure rhythmic sound denies Watt's efforts at meaning: "On. Taw ot klat tonk? On. Tonk ot klat taw? On. Tonk ta kool taw? On. Taw ta kool tonk?" The "On" stands out amid the nonsense, to register Watt's heroic persistence, but normalization registers his tragic failure: "Knot look at Wat? No. Wat look at Knot? No. Wat talk to Knot? No. Knot talk to Wat? No." Toward the end of this speech, Watt summarizes his relation to Mr. Knott: Two men, side by side.

This, however, is a late realization, and it seems to be neither reasoned nor observed. While still on the ground

52

floor, Watt observes that he and Mr. Knott are the same height. His last words about Mr. Knott describe him putting on one shoe, which brings us circling back to Watt himself, who borrowed money from Mr. Nixon for a single boot. Neither Watt nor Mr. Knott plants both feet solidly on the ground, and Sam equates the two creatures in a verbal slip: "by Knott, I beg your pardon, by Watt."

Mr. Knott has the resonances of a deity figure, as Watt has those of Christ. Religious language threads through the book: witness, abide, transgression, forgive, mansions, seeks to prosper, first was last, turn the other cheek. Mr. Knott is surrounded by "fascia of white light." He fears animals because he knew a *canon* who was kicked by a horse, a *missionary* who was trampled by an ostrich, and a *priest* who was shat on by a dove. Mr. Knott remains in bed all day Sunday; he evidently eats fish on Friday (At least the fishwife calls on Thursday.), and he changes his sheets annually on St. Patrick's Day.

The Christ-resonances of Watt are more explicit. Sam wipes Watt's face as St. Veronica does that of Christ, and he anoints Watt as Mary Magdalen does Christ. Sam quotes Watt as enunciating clearly: "Knott, Christ, Gomorrha, Cork." And Sam compares Watt to a Bosch Christ with his crown of thorns. Sam sees himself mirrored in Watt, though he does not resemble the Bosch Christ. But suffering mankind always resembles Christ.

Most critics have dwelt on the philosophic rather than fictional aspects of *Watt*. Watt's predicament has been analyzed in the light of Wittgenstein, who concludes his *Tractatus*: "Whereof one cannot speak, thereof one must be silent." Wittgenstein was addressing himself to philosophers, but Watt is a character in a novel, who is driven to speak to Sam about what cannot be meaningfully discussed, and Sam is driven to tell Watt's story to us. Though Mr. Knott cannot be reduced to language, Watt and Sam are impelled to try. Most noticeably, they (as well as Arsene and Arthur) resort to the lists, hypotheses, and permutations and combinations that make *Watt* so annoying to read. In other parts of the book, however, their styles diverge. Watt's discourse is formal, logical, occasionally aphoristic: "Obscure keys may open simple locks, but simple keys obscure locks never." "It is by the nadir that we come, and it is by the nadir that we go, whatever that means." Sam confines his aphorisms to footnotes and Addenda, but he carries the novel's lyricism. The opening pages of Part III are rich in nature imagery, unusual rhythms, and human compassion. The account of the cannibal-rats is so horrifying because Sam situates it in a Garden of Eden, and the friendship of Watt and Sam is so moving because Sam sets it against the nonbrotherly relations of the rest of the book. Sam is a writer of some range—his rendition of bouncing dialogue, the exhaustive enumeration he shares with Watt, the lyricism of Part III, the macaronic aphorisms of the Addenda.

Sam is at once the narrator and a character of the novel. He tells us that Watt does not affirm anything of himself, and Sam in turn affirms nothing important about himself. He is Watt's mirror, but a mirror of depths. Because he sympathizes with Watt's quest, we sympathize with Watt, even as we laugh or shrug at the momentum of Watt's mind. Watt, like all of us, is a creature of words, but the words we read belong to Sam. Few words are more touching than our last glimpse of Watt, stumbling backward through brambles, falling and rising, stubbornly continuing "and from the hidden pavilions, his and mine, where by this time dinner was preparing, the issuing smokes by the wind were blown, now far apart, but now together, mingled to vanish, Sam and Watt, now apart, now together, finally merge." More subtly than Murphy and Cooper, Watt and Sam are merging forms of the Beckett hero. The first couple are mind and body; later Beckett heroes will look like Cooper (as Watt already does), but they will think somewhat like Murphy. Later Beckett heroes will reason like Watt, but they will write somewhat like Sam.

Watt is harder and more rewarding than *Murphy*, as Watt is older and more profound than Murphy. *Murphy* is irrepressibly comic, but *Watt* is intermittently comic. *Murphy* ridicules time and place by punctilious precision; *Watt* ridicules time and place by deliberate vagueness. *Murphy* pivots on Murphy, who is of prime importance to the minor characters. *Watt* revolves around Watt, who is of no importance to anybody. Yet Watt resembles Murphy. Without Christian name, profession, or fixed dwelling, both Murphy and Watt dedicate themselves to the exploration of reality. For both men, meaningful reality is attained in or through the mind. But the world impinges upon Murphy's mind, and Knott's world—the absolute infinite Nothing—impinges upon Watt's mind. Both minds arrive at a mental institution, Murphy as a sympathetic attendant, and Watt as an inmate. Murphy passes into chaos from an explosion of gas; Watt systematizes inversions, like Dante's lying soothsayers. Arsene, welcoming Watt to Mr. Knott's establishment, speaks for and of all Beckett's heroes, for and of many of his readers: "For in truth the same things happen to us all, especially to men in our situation, whatever it is, if only we chose to know it."

Men in our situation, endowed with senses and reason, feel compelled to probe the meaning of life, and the probing may replace living. Or, more accurately, living becomes probing, so that other activities are mere shards—loving, laughing, working, weeping. Though events diminish between *Murphy* and *Watt*, the residue of living seems more dense. In terms of the claims that I make for Beckett's relevance to basic human experience, *Watt* is a marked advance over *Murphy*. The younger hero is an isolate of intellectual orientation, but Watt is Everyman. "The same things happen to us all," and we react to them with only minor variations. We react to our lives by trying to understand them. Like Watt, we marshal experience into name, number, and logic. Most of us disobey Wittgenstein's injunction: we cannot be silent about what we cannot speak.

So most of us utter our own kind of nonsense. But Beckett's heroes will hone their words in an effort to cut a way to the raw experience of being. They will never quite succeed in divesting themselves of language, but we will perceive, through their efforts, that, in the words of Belacqua of *Dream*: "The reality of the individual . . . is an incoherent reality and must be expressed incoherently."

3.

THE WEAKENING STRENGTH
OF FRENCH

IMMEDIATELY after the German surrender in 1945 Beckett went to see his mother and brother in Ireland. He had planned only a short stay, but he found it difficult to return to France in the postwar chaos. Upon the advice of a doctor friend, he therefore volunteered as interpreter and storekeeper for an Irish Red Cross unit that was to set up a hospital in war-ravaged Saint-Lô in Normandy. Safe and secure himself, Beckett was soon surrounded by the wounded, the hungry, the homeless. The Saint-Lô experience evoked Beckett's last poem to be written directly in English:

> Vire will wind in other shadows
> unborn through the bright ways tremble
> and the old mind ghost-forsaken
> sink into its havoc

The poem is difficult in its concentration. Artfully constructed, it holds tragedy at a distance, and it lacks the intensity that Beckett was soon to achieve in French prose. Even through the puzzling syntax, the first two lines contrast sonically with the last two. The first two lines flow, reflective of the Vire River and, implicitly, of time's continuum. The river will flow again through sunshine and shadows of a city as yet unbuilt, a new Saint-Lô. In the last two lines the heavy consonants frame the mind, which will sink into chaos after it is forsaken by its ghosts. Saint-Lô is dead, long live a new Saint-Lô, but the individual mind lives no longer than its memories.

Though most of the Irish staff stayed on at Saint-Lô for nearly three years, Beckett returned to his Paris apartment by the end of 1945. He plunged into the most productive period of his life. Between 1946 and 1950 he wrote four stories, four novels, six poems, two plays, thirteen texts, and some art criticism. All in French.

Over two decades Beckett has been variously quoted on his shift to French (translations are mine):

> Pour faire remarquer moi. (To call attention to myself.) *transition*, 1948.

> It was a different experience from writing in English. It was more exciting for me—writing in French. Shenker, 1956.

> Parce qu'en français c'est plus facile d'écrire sans style. (In French it's easier to write without style.) Gessner, 1957.

> I said that by writing in French [Beckett] was evading some part of himself. (*Pause*.) He said yes, there were a few things about himself he didn't like, that French had the right "weakening" effect. Blau, 1960.

> When I asked [Beckett] in 1962 (as everyone seems to, sooner or later) why he switched from English to French, he replied that for him, an Irishman, French represented a form of weakness by comparison with his mother tongue. Besides, English because of its very richness holds out the temptation to rhetoric and virtuosity, which are merely words mirroring themselves complacently, Narcissus-like. The relative asceticism of French seemed more appropriate to the expression of being, undeveloped, unsupported somewhere in the depths of the microcosm. Harvey, 1962.

> To myself [Beckett said] that he was afraid of English "because you couldn't help writing poetry in it." Coe, 1964.

58

[Je] me remis à écrire—en français—avec le désir de m'appauvrir encore davantage. C'était ça le vrai mobile. (I took up writing again—in French—with the desire of impoverishing myself still further. That was the true purpose.) Janvier, 1968.

If we collate these remarks, it is evident that Beckett views French as a way to strip his language to the bare essentials of his vision.

Beckett's trend toward spareness had begun as early as the 1935 English poems. With the exception of "Arènes de Lutèce," the French poems of 1938-39 are comparably spare and concentrated. Though World War II separates Beckett's first French poems from the group of six written between 1946 and 1948, the family resemblance is marked—unpunctuated lines of unequal length; simplicity of imagery and vocabulary; sound play and repetition to establish rhythm. Again, personal experience is cast in a general mold; again, macrocosm is in tension with microcosm, and death lures the persona with its release from suffering.

"Mort de A. D." was the first to be written of the six French poems of the 1940's, while the author was still at Saint-Lô. A. D. was a tubercular friend who died there. The persona is at once outraged at time that puts an end to his friend, and victimized by that very "temps irrémissible."

Three poems of 1948 were first published in *transition*, along with Beckett's English translations. "My way is in the sand flowing" introduces a sands-of-time image, but closes on a hope for peace in the receding mist of nonbeing. "What would I do without this world faceless incurious" pits everyday life in the macrocosm against the persona's retreat into the microcosm, where, however, he seeks a kindred spirit "among the voices voiceless." An astonishingly cruel and compassionate lyric closes this triad, "I would love my love to die." Only the experienced Beckett reader can realize that the persona is wishing nonsuffering in wishing for the death of his love, even as he mourns that death. The fifth poem of the group, in five lines, offers paradoxical images of the seductive power of death, "my sole season."

In contrast to these melancholy lyrics (however controlled the melancholy) is a poem that was written at the request of Beckett's friend, the painter Bram Van Velde, but that was published in the catalogue of another painter friend, Avigdor Arikha. Remarkable in this poem is its colloquial, conversational tone. Written while Beckett was at work on the trilogy of novels, the poem uses several of the same techniques—repetition, self-contradiction, interrogation, and imperatives. The final line pits the passions of living against the calm of nonbeing: "le calme l'amour la haine le calme le calme." It is fitting that Beckett's last French poem was written in the idiom of the fiction that he had come to regard as his major work.

The French fiction is a giant stride forward in Beckett's art, but its point of departure is English *Watt.* The "exteriority" of Parts I and IV of *Watt*, with its clipped and bouncing dialogue, leads to *Mercier et Camier*, and then to the drama. The "interiority" of Parts II and especially III of *Watt*, with its disjunctive immediacy, leads to the four *nouvelles* and the trilogy of novels.

Today the continuity of Beckett's fiction is generally accepted. The French fiction, like the English, is protagonist-centered, and both languages describe quests. Belacqua's aimless wandering leads to Murphy's movement toward stasis, which leads to Watt's service at Mr. Knott's house, which leads to the futile journey of Mercier and Camier, which leads to the writing/speaking of the other French heroes. Beckett's heroes—English and French—are the same and yet not the same; they are the same in questing through their lives and in verbalizing through their quests; they are not the same through variety in events, associations, and above all words.

THE PSEUDOCOUPLE

When John Fletcher attempted to date Beckett's French works, the author wrote him: "*Mercier et Camier* was the first attempt at novel in French and cannot have preceded *Nouvelles*." But Beckett's memory was wrong— or nearly wrong. Of his four *nouvelles*, *La Fin* was written first, and half of it was published as "Suite" in the July, 1946, issue of *Les Temps Modernes*. Between July and September, 1946, Beckett wrote *Le Voyage de Mercier et Camier autour du Pot dans les Bosquets de Bondy*. This "first attempt at novel in French" preceded three of the four *nouvelles*. But very soon after the swift completion of *Le Voyage de Mercier et Camier* (in substantially the form that Beckett finally published), Beckett returned to shorter fiction, writing *L'Expulsé* between October 6 and 14, 1946; *Premier Amour* between October 28 and November 12, 1946; and starting *Le Calmant* on December 23, 1946. The trilogy of novels, two plays, and thirteen texts occupied him between 1947 and 1950. For publication in book form, Beckett reordered the *nouvelles* (omitting *Premier Amour*). Only in 1970 did he consent to publish what he had come to call *Mercier et Camier*. The abridgement of the title deprives us of a clue to the meaning of the novel. "Tourner autour du pot" is colloquial French for "to detour," and the voyage of Mercier and Camier is a series of detours from their undesignated destination. The long title situates these detours in the grove of Bondy—in colloquial French a den of thieves. But though Bondy is mentioned only once in the novel—Watt refers to "Bondy métropolitain"—the book focuses on two thieves, one of whom may be saved and the other damned. The original title thus suggests that life is a detour toward an arbitrary salvation or damnation.

More than any previous Beckett fiction, *Mercier et Camier* opens *in medias res*: "The voyage of Mercier and Camier is one I can tell if I wish, for I was with them all the time." This opening sentence is the last we hear of "I," who evi-

61

dently does want to tell about the voyage, for the telling proceeds at once. We learn almost nothing about the pre-book lives of Mercier or Camier—only that Mercier is a family man and Camier a detective—but we accompany them on the voyage that they undertake after deep deliberation, "driven by a need now clear and now obscure." Unlike their predecessor Watt, or their successors Molloy and Moran, Mercier and Camier state no goal, but their voyage becomes a quest by virtue of their tenacity. In spite of a farce of missed meetings, Mercier and Camier do meet in chapter 1, and they travel together to the end of chapter 10 (of twelve). Near the beginning Mercier declares: "Today at last after years of tergiversation, we set out for an unknown destination." When they are well on their way, Camier suggests: "Let our motto be caution and circumspection, with shies to right and left and sudden retreats, as intuition's dark promptings may require. Nor should we be afraid to halt for whole days and even weeks. We have all our life before us, all at least that's left." Still later, in a bar, the two friends lift their glasses for a toast: "Camier added, And to the success of our————. But he could not complete his wish. Help me, he said. I know no word, said Mercier, or even phrase, fit to express what we think we're in the process of trying to do." And near the end of the book, Watt explains to the couple: "I too have searched, all alone, but I thought I knew for what."

Two old men meet to take a journey that ends when they go their separate ways. An invisible narrator describes the journey as though he were there. That is the substance of Beckett's first French novel.

Like the published English novels, *Mercier et Camier* has a clearly defined structure, being divided into twelve chapters. But the structure mocks itself, for each third chapter consists of a list of events in the previous two chapters—a tersely phrased, reasonably accurate, but quixotically selected list. These lists are present in the original manuscript of the novel, and they perhaps served to help Beckett himself remember incidents whose interest is only minimal. (In the published *Mercier et Camier* Beckett lists an incident, then notes in parentheses that it was eliminated; the manuscript reveals the eliminated incident.) In the novel itself, incidents are narrated only to dissolve without sequence; the caused effects of traditional fiction disappear completely, though the skeletal quest remains. Watt's troubles at Mr. Knott's house begin after his voyage, when he cannot interpret the incident of the Galls, whose plastic content seems to him a nothing that has happened. Older and perhaps wiser than Watt, Mercier and Camier make no attempt to interpret anything that happens. Their conversation tends to burnish surfaces, and yet it finally reduces incidents to nothings that happen, while insisting on the almost palpable reality of the journey itself.

Mercier and Camier of Beckett's first French novel are names of puzzling national origin, but the men seem to be Irish in a vaguely Irish setting; at least they use English or Irish money, drink Irish whiskey and stout, and are at home in a city with canals, located on an island. Though Mercier is French for a peddler of miscellaneous wares, the word has been naturalized into English. Though Camier is not a French word, it sounds like *camion*, a carrier, and Camier plays this role for Mercier. Mercier has no Christian name, but Camier has two, Francis Xavier, which could be Irish or French. Vaguely Irish, then, they set out from their town of Bondy (which contains French *bon*, good) to make a journey that will not carry them far—"with neither seas nor frontiers to cross." Except for one train trip, and in spite of their bicycle, they travel on foot, with the frequent halts that Camier notes. Wherever they are, it seems to be only a short distance to Helen's place, to which they return for rest, umbrella repair, or sexual sustenance (for Camier only). On their voyage it is always Camier who attends to practical details—buying food, making train reservations, finding an inn. And it is Mercier who sinks ever more deeply into himself, a process the narrator describes in an alogical lyricism that predicts Molloy.

Mercier and Camier are visual contrasts: Mercier being tall, gaunt, and gray of eye and beard; Camier being short, fat, and red-faced. They meet in unfamiliar, labyrinthine Square St. Ruth, named for a French marshal who was killed in Ireland. They exchange remarks with the guardian of the square and leave it, equipped for their voyage with sack, umbrella, raincoat, and bicycle—one of each for the two. The next morning they leave Helen's house without their equipment. While Camier goes to buy Mercier a cake, the latter is approached by two children who call him "Papa," and whom he drives away. Once on a train, their trip is dominated by an autobiographical monologue of M. Madden, orphan, arsonist, butcher, undertaker's man, sexton—"one corpse after another, there's my life for you." Stopping at an inn, Mercier and Camier meet the manager M. Gast and the barman George. While they sleep upstairs, a waiter Patrice dies, and a M. Conaire arrives in search of Camier. The two old men set out early and arrive at the "station of the damned." Back in town, Camier goes on an errand to Helen's house, and Mercier, sunk within himself, sees two nameless men, then recognizes the barrier-chains, with which he played as a child. Abruptly, a new chapter opens on Mercier-less Camier in a bar where the talk is of artificial insemination. Camier engages in reverie about the arrival of Mercier, which is rudely interrupted by Mercier's actual arrival, and an "embarrassed chill" settles over the cafe. Mercier recalls his marriage; the two friends recall their umbrella and bicycle. Out in the wind again they converse —"We talk too much." Tired and tired of Helen, they ask a policeman to direct them to a licensed brothel. When the policeman taunts them for this request, then threatens them, Mercier kicks him in the testicles, and Camier uses the policeman's club to beat him on the head. Leaving him for dead, they wonder if anything will change. What changes is their relationship, as fatigue erodes it. After viewing the cross of Masse, they arrive exhausted at a ruin. By chapter eleven, the last of narration, they scarcely recognize one another when Watt reunites them. Together, they abandon Watt in a bar where he has aroused wrath by cursing at life. Mercier and Camier walk a short distance along a canal. When Camier leaves him, Mercier looks at the darkening sky and listens to the rain on the water.

This summary of events neglects the texture of *Mercier et Camier.* Bright conversational gambits gradually give way to descriptions that might be landscape or soulscape. The days inevitably cloud over till the two friends walk in mist or rain, against which they do not use raincoat or umbrella. People are not quite as hostile as weather, but they view Mercier and Camier with distrust. The two friends are challenged by a park guardian, innkeepers, waiters, and policemen. They are subjected to the cruelty-obsessed M. Madden and the sex-obsessed M. Conaire—both listed as "Hors d'oeuvres" in the summary at the end of the chapter. As the love affairs of Belacqua and the encounters of Murphy serve to emphasize the isolation of those heroes, the conversations of Mercier and Camier emphasize *their* isolation, even to showing that a couple is only a pseudocouple.

Much of *Mercier et Camier* sparkles with music-hall dialogue, spoken against a background poverty. Mercier and Camier are inexplicably provided with a woman's bicycle, a sack, an umbrella, and a raincoat, but they are soon without these properties. Thieves strip the bicycle down to frame and pump. They abandon the raincoat with its pockets full of miscellaneous items—"a whole life." Later they speak nostalgically of these possessions they used to share. Near the end of the book Mercier looks at hats in a store-window, telling Camier and Watt that if he were not without desires, he would buy one *for himself.*

Mercier et Camier incorporates characters from earlier

Beckett fiction. While Camier is at Helen's house, Mercier catches a glimpse of the hero of *La Fin* with his distinctive hinged begging-board; the two men have the impression that they have seen each other before. A little later Mercier sees a man with an ass that carries sand and seashells; this man had offered shelter to the hero of *La Fin*, but he nearly knocks Mercier down, without deigning to notice him. These two characters from *La Fin* are balanced by two and a dream from *Watt*. Mercier takes an inkeeper for M. Gall, who has haunted his dreams, but the innkeeper's name is apparently Gast. Mr. Knott's gardener Mr. Graves reappears as a pastoral patriarch. Of three names familiar from *Watt*, however, only Watt is recognizable, in spite of his new preference for whiskey over milk. And yet neither Mercier nor Camier recognizes Watt, though the former admits to having known Murphy, whom Watt resembles, but who died ten years ago in mysterious circumstances. We hear nothing of Belacqua, but Mercier quotes from Dante: "Lo bello stilo che m'ha fatto onore," and style is much on Mercier's mind, since he quibbles over some half-dozen fine points of French syntax. Not until *Malone meurt*, at the center of the trilogy of French novels, does Beckett provide as much cross-reference between his works. And it may be significant that Beckett transplants from English *Watt* characters with names and speech, whereas the two characters from French *La Fin* are nameless, silent, and self-absorbed.

Both Colin Duckworth and John Fletcher have demonstrated in detail the indebtedness of *Godot* to *Mercier et Camier*: the importance of the tree and cross, the germ of Pozzo in M. Madden, a reference to the two thieves crucified with Christ. As Gogo is dependent on Didi, Camier is dependent on Mercier. To these resemblances might be added a comparable circularity of structure: at beginning and end of *Godot* the two friends wait for Godot; at beginning and end of *Mercier et Camier* the two friends are separate and alone. But it is above all the brisk exchange of dialogue that links *Mercier et Camier* to *Godot*, with phrases often arising from their immediate situation.

At the beginning of the book Mercier and Camier take shelter with two copulating dogs.

> Don't look, said Mercier.
> To hear is enough, said Camier.
> True, said Mercier.
> Patience and courage, said Camier.
> The dogs don't bother you? said Mercier.
> Why doesn't he withdraw? said Camier.
> He can't, said Mercier.
> Why? said Camier.
> One of nature's little gadgets, said Mercier, no doubt to make insemination doubly sure.
> They begin astraddle, said Camier, and end up arsy-versy.
> What would you? said Mercier. The ecstasy is past, they long to part and piss against a post or eat a morsel of shit, but they can't. So they turn their backs on each other. You would do the same if you were they.
> Delicacy would restrain me, said Camier.
> And what would you do? said Mercier.
> I would feign regret, said Camier, that I could not renew such pleasure incontinent.

By the end of the book, situation and conversation are more barren, but Mercier and Camier try to keep up some momentum. Beginning to speak simultaneously, they stop.

> Pardon, said Camier, you were saying?
> No no, said Mercier, your turn.
> No no, said Camier, it was unimportant.
> No matter, said Mercier, go ahead.
> I assure you, said Camier.
> Please, said Mercier.

After you, said Camier.
I interrupted you, said Mercier.
It's I who interrupted you, said Camier.
No no, said Mercier.
Yes yes, said Camier.

What drama usually lacks, however, is the commentary of a narrator. Though he disappears as "I" after the book's opening sentence, the narrator is, as he says, with Mercier and Camier throughout their voyage, and he does not spare us his ironies. After noting the time-table by which Mercier and Camier miss each other before they finally meet, he comments: "How that stinks of artifice." Later he characterizes his narration as "lamentable." When Camier complains of the cold, he affirms that it was indeed cold. He describes Camier's gestures and Mercier's words as "comedy." After two pages of description, he announces that this is the end of the descriptive passage; after a paragraph lasting two and a half pages, he notes that a "new paragraph" is beginning.

But in tension with such facile irony are the narrator's hints of a significance beneath or beyond the surface of the story. When Mercier and Camier look at each other, he informs us that they do not see one another. Later he tells us that it was raining in their heads. He makes them into archetypical figures by referring to them as "*les* Mercier et Camier." About a quarter of the way through the book, the narrator evokes Mercier's thoughts as a "reverie, confused and colorless, in which past and future merged unpleasantly and the present played the villain eternally drowned." Nearly two-thirds of the way through the book, the narrator glides so imperceptibly into Mercier's reverie that it is uncertain who is ruminating about man's slavery to time, which is compared both to a cramping cage and to a heap of millet grains. Listed at the end of the chapter as "Mercier's brain," this passage is already worthy of Molloy.

As the voyage progresses, the conversational verve regresses, and the narrator assumes greater importance. He has earlier entered Mercier's thoughts, limning the more quixotic friend who is also more irrational. By the time they fall asleep in exhaustion, the narrator pointedly refuses to distinguish between them: "Let him wake up then, Mercier, Camier, it makes no difference." Whichever one it is moves away, and the second to wake notices that the other is missing, but he still thinks that they may reunite. Then doubting it, each goes on alone. While one rests—"a kind of shadow Sordello"—the other approaches, but they cannot quite trust their eyes; they can no longer believe in one another's existence. In the country, replete with hedges, mud, liquid manure, ponds, rocks, cow dung, huts and an occasional "anthropseudomorph," Camier stops at a fork in the road. He turns to wave at Mercier, then takes the path to the left. When Mercier reaches the fork, he goes to the right. And the narrator concludes: "Parted! That's roughly how it must have been. The earth was laboring toward the light, the brief overlong light." Any light of life is overlong, for the darkness always menaces. Any couple is a pseudocouple, for solitude is pervasive. Mercier and Camier part. No more than the copulating dogs can they sustain their coupling. Only the voyage could bring them together, but the shared voyage was inadequate to keep them together.

The last narrated chapter of *Mercier et Camier* opens with the narrator's meditation on the problematical nature of the reality of events in time. With the re-entrance of an aged Camier, then Watt, then Mercier, the novel resumes a conversational mode. But in the final paragraph the narrator describes the silent Mercier as night falls: "In the dark he also heard better, he heard sounds that the long day had hidden from him, human murmurs for example, and the rain on the water." In the final list of chapter 12 this last paragraph merits two entries: "Mercier alone. Darkness is made perfect." The significance of the voyage of Mercier and Camier lies in their vain efforts to escape from the mist, darkness, and loneliness. Focused on the trivialities of their voyage, they lose touch with what they obscurely seek—the human and the inhuman, murmurs and rain.

Despite Beckett's distaste for it, *Mercier et Camier* is a skillful novel, but not an achieved novel. The narrator's facile ironies clash with his obscure depths. The beautifully rhythmed duets only rarely reach out for more than they seem to say, as they will in *Godot*. And Mercier's reveries are inconsistent with these duets. Incidents occur without cause, like a series of etchings, but such scenes melt confusingly into private musings of M. Gast, Camier, Mercier, and the narrator.

Toward the end of *Mercier et Camier* each member of the pseudocouple in turn reaches a fork in the road. The path on the left leads to town; the path on the right leads far more obliquely to the same town. In 1946 Beckett himself was at a comparable juncture. Behind him lay journeys through more or less traditional forms of fiction, however odd his heroes. Before him, at some indeterminable distance, lay new forms of fiction that could accommodate the formlessness of what he felt to be reality. From this juncture the oblique path is *Mercier et Camier*, with its seemingly familiar residue of incidents, characters, settings, clock-time, and dialogue. The more direct path tries to forge ahead by leaving these detours, and it is far harder to follow.

Four *Nouvelles*

Beckett chose to publish his first four French *nouvelles* in an order different from that of their composition. *L'Expulsé* (*The Expelled*), *Le Calmant* (*The Calmative*), and *La Fin* (*The End*) first appeared together in that order in 1955, a decade after they were written. Beckett told John Fletcher that they might be called Prime, Death, and Limbo. Fifteen years later, not until 1970, appeared *Premier Amour* (*First Love*); since its hero is younger than the other three, we might call it Pre-prime.

70

The four stories are linked by form. Each of them is a first-person narration: a nameless man talks about himself, his commentary punctuating a series of arbitrary and disjunctive memories. The French is at once colloquial and formal, simple but with dense resonances. In accordance with Buffon's aphorism, "Le style, c'est l'homme même." (Style is the man.) the heroes of the stories are poor, precise, and utterly unpredictable.

Events occur in all four stories, but less and less do they cohere into a plot. *Premier Amour*, however, does have a plot, which is designated by its title. The twenty-five-year-old narrator experiences the titular "first love." But it is a Beckettian love, which the narrator associates with the death of his father. Thus the love story opens at a cemetery. The woman is first called Lulu (but pronounced Loulou, since neither narrator nor woman is French), then Anna. She is cross-eyed, and she sings off key. She makes advances to the Beckett hero; she caresses his ankles, sings to him, usurps his street bench. About two-thirds of the way through the story, she takes him home with her, providing him with a room of his own, which he promptly empties of all its furniture but a sofa-bed. Like Murphy's Celia, Lulu-Anna is a prostitute but, unlike Murphy's Celia, Lulu-Anna manages to accommodate both her clients and our hero. However, she is unprofessional enough to become pregnant. The hero leaves when he hears her cries in labor. He leaves in order not to hear them. But the cries subside only when he is on the move; whenever he stops, they start again. The story ends: "For years I thought they would cease. Now I don't think so any more. I could have done with other loves perhaps. But there it is, either you love or you don't."

In *L'Expulsé*, plot thins to a sequence of relatively unrelated events. The hero is expelled from the house in which he grew up. He wanders around his native city, recognizing nothing, and being treated with scorn. Midway through the story he takes a horse-drawn taxi and spends the rest of the story with the cab, its horse, or its driver. The afternoon is dedicated to looking for a room for the narrator-hero—in vain. The cab-driver takes him home, bedding him down with horse and cab in the stable, from which the hero makes his escape through a window.

Le Calmant opens: "I don't know when I died." This is the first of many puzzling references to death in Beckett's fiction. In *Le Calmant* death brings no peace to the narrator; the word "calm" is intoned with longing some six times. The hero wanders through country and city, observing more people than the other narrators have done, most of them moving in the same direction as himself. Lying down on a crowded street, he hopes not to have to go on, but he gets up and goes on, looking for guidance from the stars that are hidden by clouds.

Le Calmant, the last of the *nouvelles* to be written, is the most densely peopled, and *La Fin*, the first to be written, is the most concretely placed. Not in terms of specific locale, but in terms of places that might house the narrator-protagonist. As in *Premier Amour* and *L'Expulsé*, the hero of *La Fin* is expelled from a building. Unlike the other two heroes, this one is very much concerned about where he will live. After much searching, he rents a basement room from a Greek or Turkish woman. (The centuries-old enemies are indistinguishable to him.) Soon he is evicted by a new proprietor who needs the room for his pig. An old friend with an ass offers him first a seaside cave, then a mountain hut, but both of these shelters displease him. He spends some time as a beggar, then does some carpentry on a boat to adapt it to his needs. His most pressing and final need is to have the water rise in the boat, apparently so that he may drown.

In spite of indeterminate chronology and episodic characters, certain patterns recur in the stories, thus acquiring the force of symbols. All the protagonists live on the margin of society, and they are aware that society scorns them. All the protagonists remember their fathers, who are usually associated with hats and with bequests of money. All the protagonist-narrators introduce animals into their stories, and all are devoted to a particular plant (hyacinth in *Premier Amour*, geranium in *L'Expulsé*, nonesuch in *Le Calmant*, and crocus in *La Fin*).

All the protagonists travel, and their journeys are juxtaposed against shelters. Even in *Premier Amour*, where the hero covers least ground, he has to leave home at the death of his father, and wanders before and after taking shelter with his first (and only) love. *L'Expulsé* opens on the hero's flight down the stairs of his home; the protagonist of *Le Calmant* seeks calm in a cathedral; the protagonist of *La Fin* is dismissed from a hospital or asylum, but he makes temporary shelters of a cave, a cabin, a shed, and a boat. The shelters do not last, and the protagonists wander compulsively—mainly around their nameless native town, which they do not know. In each story but *Premier Amour*, the protagonist is submerged in a crowd, but he also meets someone in an affectional relationship: Lulu-Anna in *Premier Amour*, the cab-driver in *L'Expulsé*, a candy-offering boy in *Le Calmant*, and an old acquaintance with an ass in *La Fin*. Except for Lulu, these offers of tenderness are linked with animals. The protagonist of *L'Expulsé* spends half his story with the cab-driver and his horse. The protagonist of *Le Calmant* is befriended by a boy with a goat, and the protagonist of *La Fin* is oppressed by a man with a pig and sheltered by a man with an ass. The French narrator-protagonists seem closer to animals than Murphy watching the Hyde Park sheep or Watt building rational edifices on the infirm base of a dog to eat Mr. Knott's remains.

More than the English heroes, Beckett's French heroes are aware of their bodies. Like Watt, two of them have remarkable gaits. They all have sore scalps, which they hide with their hats (though the hats seem to predate the pustules). The stories' heroes cannot compete in ailments with the heroes of the subsequent trilogy of novels, but they inspire horror in most observers. Even the younger hero of *Premier Amour* is constipated, cries easily, and has pains

73

that he will take pleasure in describing one day, giving us a mere sample in his corns, cramps, bunions, ingrown nails, frostbite, and trenchfoot. The hero of *La Fin* in his Limbo has crab lice, eczema, psoriasis, a cyst on his rectum, and his feet and hands feel full of ants.

In relishing physical affliction, these French heroes differ from their English predecessors. Belacqua's aching feet lead him nowhere in particular. Murphy's irregular heart is irrelevant to his life of the mind or death of the body. Watt's nonhealing wounds are neither pretext for nor subject of his assiduous speculations. But although there is nothing so simple as a cause-and-effect relationship between the ailing bodies of the French heroes and their compulsion to speak of them, a subtle link is forged between the two. Obscurely, the French heroes seek their essential selves; the body is at once an obstacle and the only path in that search. Only through physical affliction can the French heroes perhaps approach metaphysical being.

The stories are a new stylistic departure as well as a new language for Beckett. They lack exposition, climax, or dénouement. Instead, they accumulate force through their alogical immediacy. Since no reference is made to writing, the stories are apparently spoken by their narrators. Hesitation and self-correction contribute to an oral quality, and yet the sentences are grammatically correct, gathered into paragraphs. Though the sentence structure is varied, there is often no transition between sentences in the long paragraphs. *Le Calmant*, after two short paragraphs, continues in a single paragraph of seventeen pages. Rare one-sentence paragraphs therefore take on a special significance: "And yet I had done them no harm." "The scene was the familiar one of grandeur and isolation."

The French stories are meticulous in their spare detail and learned reference. Gone is the cultural range of the English fiction, and yet certain names are dropped pointedly—Racine, Baudelaire, Dante, Heraclitus, d'Aubigné, the Cyclops, Walther (von der Vogelweide), and Geulincx.

The three stories in sequence emphasize the arbitrary quality of narration, so that the overriding point of these stories is that they *are* stories. The very choice of events for narration seems to lack proportion. Thus, we never learn whether a child has been born in *Premier Amour*. In *La Fin*, the longest of the stories, the protagonist devotes a few brief sentences to his son and nearly five pages to his boat-home. Disproportionate too is the intrusion of passion into the narration, the narrators abruptly giving vent to irrational rage.

Though the stories are recognizably by the same hand, they differ in nuance. *Premier Amour* is the funniest of the four, but also the most pathetic. The basic attitude toward love as an annoying, somewhat disgusting inevitability is itself comic, as are the details of the love story: the hero has an erection when Lulu strokes his ankles, but he cannot remember his first night of love. He knows he feels love because he writes Lulu's name in cow dung. He ventures to classify the kinds of love (including Spinoza's intellectual love), and he pinpoints the moments of love's arrival and departure. Young as he is, he knows about love, but it is one of the few subjects he does know. As he says: "It's all a muddle in my head, graves and nuptials and the different varieties of motion." He also confuses orange and lemon trees, Racine and Baudelaire, fibrome and fibrone, constipation and diarrhoea. More than the other narrators, he addresses himself directly to an audience.

With his youth, love, and consciousness of words, the hero of *Premier Amour* resembles Murphy, whereas that of *L'Expulsé*, in his prime, resembles Watt. As Watt reasons in the face of the porter who has knocked him down, or while he is still semiconscious on the station floor, the hero of *L'Expulsé* tries to count the steps he is thrown down, even before he reaches the bottom. But through the rest of his story he relinquishes reason to ruminate about memory. "Memories are killing," he tells us early, and yet he continues to remember, or to comment on what he does not remember—particularly names. The incongruous entrance of memory into his observations makes for the comedy of *L'Expulsé*, less sustained than in *Premier Amour*. The two stories end in evasion: the hero of *Premier Amour* leaves cries of labor pain, and the hero of *L'Expulsé* leaves the womblike stable, for birth inevitably leads to death.

Le Calmant and *La Fin*, in contrast to the other two stories, intrude humor into sadder narrations, the one opening on death and the other closing on a wish for drowning. In *Le Calmant* fear seems to be the very foundation of narration, which *is* the calmative to combat fear. The narrator tells of three other narrations—a man surrounded by women, his father's story of Joe Breem or Breen, a man's story of a woman, Pauline. More than the other heroes, then, this one depends upon fiction. Early in his account he announces tersely: "We are needless to say in a skull," but even earlier he ruminates in leisurely fashion, so that the very rhythms seem to gather courage for the struggle of the imagination. "But it's to me this evening something has to happen, to my body as in myth and metamorphosis, this old body to which nothing ever happened, or so little, which never met with anything, loved anything, wished for anything, in its tarnished universe, except for the mirrors to shatter, the plane, the curved, the magnifying, the minifying, and to vanish in the havoc of its images." These short phrases, separated by commas, referring to the subject, body, are a long syntactical leap beyond *Watt*. The basic image is arresting—a body reflected in distortions, wishing for the glass to break, in order to annihilate the body. Beneath the balanced phrases lies the traditional association of broken mirrors with bad luck, and the implication that man exists only in what reflects him. Moreover, this body is strangely mental in its wish (even linked to the word "havoc" that Beckett associated with the mind in "Saint-Lô").

Comparably poetic prose is rare in *La Fin*, the flattest of the four stories. (So unclimactic is *La Fin* that *Les Temps*

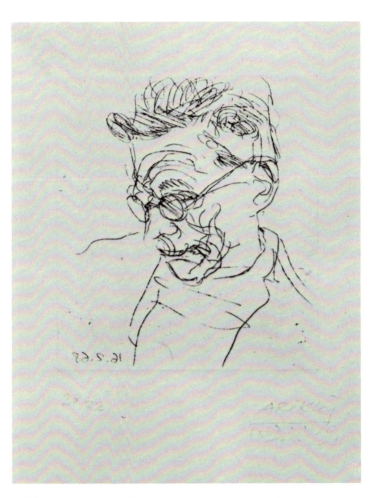

Arikha Etching of Beckett, 1968. (PHOTO LATHROP)

Arikha Etching of Beckett, 1970. (PHOTO COLLINGWOOD)

Modernes, which published the first half of it, saw no reason to publish the second half.) The prose of *La Fin* seems to gather no momentum as it describes town and country, seaside and mountains, and various people. The only authorial intrusions are "That's all a pack of lies, I feel." and "—no, I can't." But despite these disclaimers, the end of *La Fin* accomplishes an amazing creative feat. After dissatisfaction with the seaside cave and the mountain cabin, the narrator makes his berth in an abandoned boat in a shed on a large estate. By sheer imagination—the narrator calls it a vision—he creates a liquid world for that boat, and he closes his story with preparations for drowning. In the ending sentences only, minute observation dissolves into cosmic reach: "The sea, the sky, the mountains and the islands closed in and crushed me in a mighty systole, then scattered to the uttermost confines of space. The memory came faint and cold of the story I might have told, a story in the likeness of my life, I mean without the courage to end or the strength to go on." Vision embraces both courage and strength in these sentences that are at once pantheistic, solipsistic, and familiarly poetic. By "familiarly poetic" I mean that the sentences poetically render familiar sensations. We have all known moments in which we seem to reflect the natural world, and the natural world seems invested with our own emotions. Out of such moments grew the attitudes of pantheism and solipsism. The first of the quoted sentences captures that romantic moment for fiction, but the last sentence annihilates the moment through the reality of transience. *The End* thus denies an end.

Much of Beckett's subsequent fiction will contain the stuff of poetry, and all of it will be haunted by treacherous time. As early as 1931 he wrote in *Proust:* "The most successful evocative experiment can only project the echo of a past sensation, because, being an act of intellection, it is conditioned by the prejudices of the intelligence which abstracts from any given sensation, as being illogical and insignificant, a discordant and frivolous intruder, whatever word or gesture, sound or perfume, cannot be fitted into the puzzle of a concept. But the essence of any new experience is contained precisely in this mysterious element that the vigilant will rejects as an anachronism. It is the axis about which the sensation pivots, the centre of gravity of its coherence." Poems are often such evocative experiments, but, beginning with the *nouvelles*, and to a lesser extent *Mercier et Camier*, Beckett conducts these evocative experiments in fiction by dispensing with many conceptual details of traditional storytelling. Though the *nouvelles* suffer by comparison with the trilogy of novels, they prepare its terrain by reducing plot, simplifying character, generalizing setting, and escaping from the vigilant will of author and reader. It is by these means that Beckett reaches toward being, but the process of reaching is always experiential, never abstract.

A Trilogy of Novels

"Strength was certainly needed to stay with Camier, as it was needed to stay with Mercier, but less than was needed to fight the battle of soliloquy." It is the "battle of soliloquy" that engages the energies of the four narrators of Beckett's French trilogy—Molloy, Moran, Malone, the Unnamable. Strictly speaking, the four *nouvelles* are also soliloquies, since the narrators apparently *tell* their tales. However, those tales are not battles so much as passionate rambles. The narrators of the trilogy of novels, in contrast, seem to wrest words from recalcitrant matter. The soliloquies are battles for words and with words, which three of the narrators explicitly commit to writing.

Beckett's trilogy of novels forms a unique sequence. At the most obvious level, the novels do not move characters through a chronological progression as in the Victorian three-decker or the French *roman fleuve*. Named for their narrator-protagonists—*Molloy, Malone meurt,* and *L'In-*

78

nommable—the three French novels probe with increasing intensity into the nature of man. In order to explore through his fiction, Beckett cuts through the circumstantial detail of fiction, down to the "I" who tries to talk about himself. Except for Moran, the protagonist-narrators meet fewer people and visit fewer places than in the *nouvelles*, and yet the novels, like the *nouvelles*, might be subtitled Prime, Death, Limbo. As the pages fill with words, the focus narrows down to a word-uttering being in limbo, but the process of narrowing concentrates the breadth and depth of human experience. "Breadth and depth of human experience": the critic summarizes with a pat phrase, but the artist, Beckett, suggests the experience with excruciating concreteness, if only to dispense with it as finally irrelevant to basic being.

Molloy

The trilogy starts with the here-and-now of the narrator-protagonist: "I am in my mother's room. . . . There's this man who comes every week. . . . Yes, I work now. . . . What I'd like now is to speak of the things that are left, say my goodbyes, finish dying." Molloy does not finish dying in his novel, but he recalls certain adventures in living-dying.

The opening paragraph of *Molloy* is a prelude to the unparagraphed associations of the rest of Molloy's soliloquy, and its style is atypical of the novel—shorter sentences, simpler syntax, and closer adherence to factual detail. Its themes fall into an approximation of sonata form. At the beginning and end is the theme of writing, but the large middle section rambles over the theme of fellowmen— collector of the writing, Molloy's mother, his possible son, an unnamed chambermaid, his true love, and back to the collector of the writing. This introductory three-part division is neither neat nor pat, but it prepares us for the novel to come—Molloy and his fellowmen rendered through his writing.

79

The book's second paragraph contains Molloy's account of his travels, about half of Beckett's novel. The first sentence of the second paragraph introduces the whole trilogy: "This time, then once more I think, then perhaps a last time, then I think it'll be over, with that world too." The three "time"s are the three novels of the trilogy; the repeated "I think" is in trilogy-long tension with "that world." But we are beyond the simplistic Murphyan conflict between macrocosm and microcosm. In *Molloy* "that world" materializes in disparate, unpredictable elements, as in memories or dreams. Thought, too, erupts in elemental forms— the rational constructs of Western man and the irrational reactions of all men.

Imperceptibly, the narrator—we do not yet know he is called Molloy—graduates from difficulties in narrating, even in thinking, to the beginnings of a story: "A and C going slowly towards each other, unconscious of what they were doing." Most fiction and much experience are subsumed in that slow approach. Would two people ever meet if they could foresee all the ramifications and repercussions of meeting?

Gradually, Molloy surrounds A and C with an environment that is a singular combination of precision, reflection, and rhythm: "From there he must have seen it all, the plain, the sea, and then these self-same hills, that some call mountains, indigo in places in the evening light, their serried ranges crowding to the skyline, cloven with hidden valleys that the eye divines from sudden shifts of colour and then from other signs for which there are no words, nor even thoughts." Molloy rarely manages an objective sentence; descriptions lead inevitably back to his mind: "Perhaps I'm inventing a little, perhaps embellishing." Nevertheless, he does produce eight pages about A and C, making himself increasingly evident as their observer.

Abruptly A and C disappear, and Molloy is alone, craving for a fellow: "But talking of the craving for a fellow let me observe that having waked between eleven o'clock and midday (I heard the angelus, recalling the incarnation, shortly after) I resolved to go and see my mother." As the angelus announces the incarnation, God made flesh, it seems to announce Molloy's words made flesh. He is incarnated in his story. And though Molloy will often digress from that story, he will return to its main line: he is en route to see his mother. That is the fellowship he craves, with its memories of intense love-hate; that is the journey he undertakes, toward communion.

Like Mercier and Camier, Molloy finds a bicycle to begin his voyage. With it and later without it, he travels toward his mother, however many circles he may describe. So, the first description of the bicycle circles Molloy back to "her who brought me into the world, through the hole in her arse if my memory is correct." Setting out on what he calls an "unreal journey" to his mother, Molloy lyricizes about their names Ma-g and Da-n.

Against the stable background of this journey, different events claim Molloy, and they happen more mysteriously than did the incidents of *Mercier et Camier*. After a flashback to Molloy's life with mother, we read of his arrest and release, his awakening under the eyes of a shepherd and his dog. About a third of Molloy's narrative takes place in Lousse's territory, and Lousse herself causes Molloy to recall his love affair with Ruth-Edith-Rose. After leaving Lousse, Molloy spends time near the sea, where he distributes sixteen "sucking-stones." In a forest he assaults a charcoal burner. Finally, within sight of his town, he lies in a ditch and hears a voice. These events bear no causal relationship to one another. Vivid in themselves, they cohere in no context, but they resonate with mythic echoes. Beckett's verbal mastery blends Molloy's passionate immediacy with subliminal reminiscences of the legends of our culture.

In discussing the *nouvelles*, I isolated a few sentences to show their poetic density, but such quotation is distortion because poetic density depends upon context. In *Molloy* such quotation is even more misleading, for occasional aphorisms thread through involved complexities, in which words mean more than they seem to say: "And once again I am I will not say alone, no, that's not like me, but, how shall I say, I don't know, restored to myself, no, I never left myself, free, yes, I don't know what that means but it's the word I mean to use, free to do what, to do nothing, to know, but what, the laws of the mind perhaps, of my mind, that for example water rises in proportion as it drowns you and that you would do better, at least no worse, to obliterate texts than to blacken margins, to fill in the holes of words till all is blank and flat and the whole ghastly business looks like what it is, senseless, speechless, issueless misery." The use of the first person identifies reader with writer. The subtle shift from first to second person gives a sense of dialogue, and the final generalization summarizes the gap between exploration of self and language ill suited for the task. The very structure of the sentences conveys the enormous difficulty of writing a sentence. Molloy's hesitations and self-contradictions are a concentration of Western intellectual anguish: What am I? Where does my self begin and end? Where does my freedom begin? Are there any laws for my mind? Or is it submerged in the words I learn? Molloy's implication of the inadequacy of words is familiar to anyone who has worked with words. More importantly, however, words are inadequate for all of us, who try to make them serve in situations that shatter us—guilt, love, death. Molloy's "no . . . no . . . yes . . . to know" seems to do what his mind glances at—fill in the holes of words, even while his rhythms evoke a misery that is far from senseless or speechless.

Molloy offers us speech and sense, expressed in some of the most lyrically suggestive sentences of the language (in two languages, French and English translation). On first reading especially, it is the shape of Molloy's sentences that is so arresting. Molloy himself sometimes hears words as pure sound, but Beckett shapes sound into meaning. Unlike sentences of conventional fiction or even of some poetry,

Molloy's sentences force us into awareness of how sounds build words build phrases build sentences. Unlike Chateaubriand's poetic prose, however, such sentences tell stories and create characters. The sentences add up to Molloy and his adventures.

A first reading of Molloy's account may leave us somewhat hazy about what happens to him, but we are clear that it happened to a figure of mythic size. Molloy says he is en route to see his mother, and though his journey stops short of its goal, he passes through such womb-places as ditches, caves, alleys, to arrive in his mother's room. Molloy reminds us of the archetype of the fabulous voyager, and in Western culture this suggests Ulysses, Aeneas, Dante, Christian. Like them, Molloy is beset with obstacles, which he lumps together as "they." Molloy claims to have killed the Aegean in himself, but the ghost of Ulysses shadows him on his odyssey: he is mollified by Circe's moly rather than using it to ward her off; his Nausicaa woos him in a rubbish dump; a Cyclopean policeman causes him to be fed rather than threatening to eat him; his Penelope is a senile mother rather than a faithful wife; violent though he is, Molloy slays no suitors. But the wily voyager forges ahead, somehow reaching Ithaca, since he begins his account in his mother's bed.

Molloy has been compared to Christ as well as to Ulysses, and, similarly, the association is partial and ironic. Molloy occasionally invokes Christ as an expletive: "Jesus-Christ, it's much worse than yesterday." "Christ, there's crawling." (Both were added only in Beckett's translation into English.) Molloy refers to A and C as his two thieves, he associates the angelus with the incarnation, he steals a silver object in the shape of a double cross, and he writes of his journey as "a veritable Calvary with no limit to its stations and no hope of crucifixion, though I say it myself, and no Simon." When Molloy assimilates the women in his life—Ruth-chambermaid-Lousse-mother—he says it is "like being crucified, I don't know why and I don't want to," but we can discern the shape of a Pietà. Sam compelled us to view Watt seriously as Christ, with his crown of thorns, but Molloy chronicles his own suffering, so that we see him as both Christlike martyr and fool.

Molloy is a fabulous writer as well as voyager; he writes his own fable or epic, but like most writers of fable or epic, he has no sense of humor. And that is a major source of the exquisite humor of his soliloquy. With persistence that becomes comic, Molloy dwells on the miseries of his body and the malevolence of his world. Almost invariably, his direct quotations of dialogue are incongruously comic, but he seems innocent of that. His three r's are rage, reason, and resignation, and they are evidenced with hilarious disproportion. For example, Molloy rages at charity, he reasons the distribution of his sucking-stones, and he is resigned to making love. He sees nothing funny in any of these descriptions, but their humor comments on our habits. In raging at charity, one of the three theological virtues, Molloy implies such questions as: What is the real motive of the dispenser? What becomes of the dignity of the recipient? In Molloy's symmetrical distribution of sucking-stones lies doubt in the scientific method. In Molloy's resignation to love, Beckett repeats a parody of love that began in the unpublished *Dream*, was taken up in moments of *Murphy*, appeared briefly in the Watt-Mrs. Gorman interlude. Grotesque as these couplings are, they are somehow familiar, and they question the Western tradition of romantic love, from the Provençal poets on. As opposed to the comedy of *Murphy*, whose learning was often gratuitous display, or of the Mercier-Camier dialogues, focused on the immediate situation, the profound comedy of *Molloy* reflects on the very bases of Western culture. In addition, Molloy's own prose is punctuated by such laughter-arousing devices as disjunction ("Molloy, or life without a chambermaid"), incongruity ("Is it true love, in the rectum?"), and paradox ("My waking was a kind of sleeping.").

For all its humor, *Molloy* is not primarily a comic novel,

84

but one of verbal and human exploration—human because
verbal. Through the words with which Beckett endows
Molloy, he attempts to penetrate to depths that have not
before been penetrated by words. In the stories there already was an effort to capture the feeling of being part of a
larger harmony or discord, which did not depend upon any
supernatural power. That effort is more intense in *Molloy*,
so that the hero emerges as a romantic force: "Yes, there
were times when I forgot not only who I was, but what I
was, forgot to be. Then I was no longer that sealed jar to
which I owed my being so well preserved, but a wall gave
way and I filled with roots and tame stems for example,
stakes long since dead and ready for burning, the recess of
night and the imminence of dawn, and then the labour of
the planet rolling eager into winter would rid it of these
contemptible scabs. Or of that winter I was the precarious
calm, the thaw of the snows which make no difference and
all the horrors of it all all over again. But that did not happen to me often, mostly I stayed in my jar which knew
neither seasons nor gardens." After reading this passage
perhaps a hundred times, I do not pretend to understand
it, but I feel it, and I think it is not an uncommon feeling—a
timeless-jar defense against aging and death, contrasted
with the vibrant desire for and the ecstatic pain of the rare
crumbling of that defense.

To recapitulate and summarize the achievement of Molloy's monologue: out of the very words that Molloy
questions, he builds sentences of varied shape, rhythm, imagery, and significance. In small groups, the sentences are
sometimes woven into comic tapestries, which have been
compared to the *lazzi* of *commedia dell'arte*, commenting
upon aspects of our civilization. Through the course of his
account, his sentences finally accumulate into a "fabulous
being" who rages and reasons his way toward his mother.
Molloy has shed most of his education as useless, so that he
approaches people and things without learned attitudes.
Though Molloy still retains many of our habits—the habits

85

of 2500 years of Western civilization and the habits of 200 years of industrial life—he also is ready to shed habits, and he reacts directly to things, people, and animals. His unmediated reactions bring us closer to the suffering of being. He introduces the rolling planet into our sealed jars.

Moran

After Molloy, Moran is a pygmy, as he is meant to be. If Beckett had begun *Molloy* with Moran's report, we would have been in a satirized small-town world. As is, when we read on the first page of Moran's report: "I remember the day I received the order to see about Molloy," we can guess that Molloy is not easily seen about. Molloy has claimed to be "no enemy of the commonplace," but it is Moran who writes in commonplaces. As Olga Bernal has shown, Moran defines himself by his possessions, including his language. Neat paragraphs reflect the neat life of Moran. When Moran focuses on Molloy, however, possessions become nonfunctional and language becomes untrustworthy. Moran, suddenly detached from his comfortable Sunday surroundings, writes: "Unfathomable mind, now beacon, now sea." These Molloyan phrases sound strange from Moran, and in retrospect we can understand why it takes Moran nearly half his report to leave his house, where his mind is a beacon, and dare a journey in which his mind becomes as deep and tempest-tossed as the sea.

The first part of Moran's report is a skillful sketch of himself as "cold as crystal and as free from spurious depth." He swiftly evokes his lazy provincial town and his well-ordered house, in which light is obtained by a mere flick of the switch. After the depths of Molloy's soliloquy, such skill seems facile, and Beckett subjects us to it only briefly. Even before Moran sets out on his quest, he begins to think *like* Molloy, in thinking *about* Molloy. Like Molloy, Moran assimilates himself into nature, and at the same time seeks to differentiate himself from nature. In a page of poetic prose

86

that recalls Molloy's self-exploration, Moran conjures a vision of Molloy that predicts his own descent into mystery: "His life has been nothing but a waiting for this, to see himself damned, blessed, to fancy himself everyman, above all others." The antithesis of Everyman and Elected Man is Molloy, will be Moran, and has been every man who thinks about himself.

Toward the end of this meditation, Moran declares: "For where Molloy could not be, nor Moran either for that matter, there Moran could bend over Molloy." The exploration of the boundaries of a human being can take place only outside the boundaries of everyday existence, and, knowing this, Moran is aware that he is investing Molloy "with the air of a fabulous being." When he focuses specifically on Molloy, Moran describes him in words whose veracity seem striking; hirsute, hunted or imprisoned, and hulking, Molloy moved constantly, and "his whole body was a vociferation."

However, Moran cannot sustain such meditation on the unknown, and he returns to the proper and preposterous preparations for his voyage. Even after he leaves home, Moran appears as a respectable citizen. A farmer offers him a lift, which he politely refuses. Moran eats the canned food of our industrial world, which his son purchases in the nearby towns. But while his son is off in Hole buying a bicycle, Moran is confronted by his violence and fear. He gives bread to a dim stranger with a club or stick, and he is surprised to find that the stick is light. When he meets another man, correctly dressed and resembling him, Moran bashes in the man's skull. Moran has faced two aspects of himself—irrational threat (the man with a club) and smug order (the man with the blue suit); he has nourished the one and slaughtered the other.

But like his Molloyan meditations at home, Moran's generosity and violence do not last. When his son returns, Moran reverts to the hypocritically sadistic father. Only when he is deserted by the son who has catered to his material needs does Moran gradually approach the Molloy he seeks. A shepherd gestures rather than speaking with him; a farmer—perhaps the same who once offered him a ride—is suspicious of him. In the forest Moran eats the fruit of trees. With clothes decayed, he crawls close to the earth, so that he becomes a virtual reptile, like Molloy at the end of his voyage. But man is not reducible to mere animality. Molloy is presumably rescued from the ditch, and Moran is ordered out of the forest. Once on his way home, the old Moran begins to surface—asking questions, making lists, aware of time and specific place. When Moran meets the second farmer, he has resumed the hypocritical duplicity of his religion. But at home all is in ruins, and Moran writing knows that his home can no longer contain him.

Only after we have finished the whole novel can we realize that Molloy has devoured Moran. Our first impression is rather of their opposition: barbarian and bourgeois, poet and accountant. Molloy early announces, "All grows dim"; Moran depends upon memory: "I remember the day. . . ." Moran in Turdy distinguishes people and objects by name; Molloy confuses objects and persons, and he even has trouble remembering his own name. Moran recognizes that Molloy is "Just the opposite of myself." But slowly, Moran comes to resemble Molloy. The capacity for such resemblance was present from the start: their seemingly Irish names, beginning with M, thirteenth letter of the alphabet, have the same root except for a liquid consonant, and that root *mol* means soft or pliable in Latin. It is Moran who proves malleable into Molloy, but both are malleable to the exigencies of an inner voice.

In spite of the surface antithesis of Molloy and Moran, similarity of name is immediately apparent, and other similarities are subtly suggested: they are both family men in their own way—the one haunted by his mother and the other obsessed with his son. They both receive a thirsty messenger, and they both undertake questing journeys. Both have hazy senses of direction, even to confusing right and left. Both own bicycles, which they describe in rhapsodic detail and which they ride with allowances for their infirmities.

Probably the most marked similarity between Moran and Molloy is their physical decrepitude. Molloy begins his voyage on crutches and ends it, after crawling in circles, at the bottom of a ditch. Moran begins in health, sets out after a first pain in the knee; on his voyage his knee grows so stiff that he cannot kneel, and he finds it hard to sit—Molloy's condition. Stiff legs are not the only afflictions shared by Molloy and Moran: they both have low-hanging testicles and few or no teeth. Both have good hearing and bad sight, and both confuse blue and green. Each is inordinately fond of his hat, which Molloy attaches to his buttonhole and Moran ties under his chin; both jam their hats so hard upon their skulls that the hat becomes a virtual part of the body (though Moran loses his straw in spite of this). Given their physical problems, it is not surprising that both wax lyrical about lying down. Both expand, too, on the less savory habits of their bodies.

In their respective monologues, they describe a similar external environment. Both Molloy and Moran come from a nearby town situated near the country. Molloy thinks that the name of his town begins with B or P, and Moran affirms that it is Bally (suggestive of Ireland). Townsmen though they may be, they travel through pastures and forests. In the lives of both, a garden with a wicket-gate is of some importance. Both hear a gong—ominous to Molloy, merely announcing the time to Moran. Both Molloy and Moran meet a shepherd with a dog and a flock of sheep, and for both voyagers this encounter evokes a reference to the deity, the traditional Good Shepherd: Molloy's "Good God, what a land of breeders," and Moran's "What a pastoral land, my God." During times of crisis, both Molloy and Moran note that the weather is fine, but their self-explorations seem to take place in mist or rain (as do those of Mercier in his novel). Violent at times, both fear the violence of others. Both

Molloy and Moran meet a man with a stick, and both attack someone. Both take part in the burial of their victims— Molloy of Lousse's dog and Moran of the man who resembled him—and, for both, the burials are in some sense their own.

I have been playing with what I might call circumstantial evidence linking Moran to Molloy. Though such evidence takes some searching, its subtle effect cements their final resemblance as writers. Both Molloy and Moran write in a room, but they begin in different styles. Moran's report opens like a parody of the realistic novel, whereas Molloy plunges us almost at once into poetic mystery. This is the heart of their difference until differences dissolve in the forest where Moran comes to resemble Molloy. In their writing as in their lives there is circumstantial evidence of similarity: both confuse certain words regularly—fundamentals and accidentals, induction and deduction, mongrel and pedigree for Molloy; canton and commune, affections and afflictions for Moran. Both are particularly concerned with verbs; Molloy speaks of the pluperfect and the mythological present, and he worries about a tense for his life, which is at once continuous and over. Moran reproaches his son in the prophetic present, and though he resolves to write in the past, he actually uses the present. Both writers discuss imperatives at some length.

Both soliloquies are written compulsively, outwardly in subservience to a thirsty messenger, actually in obedience to an inner voice. Both soliloquies report a hunter in search of human prey, and each of them writes of failure, without acknowledging failure; Molloy does not find his mother, and Moran does not find Molloy. However, Molloy in his mother's bed *is* in a sense his mother—the genealogical race continues. Moran in the forest *is* in a sense Molloy—the cultural race continues. Molloy writing in bed *is* in a sense Moran writing at his desk—the writer's race continues. Moreover, Moran's closing words contradict the facts of his opening words. He has learned to imagine or lie; he has learned that words tell truth through lies.

It is while Moran is alone in the forest that his account comes to resemble that of Molloy: it abandons paragraphs, it minimizes sequence, it selects arbitrarily, and it rambles into highly imaged, delicately rhythmed meditations that distinguish *Molloy* from most fiction. Like all fiction, the voyages of Molloy and Moran are imaginary; unlike most fiction, the act of imagining becomes the primal human act.

Malone meurt

Malone dies. Not on a battlefield but in bed. And yet he carries "the battle of soliloquy" further than Molloy or Moran. His name, Malone, contains "alone," and unlike Molloy or Moran, he is alone in his world—without son or messenger, and with only a blurred memory of mother. His human contacts are limited: a gaunt hand delivers and removes his pots (for about two-thirds of his dying time); a couple is dimly discerned in another building; a black-suited visitor strikes him on the head. These people are nameless, fleeting, scarcely worth noting. What *is* worth noting, Malone informs us early, are stories. And he turns to them with a will, with the will not to dwell upon his life that is a process of dying, like all life.

The three fictional writers of Beckett's trilogy open their soliloquies with a kind of prelude. Molloy and Moran give us specific information as to their location, but Malone guesses at the time he will *not* be, at the holidays he will *not* have to suffer through. In other words, Molloy and Moran immerse us in life, whereas Malone absorbs us in death. While dying, Malone writes in an exercise-book. No Youdi, no Gaber, no mysterious messenger requires a report from him, but he will nevertheless write to fill the time of dying. As befits the requiem occasion, his stories will be calm: "there will be no ugliness or beauty or fever in them any

91

more, they will be almost lifeless, like the teller." And yet, to combat a lifetime of gravity, he hopes for gamesmanship, the spirit of play. Almost lifeless as he predicts his stories will be, they will feed on life, since one will concern a man and a woman, one an animal, and only one will be about a lifeless thing. Lest the stories not last his remaining life, however, Malone will kill time with an inventory of his possessions. Almost as an afterthought, he decides that he might as well briefly summarize his present state. The program being determined—"Present state, three stories, inventory, there."—Malone nevertheless fears an occasional interlude.

He is right to fear. In his very first description of his present state Malone meanders into memory and speculation. And yet his present state is vividly particularized: hatted but otherwise naked in his bed by the window, he eats from and excretes into pots that are delivered and removed as needed. Like Molloy, Malone is ignorant of how he arrived in this bed in this room, but unlike Molloy, Malone is quite confident that he will die there, absent from "that world." (The original title of this second novel of Beckett's trilogy was *L'Absent*.) And indeed the facts as noted by Malone seem to bear out his premonition of an imminent death: sight and hearing are dim, legs are paralyzed, and arms are nearly powerless. Only fingers still serve, figuring in his writing and physically accomplishing that writing. Malone implies that there will be two styles in his writing, the empirical enumeration of his present state and the omniscient narration of his fiction. But both styles will escape his control and merge into poetic rumination.

As circumstantial evidence links Moran to Molloy, a few details link Malone to Molloy. Like Molloy, Malone has a large hirsute head, and he secures his hat with a string. Like Molloy, Malone does not reveal his name till well into his narrative. Malone's possessions recall Molloy's adventures—a bicycle bell, a blood-stained club, a silver knife-rest, part of a crutch. Both Malone and Molloy write in a bed in a room, without knowledge of how they came there. Both are toothless and partly paralyzed, with memories of vigorous movement, in part through a forest. Like Molloy and Moran, Malone compensates for ailing limbs with an extension of those limbs—Molloy's crutches, Moran's umbrella, and Malone's hooked stick. Like Molloy and Moran, the mind of Malone grinds more furiously because his body is still. Like Molloy and Moran, Malone writes. However, this circumstantial evidence does not quite account for our impression that Molloy has grown into Malone, still seeking the limits of his world and his self:

> [Thought] too seeks me, as it always has, where I am not to be found. It too cannot be quiet. On others let it wreak its dying rage, and leave me in peace. Such would seem to be my present state.
> The man's name is Saposcat.

There is no transition between Malone's present state and his story, except for a space on the page. Carefully characterized not to resemble his creator, Saposcat contains his paradoxical nature in his very name, combining soap and dung. Once created, however, he is called "Sapo," a diminutive of Latin *sapiens* and cognate of English "sap," the opposite of *sapiens*. Educated to bourgeois values, Sapo is soon invaded by fears and longings that reflect those of Malone himself: "And a little less well endowed with strength and courage [Sapo] too would have abandoned and despaired of ever knowing what manner of being he was, and how he was going to live, and lived vanquished, blindly, in a mad world, in the midst of strangers." Misanthropic as the sentence sounds, it centers on delving into the self, not on hating others.

In Malone's own fiction, he tries to focus on a fictional world, rather than himself. But not only do his own obsessions—with being and death—intermittently obsess his

93

characters; he also parallels his stories with his own story in his own world. Thus the loss of Malone's exercise-book looms as large as the career of Sapo.

When Malone's thoughts threaten to engulf Sapo, the author shifts abruptly to the Lamberts (in the French original "les Louis"), whose name comes from Balzac's realistic novel *Louis Lambert*, about an unrealistic character. Malone tries to hew to realistic detail, but his failure is more subtle than in Sapo's family. Rather than meandering into Sapo's mind, Malone harps on the Lamberts' proximity to death. Papa Lambert is a skillful slaughterer of pigs, but other animals die or are killed on that farm that reflects our world—rabbits, hens, pigeons, goats, mules. Big Lambert rescues animals from a quick death to subject them to a slow death: "The slaughter-house, said Lambert, that's where I buy my beasts." Like old Madden in *Mercier et Camier*, Big Lambert is a horrifying portrait of man's inhumanity to beast and man—"one corpse after another."

The Saposcat family is at once laughable and pitiable in its limitations, but the Lambert family stupefies us with the brutality of its life. And yet we belong to both families— the earnest bourgeoisie and the equally earnest peasantry that feeds on, lives off the suffering and death of living beings. Despite Malone's determination to remain calm in his narration, a number of phrases reveal his disturbance at death: "[Mrs. Lambert] began to cry out and gesticulate, the last of all the living as likely as not and dead to what was going on about her." "For among those who must have known, some are dead and the others have been forgotten." "For he knew how the dead and buried tend, contrary to what one might expect, to rise to the surface, in which they resemble the drowned." "It won't kill them, she said." At what proves to be the end of Malone's first story, he blends Sapo's departure from the Lamberts into his leitmotif of death: "Then, as people do when someone even insignificant dies, they summoned up such memories as [Sapo] had left them, helping one another and trying to agree. But we all

94

know that little flame and its flickerings in the wild shadows. And agreement only comes a little later, with the forgetting." Even death is less obscene than the terrible brevity of mortal memory.

After an interlude in which Malone loses his pencil and is absorbed by "all this ballsaching poppycock about life and death," he encounters Sapo again, years older. Unlike young Sapo, smothered in realistic detail, old Sapo, soon renamed Macmann, evokes an imaged elegy on aspects of man's mortality. If young Sapo is Malone's effort at realistic fiction, old Sapo is his lapse into prose poetry. Unlike the lyrical sentences of Molloy, those of Malone are too sustained for excerpt. Dwelling on death, Malone decides that his own death is near at hand, and it is in connection with his own death that he names other fictions: "Then it will be all over with the Murphys, Merciers, Molloys, Morans and Malones, unless it goes on beyond the grave." The implication is that all these fictions are alike, fitting into the same grave as their creator, but it is Malone and not Beckett who poses as their creator. And Malone dying sees not a grave but a window at his bedside, through which he distinguishes a couple making love. Beckett's story of first love opens at a cemetery, and Malone's talk of a grave gives him a view of love that looks like pain, and that may lead to the pain of birth.

The son of man was born to suffer, and Malone rechristens an aged Sapo as Macmann, son of man: "Macwhat? . . . Mann, his name is Macmann." Macmann seems to attract a biblical flood to himself as he lies first prostrate, then supine in the crucifixion position. Macmann looks and dresses like Molloy, and into Macmann's mind Malone puts some Molloyan reasoning about his suffering, "ill-fitted [though he is] for pure reason." With apparent relief, Malone shifts Macmann from thinking to moving; Macmann rolls toward a plain, as Molloy only dreamed of doing. After a long interlude of inventory and its concomitant memories, during which Malone loses his stick, we find

Macmann firmly immured in an asylum. He has arrived there as mysteriously as Molloy and Malone in their respective rooms. And suggested perhaps by Malone's view of a copulating couple, Macmann is allowed to copulate with Moll, in Beckett's most savage parody of love, whose words and gestures are appallingly familiar to most of us. But possession diminishes desire, and Macmann scarcely notices the death of Moll. Moran's home life centered in his garden; Molloy's intercourse with Lousse took place in her garden; but Malone enjoys the asylum garden only after Moll's death. Like the hero of *Premier Amour*, and Molloy with Ruth-Edith-Rose, Macmann knows love only in a room. In the open spaces death reigns.

Before death dominates Malone's story, he receives a visit that frightens him into a revised plan on how to spend his remaining time: "Visit, various remarks, Macmann continued, agony recalled. Macmann continued, then mixture of Macmann and agony as long as possible." Ambiguous is *whose* agony. With the exception of a single paragraph's return to himself—"I shall say I no more"—Malone clings to the Macmann story for the remainder of his life.

On Easter weekend "spent by Jesus in Hell," six asylum inmates go on a picnic. On an island the keeper Lemuel (an alternate form for Samuel, from *Ecclesiastes*) kills two sailors with his hatchet, then sets out to sea with his charges, including Macmann. The novel's last broken phrases blend not Macmann but Lemuel into Malone's dying. Lemuel raises his blood-stained hatchet, but he will not hit anyone any more

> or with it or with his hammer or with his stick or with his fist or in thought in dream I mean never he will never [mixture of the weapons of Lemuel, Malone, and Malone's visitor]
> or with his pencil or with his stick or [Malone's weapons]
> or light light I mean [metaphor for life]

never there he will never [negative future for all
mankind—]
never anything
there
any more

We assume that Malone has died into the end of his
story, as Everyman dies in any story that goes on long
enough. The process of Malone's dying has penetrated his
story, but the fragmentation of the prose at once reflects
Lemuel's chopping action in Malone's fiction and the
chopped-off quality of Malone's, and all, life.

Unlike Molloy and Moran, the bulk of whose writing is
about the past, Malone often intrudes remarks about his
present. He calls it his present *state*, but it is not a stasis,
for there are notable events in his present: he loses and
finds his exercise-book, he loses and finds his pencil, he sees
a copulating couple, he loses and does not find his stick, he
is struck on the head and observed by a visitor. An important non-event is the cessation of attention to his bodily
needs; after he invents Macmann, the hand no longer sup-
plies and removes his pots. Anyone who has been bedridden
will appreciate how momentous such events can be; meals
and bedpans resonate with adventure. Anyone with imagination can appreciate how symbolic such events may seem.
At one point Malone declares: "This exercise-book is my
life." Rather than Prufrock's coffee-spoons, Malone measures
out his life in exercise-book and pencil, so that his two losses
are warnings of the imminence of death, even though
Malone retrieves the objects. The stick, on the other hand, is
an extension of Malone's body, with power to search or to
harm. When it is lost, the body is virtually dead, but the
mind lives on a while in the writing fingers. The copulating
couple and the assailant in morning clothes suggest birth
and death, the limits of mortality, and it is his mortality
that obsesses dying Malone.

Dying, Malone grasps at his possessions, as we see the

97

dying do, on all sides of us. And if his possessions are useless and poor—hat, notebook, pencil, boot, three socks, pipe-bowl, packet wrapped in newspaper, needle between two corks, photograph of an ass, top of a crutch, bloody club, and cap of a bicycle bell—they comment all the more pointedly on our apparent wealth. Among Malone's possessions, he remembers a Venus pencil, but he may be sentimentalizing something that never existed, for he does not locate the erotically named Venus pencil in his bed. Again a pointed commentary on our inventories of castles in Spain—with luscious inhabitants.

Malone's seemingly reduced life thus mirrors much of the life of our middle-class culture, fearing death, magnifying events, clinging to possessions. Where Malone's life differs from the average is in the intensity of his feelings. As he approaches death, he experiences certain unexpected sensations. Midway through the novel Malone has the impression of dilating enormously, while he remains ensconced in his head. And toward the end of the book he feels extraordinary heat "which has seized on certain parts of [his] economy." Malone's last explicit reference to himself is as a giant foetus, being born into death. Though he resolves to leave himself—"I shall say I no more"—he intrudes his first person three times into the last pages of his story: "I remember . . . I mean . . . I mean."

The three phrases summarize an author's relation to his novel, and Malone's fiction forms a parodic history of the novel, that middle-class genre. Molloy, "fabulous being," was epic in dimension, but Malone's characters are mired in the middle class—the Saposcat family in town, the Lambert family on the farm. Even unaffiliated Macmann is attacked by psychology, Christianity, romantic love—familiar today in middle-class habits. But Malone, distant and omniscient as the Creator, is bored by his realistic creatures. "I can't" and "What tedium" are his refrains. Nevertheless, he can and does capture his characters with economy and even sympathy.

98

Of all Beckett's characters Malone is the most explicit creator of fiction, and his book contains many references to Beckett's own fiction. Malone implicitly refers to Beckett's pre-trilogy books when he declares: "At first I did not write, I just said the thing." Belacqua is absent from Malone's writing, but he refers to Sordello, whom Molloy confused with Belacqua. Like Murphy, Malone has gazed at the London stars, and like him, he has failed "by a hair's breadth" with the insane. Malone mentions in passing Mr. Quin whom Watt evoked in *Mercier et Camier*, and he mentions Watt himself. Malone at one point enters the mind of a cab-man, who might be the driver in *L'Expulsé*. Like Moran, Malone's visitor carries a tightly rolled umbrella. Reminiscences of Molloy have been cited. Like Vladimir in *Godot*, Malone muses about the two thieves. Malone refers to Murphy, Mercier, Molloy, and Moran, and then asks himself how many he killed. He specifies that one was hit on the head, and we recognize Moran's victim in the forest. Another was burned to death, and this is of course Murphy. No causes are given for two other deaths, but Belacqua died on an operating table, and a policeman was a victim of the blows of Mercier and Camier. Malone then recalls the butler in *Murphy*: "I cut his throat with his razor, that makes five." Malone is most preoccupied with mortality, and it is fitting that he should toll Beckett's dead.

But we can enjoy *Malone* without knowing any of Beckett's other works. *The Unnamable* will refer to Malone's "mortal liveliness," and that is the source of his charm. Murphy attracted us by his "surgical quality," which I interpret as the incisiveness of his mind. Watt's mind was blunt but impressive in its persistence, and the dialogue of Mercier and Camier is riotously readable. Molloy was awesome when alone, amusing in company. But Malone, who is almost always alone, is utterly endearing in his singularity and in his proximity to death.

Imbedded in one of Malone's self-examinations is a transition to *L'Innommable*, the last volume of the trilogy: "But my fingers too write in other latitudes and the air that breathes through my pages and turns them without my knowing, when I doze off, so that the subject falls far from the verb and the object lands somewhere in the void, is not the air of this second-last abode, and a mercy it is." The last abode will be *L'Innommable*.

But the second-last abode is a rich mansion beneath its mean surface. Far from the lifeless tale that Malone predicted when he started, his stories are vigorous and economical. Though they parody the realistic novel, that genre is imitative of everyday familiar life, so that we see ourselves reflected in it, and because of Malone's tart humor, we see our absurdity. Malone is sardonic about himself, and we often laugh at his body or his surroundings. But when, in spite of himself, he reaches into his mind, humor tends to disappear, and we find ourselves in darkness. For it is only when Malone is alone, unable to summon objects or characters, that we feel the full measure of human loneliness.

Most critics have analyzed *Malone meurt* as a fiction about fiction, and it is certainly and brilliantly that. But it is more important than that. It is fiction about the brave mind of a dying animal, to whose species we belong.

L'Innommable

Not only is the Unnamable nameless; he is placeless, timeless, and he often feels languageless through all his talk. But like his predecessors with location, age, and name in Beckett's fiction, he uses words. Moreover, he is more conscious of his predecessors than is any other Beckett protagonist; the Unnamable makes several references to Murphy, Watt, Mercier-Camier, Molloy, Moran, and especially Malone. Singly and collectively, Beckett's fictions have contributed to the confusion of the Unnamable. From the beginning of his narration the Unnamable assimilates himself into them: "I believe they are all here. . . . I believe

100

we are all here." Sporadically but consistently, he tries to define himself through them, and, gradually, in spite of them. Finally, however, the Unnamable arrives at no definition, and the Unnamable comes to mean the undefinable.

But this is to begin at the end of the third volume of the trilogy. In spite of Beckett's title, in English *The Unnamable*, we have to finish the book before we know that the protagonist *remains* unnamable and indefinable. (Beckett himself arrived at namelessness through writing; the original title of the third volume of the trilogy was *Mahood*.) The Unnamable's "battle of soliloquy" is a series of skirmishes intended to trap an elusive self. As never before, the hero announces and insists that he alone is the subject of his story that is not a story, and that will renounce fictional devices. Though the Unnamable claims to be on his guard against fiction, though he explicitly banishes Beckett's fictions as "sufferers of my pains," he too slips into fiction, even foisting names on three of his heroes. Successively, he admits Basil, Mahood, and Worm, whose meaning may be seen to summarize man's conceptions of himself—Greek *basileus*, king; Mahood, manhood; and Worm, the inhabitant of graves. But Basil is also basilisk-serpent, as is Worm. Thus the Unnamable moves sequentially from king to grave, but circularly from serpent to serpent, with attendant biblical resonance. Worm also suggests larva and maggot; the Unnamable's Worm hovers at the edge of being—a larva conceived but not quite born, a maggot buried but not quite dead.

Beckett indicated that his story *La Fin* could be subtitled Limbo, and the word is at least as suitable for *L'Innommable*. In the original Latin, limbo is a border or edge, and its Christian meaning is the edge of Hell, to which the unbaptized are condemned, but by extension limbo has come to mean the edge of nowhere or oblivion. When man seeks to define himself by rejecting his surroundings, his memories, and even his habitual language, he is at the edge of nowhere. The place is unbearable, and the Unnamable

101

accepts it only gradually, and then tentatively, after exhausting all alternatives.

Though Beckett's protagonist-narrator proves to be unnamable, he himself invents names to carry his heavy burden, and the burden is all the heavier because names can summon only the frailest portraits. But the Unnamable's stories are carrying me away from him, who stamps his personality upon us, however much he denies himself. The Unnamable seems to issue from Malone, as Malone issues from Molloy, but the three are also distinct. Molloy's restless ingenuousness differs from Malone's spirit of method, and both fictional characters differ from the Unnamable, who jogs us dizzily through his evanescence.

Molloy and Malone wrote little preludes before launching into their narratives. The Unnamable writes or speaks pages of what he specifically calls a "preamble," and he is therefore slow to reach his narrative. He does not use his preamble to situate himself in space and approximate time, as do Molloy and Malone. Instead, his first paragraph asks questions, makes hypotheses, negates affirmations, and claims that it is impossible to know anything. Three opening questions are followed by "Unquestioning." "I, say I. Unbelieving." is parallelled by "It, say it, not knowing what." Neither self nor world, which have been in opposition since Beckett's *Murphy*, are knowable through words, and yet we have only words with which to know.

After a second paragraph of doubt about people and things, the Unnamable affirms that Malone revolves about him, who is seated and crying, who sees irregular lights and hears miscellaneous noises. He recalls an encounter between oblong shapes, like men. He then doubts his affirmations, erects hypotheses upon or against them, but nevertheless comes to accept them. Given the paucity of his information, the Unnamable early begins to rail against a "they" who filled him full of information about the world we know, about events we recollect from the first two volumes of the trilogy. Of "them" the Unnamable is most rancorous against Basil. When Malone continues to revolve around him, so does "the other," who does not meet Malone, and soon there are several others, so that the Unnamable beats a hasty retreat to loneliness: "Me, utter me, in the same foul breath as my creatures?" He tries to make statements about his immobility, about his inexplicable ability to write. Unable to speak, he will speak in order to stop speaking. He does not, like Molloy or Moran, claim a goal; he does not, like Malone, dwell on death. He wants only to end the discourse, to achieve silence: "Yes, it is to be wished, to end would be wonderful, no matter who I am, no matter where I am." And in order to reach an end, the Unnamable dreams of saying nothing. He denies whatever he or others have said—the Murphys, Molloys, Malones, and the figures of the novel up to this point: "no one wheels about me, no one comes towards me, no one has ever met anyone before my eyes, these creatures have never been, only I and this black void have ever been." And yet, in the first sentence of the long paragraph that follows the preamble—the paragraph that contains the remainder of the book—the Unnamable summarizes what he has already affirmed and denied: "I, of whom I know nothing, I know my eyes are open, because of the tears that pour from them unceasingly." He knows nothing, but he knows something, and he soon denies this too, declaring himself to be a talking ball. Only a voice is sure. To keep it talking "another fairy-tale" may be necessary, especially since he may have learned a few techniques in finishing "with [his] troop of lunatics." The Unnamable feels himself slipping "towards the resorts of fable," and soon he has slipped. Suddenly, Basil is important, and he is renamed Mahood, with all attendant risks: "It was he told me stories about me, lived in my stead, issued forth from me, came back to me, entered back into me, heaped stories on my head." But by the timeless time of *L'Innommable* the stories dwindle to four, occupying less than one-fifth of the pages of the novel.

As might be expected, the stories of the Unnamable bear

a resemblance to earlier Beckett stories—"it must be a sinecure handed down from generation to generation, to judge by their family air." The first story features Mahood, who is as active as Molloy or Moran. Like them, he makes the archetypical voyage home, in spite of physical handicaps (lack of a leg and the homologous arm); he retains just enough limb and life to manipulate crutches toward his arena-home. As if to compensate for a maimed body, Mahood is liberally endowed with family—father, mother, wife (alternately called Ptomaine and Isolde, each name ironic in its own way), and eight or nine offspring, all of whom focus on Mahood's journey toward their collective bosom. The larger the family, the greater prey to mortality; death comes wholesale through botulinus poisoning, and Mahood reaches home, only to find it full of the putrid flesh of his near and dear ones. But he doesn't stop there. Mahood is no Malone tale of mortality, but a metaphysical fable of the need to be witnessed. So Mahood plunges his crutches into the corpses of his family. In vain. No one is alive to testify to his existence. He is compelled to turn his words full force upon himself. Mahood might as well be the Unnamable, and creature dissolves into his creator, first-person pronoun and all.

Within a page or two, the Unnamable embarks on a new story, its immobile hero reminiscent of immobile Malone. Still named Mahood, this limbless hero is supported in a jar. In spite of this static position, he has a few perspectives on the outer world; he advertises a restaurant in whose background is a slaughterhouse—"Here all is killing and eating." Like Malone, like Macmann, Mahood is tended by a woman, the restaurant-owner alternately called Marguerite and Madeleine (both containing the syllable Ma, about which Molloy was so lyrical). The Unnamable soon shifts to the first person for this story too, gliding imperceptibly into his own obsessive search for the boundaries of his identity. Adopting the name and stance of Mahood as schoolboy, the Unnamable engages in a dialogue with mysterious mentors. But suddenly the Unnamable christens Worm, "the first of his kind." It is in the effort to pinpoint Worm, that minimal being, if being it is, that the Unnamable discovers himself back in Mahood's story in the first person. With the passage of time, the attitude of Marguerite-Madeleine has changed. Malone's ministering woman helped kill him by neglect, but Mahood's ministering woman helps kill him by assiduous attention. Because Mahood commands no credence, either from passers-by or even passing flies, the woman multiplies her cares, struggling against her doubts about Mahood's existence, but failing in her struggle. After a long excursus on himself in Worm and Worm in himself, the Unnamable finds Mahood again, only to abandon him "stuck up to his skull in his vase, opposite the shambles, beseeching the passers-by, without a word, or a gesture, or any play of his features, they don't play, to perceive him ostensibly, concomitantly with the day's dish, or independently, for reasons unknown, perhaps in the hope of being proven in the swim, that is to say guaranteed not to sink, sooner or later, that must be it, such notions may be entertained, without any process of thought." Fiction proves frail, and Beckett's hesitant phrases mirror the frailty. The effort at description precipitates into anguished literalness— "any play of his features, they don't play," "in the swim, that is to say guaranteed not to sink." Qualifiers conceal rather than reveal meaning—"ostensibly, concomitantly with the day's dish, or independently." Each phrase adds a notion, but the notions do not cohere in a conception—"without any process of thought."

Mahood, the type-character of manhood, has been propelled through two stories that summarize and parody the first two volumes of Beckett's trilogy (and much of human action)—the inventive voyager that is Molloy and the invalid waiter that is Malone. There all is voyaging or waiting. In neither story has the Unnamable succeeded in creating a second character, a witness who believes in the existence of his hero. The Mahood stories reflect the situation of the Unnamable, and they reflect the human situation of trying to define the boundaries of the self. Though I have tried to summarize the stories of the Unnamable (who calls them Mahood's stories), they are narrated murkily. The Unnamable lacks Malone's spirit of method, and his aporia intrudes upon and disintegrates his stories, which become nothing more than impenetrable words. The discourse continues, but who is saying what to whom?

This question riddles the Unnamable's book, his soliloquy, and since fiction gives no answer, the second half of the book is virtually empty of fiction in the form of story. The character Worm was created to be without character, almost without characteristics—"all-impotent, all-nescient." He will supply knowledge through ignorance, meaning through silence. By the terms of his creation, he has no story, he cannot note, and he is mute. With a single (tearing) eye and an inexplicable ability to hear, Worm is a sponge of words. He neither thinks nor feels but simply absorbs. And yet, intermittently through the second portion of Beckett's novel, Worm becomes interchangeable with, indistinguishable from, a powerfully thinking and feeling Unnamable.

Though Mahood's stories have failed to delimit his creator, though Worm is designed to be the anti-Mahood, the Unnamable tells two more brief tales—so brief that they seem to be a residual momentum of the story-telling habit of words. The first is a tale of a task, filling one container and emptying another, as happens in *Watt* and *Malone meurt*. Though the container has shrunk to a thimble, the narrator begins to build a system of pipes and taps, of hope and zeal. He forces himself to distance his little story into the third-person pronoun, who loses his thimble and then himself. The story is over.

The Unnamable's last story is equally brief and even more distant. A pronominal protagonist dies several times in several ways, so that his wife and mother (or mother-in-law) can react with emotion. But the Unnamable can summon no emotion for his story, whose nameless characters merge into one another: "there's a story for you, I thought they were over, perhaps it's a new one, lepping fresh, is it the return to the world of fable, no, just a reminder, to make me regret what I have lost, long to be again in the place I was banished from."

The whole of *L'Innommable* is only a token "return to the world of fable," for fable occupies less than one-fifth of the book. Malone told his own story while telling his fables, so that the texture of his soliloquy consisted of "fact" in tension with fiction. But the fabric of *L'Innommable* is at once thinner and more intricate, alternating the narrating "I" first with Mahood, then with Worm, to conclude in a torrent of phrases washing over the self. Mahood is the Unnamable's only fiction to figure in stories, but Mahood is also at times the manipulator of the Unnamable's thoughts. Worm figures in no stories, but he is at times the victim of the same Protean "they" who oppress the Unnamable. Mahood and Worm are very different characters from Sapo and Macmann, but they are also different from one another, as the Unnamable points out with himself at the center: "Since I couldn't be Mahood, as I might have been, I must be Worm, as I cannot be." "Mahood I couldn't die. Worm will I ever get born?" Sapo and Macmann reflect Malone's world and ours. The Unnamable has no world, but Mahood still retains images of ours. Unworldly, anti-worldly Worm makes frenzied plunges into the depths of the self, refusing words even as he breathes them. Finally as initially, and how much more frustratingly, the Unnamable is reduced to words to examine his situation, which rejects all residue of a familiar world, even language. Distrusting words, the Unnamable uses words, still trying to mark the boundaries of his imagination: "What am I doing in Mahood's story, and in Worm's, or rather what are they doing in mine?"

The Unnamable's unparagraphed rush of words is difficult to read and more difficult to pierce. The Unnamable himself is aware of the mounting accumulations of words—a thousand on memory, ten thousand as a pensum, and a blush of

107

shame every thirty or forty thousand, because speech does not yield definition. The larger the heap of words, the smaller the Unnamable's belief in them. More and more, his words are about little more than words, but that is ultimately a great deal, since he claims to be composed of words.

The Unnamable seeks himself, and by extension the essence of all selfhood, in words that he disclaims. If not his, whose? That question becomes a musical and meaningful theme of the book. Early and late, the Unnamable assigns all words to "them" a pronoun of diverse antecedent. Molloy's "they" were the malevolent inhabitants of society, but the Unnamable's "they" embrace people who have become forces and fictions—my delegates, a meeting of deputies, these gentlemen, a college of tyrants, low types, poor bastards, paltry priests of the irrepressible ephemeral, my tempters, the same old gang, my tormentors, my purveyors, poor devils, fake maniacs, voluble shades, charnel-house of renegades, herd of shites, clowns, the same foul brute . . . pretending to be a many. Creators or creatures, "they" serve the Unnamable so that he denies responsibility for the words he offers us.

Early in the novel, when the Unnamable still feels that the words emanate from him, he describes himself as a talking ball. But soon the *talking* is more certain than the *ball*, and then the Unnamable finds himself listening to a voice he no longer claims as his. The utterance of this voice—the body of the book—has an oral quality that is unique in written literature. And yet the Unnamable comments upon his composition as if he were the editor of a written manuscript. He remarks on parentheses, an ocean of commas, metaphors and apostrophes, verb tenses (including a wish for nonexistent future and conditional participles). He is aware of ellipsis, rhetoric, and types of discourse—"Orders, prayers, threats, praise, reproach, reasons." More than any previous Beckett narrator, he is troubled by pronouns because he is dubious about their ante-

Samuel Beckett's Birthplace in Foxrock, Ireland. (PHOTO M. N. JACOB)

Samuel Beckett's Apartment at 6 rue des Favorites, Paris, 1938-1961. Top story left of angle are Beckett's windows. (PHOTO HELMER)

Scene from original production of *En attendant Godot*, Paris, 1953. (PHO BERNAND)

cedents. Thus he calls the first person pronoun "cursed" or "farcical"; he regards as synonymous "I say to myself, they say to me, Worm says to me." And he inveighs against the very order of grammar: "In the meantime no sense in bickering about pronouns and other parts of blather. The subject doesn't matter, there is none. Worm being in the singular, as it turned out, they are in the plural, to avoid confusion, confusion is better avoided, pending the great confounding."

Despite these imprecations, despite his doubt about how he manages to write, the Unnamable does write with opaque coherence about chaos, even while he mirrors chaos through repetitions and rhythms of near hysteria. As early as the opening paragraph of the book, we find the rhetorical patterns that will recur—questions, hypotheses, affirmations, negations, resolutions, contradictions. Each rhetorical form seems to acquire its distinctive rhythm as the book progresses. Imagery, however, is unusually spare, even for Beckett's French fiction. The opening paragraph has only one image, forecasting the comparative nudity of the rest of the book. Into the generalizations of the first paragraph flies a single shitting bird. In the last 1500-word sentence of the book, the several images close on a door. Between birdshit and door are repeated images of darkness and silence as opposed to light and voice. Intermittently echoic are images of birds and rats, regurgitation and tears, an eye, an ear, and more rarely, a mouth. It is rhythm, more than imagery, that conveys the agony of the Unnamable—the agony of stripping away a physical, reasonable, or emotional world in order to find the essence of self, neighbor to nothing.

Through the body of *L'Innommable* monosyllabic interrogatives, negatives, and pronouns beat like a tomtom through a forest of abstraction. Occasionally counterpointed against them is a residue of polysyllabic erudition—aporia, ephectic, facetiae, naevi, infundibuliform, wistiti, hippophagist, Botal's Foramen, circumvolutionisation, succedenae, sargasso, paraphimotically, apodosis, the Abderite.

109

Molloy arrests the reader with certain sentences of poetic prose, and *Malone meurt* with obliquely relating paragraphs. In *L'Innommable* phrases gather into hypnotic rhythms. At the beginning of the book paragraphs compose the preamble, but phrasal rhythms soon break down the well-formed sentences, and eventually replace them. The discourse takes on a jerky rhythm of short phrases, with one or two accents to the phrase: "These things I say, and shall say, if I can, are no longer, or are not yet, or never were, or never will be, or if they were, if they are, if they will be, were not here, are not here, will not be here, but elsewhere." A primer of tenses, the accumulated phrases deny time and seem to deny meaning too, but that seeming denial *is* their meaning. Like hiccups, the phrases are at once painful and comical, Beckett often burying a pointed joke within the pain:

> the question may be asked, off the record, why time doesn't pass, doesn't pass from you, why it piles up all about you, instant on instant, on all sides, deeper and deeper, thicker and thicker, your time, others' time, the time of the ancient dead and the dead yet unborn, why it buries you grain by grain neither dead nor alive, with no memory of anything, no history and no prospects, buried under the seconds, saying any old thing, your mouth full of sand, oh I know it's immaterial, time is one thing, I another, but the question may be asked, why time doesn't pass, just like that, off the record, en passant, to pass the time. . . .

To pass the time, one asks the question of why time doesn't pass!

The book's opening sentences are questions: "Where now? Who now? When now?" And denials of what it is doing: "Unquestioning." The book continues with an ambiguous imperative: "I, say I." And undercuts the command: "Unbelieving." The long last sentence is still trying to answer the opening questions, trying to formulate new imperatives, trying to deny the denials. After all the effort, a voice of unknown origin concludes with a hopeless hope for a beginning: "perhaps they have carried me to the threshold of my story, before the door that opens on my story, that would surprise me, if it opens, it will be I, it will be the silence, where I am, I don't know, I'll never know, in the silence you don't know, you must go on, I can't go on, I'll go on."

The quandary of the Unnamable has been compared to that of Sartre's consciousness in *Being and Nothingness*, which should more properly be entitled *Nothingness vs. Being*. Being's main attribute is being there, in itself. Consciousness, which alone can be aware of Being, is therefore not Being, or Nothing. As Sartre summarizes the paradox in an often-quoted sentence: "Nothingness lies coiled in the heart of being—like a worm." But Beckett's Worm, the Unnamable's Worm, does not lie coiled. Sluggish as a tapeworm, he battens briefly on the unnamable being of the Unnamable, only to disappear into the wordy nothing he is.

L'Innommable embodies the paradoxical achievement of creating something that skirts nothing. Beckett has agonized over a philosophic problem in such a way that nonphilosophic readers can recognize it as their own. He has forged a distinctive voice in a bodiless narrator who denies the voice. By far the most difficult of the three volumes of the trilogy, *L'Innommable* may seem to undermine my argument for Beckett's relevance to broad areas of human experience. Three of the Unnamable's four stories swiftly dispense with forms of love, and the fourth story belittles invention. The bulk of the book dissolves the world in order to define the self. And yet the very urge to define has been *earned* through living in a human suffering world. Where *now*, after committing worlds to fiction in order to apprehend them with feeling? Who *now*, after figuring in relationships that thrive on emotion? After living intensely, and distilling that living into fiction, *I'll go on* refining that distillate, seeking an asymptotic proximity to an axis of

111

lonely experience—for what is excruciatingly intimate proves to be astoundingly common. *L'Innommable*, which concludes the three-volume portrait of a word-user, is relevant to all who play and work with words. The Unnamable digs toward himself through his fictions as we dig toward ourselves through our lives, with words as the principal undependable tool.

The Trilogy

Beckett did not preconceive of the trilogy as a trilogy. Before writing his first French novel *Mercier et Camier*, he produced a *nouvelle*. Then, dissatisfied with *Mercier et Camier*, he returned to *nouvelles* to strengthen the weakening effect of the French language on his prose. In 1947 he began another French novel, which became *Molloy*. Then, stepping back from *Molloy*, which seemed to demand continuation, he wrote the play *Eleuthéria*. Though there is almost no connection between the play and the fiction, the completion of the drama enabled Beckett to produce the second volume of the trilogy, *Malone meurt*. Again he was stopped, with his protagonist apparently dead. And again Beckett sought relief in a play, *En attendant Godot*. Freed again for fiction, he continued and completed the trilogy with *L'Innommable*. Looking back on the process, he has said that he wrote the three volumes with difficulty. "But with élan, in a sort of enthusiasm. . . . *Malone* came from *Molloy*, *The Unnamable* came from *Malone*." None of the novels was sent to a publisher until the three were completed, at which time Beckett stipulated that a publisher had to accept all or none. Some six French publishers rejected the trilogy before Jérôme Lindon of Les Editions de Minuit agreed in 1951 to publish the three "as soon as possible."

A trilogy of novels would seem to be anachronistic, a century after the heyday of the Victorian three-decker or its

112

French counterpart. These productions for leisurely reading, innocent of the competition of mass media, lasted longer in France than in England, for the twentieth century saw publication of the *romans fleuves* of Roger Martin du Gard, Jules Romains, Romain Rolland, and of course Marcel Proust. Unlike these novels, however, Beckett's trilogy has no apparent continuity in time. And unlike the tetralogy of Lawrence Durrell, Beckett's works do not supply different perspectives on the same events. Rather, his trilogy mounts in concentration and intensity through its three volumes. In *Molloy* the present is in tension with the past. In *Malone meurt* the writer's present state is in tension with a world of fiction. In *L'Innommable* the microcosm is in tension with its own inability to apprehend a macrocosm. All tensions rest on the frenzy of their protagonist-narrators.

In the trilogy Beckett centers his fiction on protagonist-narrators who are acutely conscious of narrating. Through changing names, each protagonist-narrator assimilates his predecessor, binding the three novels into a trilogy. Their successive adventures do not constitute a plot; their successive encounters do not describe a society; their successive styles do not display an organic development. The continuity of the three novels is most apparent in progressive reduction—places, people, events, things, and words themselves (the variety rather than the quantity of the last). From a room in a house to a room in an indeterminable building, the protagonist is moved to a place that is nowhere. From moving among people with name and function to meeting briefly with nameless figures, the protagonist withdraws within his problematical self. From volume to volume of the trilogy, the protagonist-narrator concentrates more demandingly upon himself, and each one is ready to consign his predecessors to oblivion: Moran—"What a rabble in my head, what a gallery of moribunds. Murphy, Watt, Yerk, Mercier and all the others." Malone—"Then it will be all over with the Murphys, Merciers, Molloys, Morans and Malones, unless it goes on beyond the grave." And the Unnamable—"then he says Murphy, or Molloy, I forget, as if I were Malone, but their day is done."

From Murphy on, Beckett's protagonists have been engaged in compulsive quests, but increasingly for Molloy, Moran, Malone, and the Unnamable the narration becomes the quest. All fictional quests are conveyed through words, but the quests of Beckett's trilogy gradually become the words of the trilogy.

In the first novel this is not immediately evident. We learn at once that Molloy and Moran are writing words, but there is discrepancy between the immobile writer and the clumsily mobile protagonist he writes about. The first volume of the trilogy is peopled with characters who answer to proper names. Jacques Moran seems to know the name of everyone in his home town of Turdy. Molloy, who looms into epic dimension, is not so definite of name, and yet he ventures a few—a woman who shelters him is Sophie, Lousse, or Loy (and her dead dog is Teddy); the woman he loved is Ruth, Edith, or Rose. With more indefiniteness, Molloy elides both women into his mother, who shares his name, Molloy. At the beginning of Molloy's story, his strangers have initials rather than names, but as he continues his voyage, he meets mere common nouns—a policeman, a shepherd, a charcoal burner. Similarly, Moran in quest of Molloy meets people whom he designates merely as a farmer, a dim man, a shepherd, another farmer (or perhaps the same one). Moran at first communicates with people in direct address, but Molloy has trouble making himself understood through words, and he does not use them to his mother or his messenger.

In the second volume of the trilogy names are not part of Malone's present state, which is reduced to a gaunt hand carrying a pot, the shadow of a couple making love, and, late in the book, a visitor in a black suit. Aphonic Malone addresses words to no one. In the third volume of the trilogy the Unnamable begins in questions and ends in resolutions—two rhetorical forms he renounces in vain. He half-heartedly gives names to his inchoate characters, but he himself is nameless and unnamable. His world is bounded only by his words—from the initial revolutions of Malone to the final sourceless voice.

In the three volumes the novel world is a reflection of the protagonist-narrator, each more unprepossessing than his predecessor. Not only do they lack ambition and achievement, but they are physically decrepit, so that they virtually crumble as we read. The sequence is graphic: Moran and the increasing pain in his legs, Molloy and the increasing paralysis in his legs, Malone and the total paralysis of most of his body, and the bodiless Unnamable. Though all four protagonists are immobile at the time of their narrations, motion plays a significant role in their stories: Moran most active, Molloy most versatile, Malone with vivid descriptions of locomotion, and the static Unnamable about whom all moves.

Since motion is defined by space and time, these two ordinates dwindle too. Moran knows that he lives in Turdy and that he seeks Molloy in Bally; on his voyage he notices the seasons of the year and, occasionally, the days of the week. Molloy seeks a nameless native town, and his awareness of the seasons is disproportionate to their length. Malone's space is confined to his room, but he still retains knowledge of the calendar, if not of passing time. For the Unnamable time and place have no reality; all he knows is that he is now in an unlocatable "here," where he has been forever. His opening questions "Where now? Who now? When now?" are never answered, but they are asked in many different forms. During the course of the trilogy there is narrative movement from and toward these questions. The trilogy as a whole moves from quest to questions.

Molloy early warns us of the discrepancy between events and narration: "And when I say I said, etc., all I mean is that I knew confusedly things were so, without knowing exactly what it was all about. And every time I say, I said this, or I said that . . . I am merely complying with the convention that demands you either lie or hold your peace. For what really happened was quite different." And similarly, Malone: "Misfortunes, blessings, I have no time to pick my words, I am in a hurry to be done. And yet no, I am in no hurry. Decidedly this evening I shall say nothing that is not false, I mean nothing that is not calculated to leave me in doubt as to my real intentions." For the Unnamable, all is doubt, all is lies.

All four narrators of the trilogy convert their doubt and lies into fiction, in the hope of lessening doubt and lies. In *Molloy* the main story threads may be fiction—search for a mother, search for Molloy. In *Malone meurt* fiction is obvious artifice—the education of Sapo, the love affair of Macmann. In *L'Innommable* the fictions dwindle to parody-sketches—Mahood's voyage home, his state of containment. Thus summarized, the fiction of the trilogy loses its comparative texture: that of Moran is still quite dense; he peoples a house and a town; he has a wardrobe and garden; even alone in the forest, he behaves like a man of means. Molloy is at once impoverished and liberated: only one town is on his horizon, and all people are strangers; possessions are profitless, and events disjunctive. Malone's fictional world is in tension with his real present state, and coherent people exist only in the former, where events can still be managed to happen swiftly and violently. For the Unnamable, fiction loses all force. Thus, Malone can distinguish clearly between the adolescent Sapo and the middle-aged Macmann, but the Unnamable uses the single name Mahood for his crippled traveler and his immobile trunk. He creates Worm to be without character, and he tells his last brief tales about nameless characters, dissolving nouns into pronouns. From Moran to the Unnamable, narrated events give way to narrated fictions, and fictions give way to discourse about the self, whoever that may be. A stream of consciousness flows on about a consciousness so general that it might belong to any one of us.

116

In the trilogy the movement is from crowd to aloneness, mobility to stasis, landscapes to ubiquitous gray, conversations to aphony, names to namelessness, Western civilization to the shards of words. Beckett's own words for these processes are energetically rhythmed. The trilogy is tensely poised between the mounting anguish of verbal rhythms and the dying sense of a civilization.

Keenly intelligent, the narrating protagonists are aware of language, and they variously try to impose some method on the flow of words. Moran is syntactically sound: his thoughts begin in conventional paragraphs, each introduced by its topic sentence. His narration is neatly divided into dialogue and description, the former properly introduced by such verbs as "said," "exclaimed." Even after he sets out in search of Molloy, it is some time before he begins to narrate in an unparagraphed sequence of impressions—a style with which we are familiar from the Molloy part of the novel. Both Molloy and Moran, writing of motion, are conscious of verbs, their tenses and moods. Malone is more systematic than either Molloy or Moran, ordering his narration before he begins: present state, stories, inventory. And he begins all three subjects with lucid measured prose, seeking precision in nouns and verbs. But the tripartite division cannot be sustained; questions and interjections disturb simple declarative grammar, and grammar becomes cause and technique of much of the booklong anguish of the Unnamable. How can one frame the simplest declarative statement: I, say I. It, say it. Me, utter me. Most often, the Unnamable makes a statement, then immediately denies or qualifies it. Some of his sentences read like verb charts through various tenses, and others like conjugations through various pronouns, without hope of establishing an antecedent.

In Beckett's trilogy energies are running down—events, characters, names, images, but not words. As people and things recede into words, the carrier of the words plays an increasingly large role, and the carrier of human words is a

117

voice. As early as *Murphy* the protagonist heard words "demanding so strongly to be spoken that he spoke them." During the harangue of Mr. Spiro in *Watt*, "Watt heard nothing of this, because of other voices, singing, crying, stating, murmuring, things unintelligible, in his ear." After Watt's departure from Mr. Knott's house, while he is reclining on his back in the darkened station, "In his skull the voices whispering their canon were like a patter of mice." The inner voice of Camier focuses on a sack, whereas that of Mercier quotes from Dante. But these are mere foreshadows of the voices of the trilogy. When Molloy first hears a voice—a whisper—he devotes a page of description to it, beginning: "I listen and the voice is of a world collapsing endlessly. . . ." Later in the novel, the voice seems to speak for Molloy's feelings; then it deserts him abruptly but finally urges him not to fret. In the Moran part of the novel Gaber's orders are replaced by an inner voice: "I have spoken of a voice giving me orders, or rather advice. It was on the way home I heard it for the first time. I paid no attention to it." But by the end of the book, Moran is all ears, for it is the voice that has commanded him to write the book he has just written.

It is in *L'Innommable*, however, that the voice dominates, seeming to speak rather than write the novel. Inconclusive as the Unnamable is about his physical construction, he intermittently knows that he has a voice: "This voice that speaks, knowing that it lies, indifferent to what it says, too old perhaps and too abased ever to succeed in saying the words that would be its last, knowing itself useless and its uselessness in vain, not listening to itself but to the silence that it breaks and whence perhaps one day will come stealing the long clear sigh of advent and farewell, is it one? . . . It is not mine, I have none, I have no voice and must speak." Whether the voice is his or not, whether it is a voice or not, the Unnamable keeps on evoking it, listening to it, hoping for it to go quiet, throughout the book, on to

118

the last page: "it will be the silence, the one that doesn't last, spent listening, spent waiting, for it to be broken, for the voice to break it," as the voice has broken silence, even while seeking it, throughout the trilogy.

Hugh Kenner has made one of the most succinct summaries of Beckett's achievement in the trilogy: "A bodily career, then (2) an immobility, then (3) a writing, then (4) a writing about the writing, along with (4a) a fiction arising from and paralleling the writing, then (5) a writing become a writing: this is not only the shape of the trilogy, and by inference Mr. Beckett's Pocket History of Western Thought from Homer to The Unnamable, it has also become an archetypal intellectual career." But Kenner's summary, as I believe he would admit, skirts the central achievement of the trilogy. Beckett abandoned his own intellectual career almost before he had started it, and about the trilogy he told an interviewer: "I conceived *Molloy* and what followed the day I became aware of my stupidity. Then I began to write the things I feel." I think he meant this literally. After absorbing much knowledge, Beckett became aware that one can know too much to know, that one must return to the innocence of stupidity in order to feel.

If the trilogy is Beckett's Pocket History of Western Thought from Homer to the Unnamable, it is that in spite of its author. In the trilogy Western Thought comes to us in fragments—Homer, Democritus, Aquinas, Dante, Descartes, Geulincx—but "the things I feel" are passionately present on every page. The trilogy heroes do not indulge in Murphy's snobbish solipsism; they try to communicate, not only through words but through love. Molloy's emotional life is the richest—Mother Ma-g, Sophie-Loy-Lousse, Ruth-Edith-Rose. Malone has to imagine love—Macmann and his Moll. The Unnamable can imagine it more slenderly—Mahood moving toward Ptomaine-Isolde or witnessed by Marguerite-Madeleine. Deliberate uncertainty as to the

119

name of the beloved undercuts the romantic tradition of a one-and-only, and for all the authentic details of tenderness, love provides no enduring witness or communication.

Tenderness dissolves in suffering. Torture and death are reserved mainly for animals, but the resonances are human. People are subjected to smaller tortures and temporary deaths: Molloy's sojourn in prison, Moran's vexations with his faith, Malone's slow starvation, and the ubiquitous uncertainty of the Unnamable. All four narrators hope that fiction will be a life raft on an ocean of doubts. In vain. For fiction disintegrates into the words that compose it.

At the level of literary history, details of the trilogy are rooted in Beckett's life. Landscapes are vaguely Irish, and Molloy's native town, according to Moran, is Bally. Sapo has pale blue eyes, like Beckett's own. Moran's neighbors, the Elsner sisters, are named for Beckett's kindergarten teacher, and Big Lambert is based on a man Beckett knew in the Vaucluse. Macmann is incarcerated in the House of St. John of God, the actual name of the insane asylum near Beckett's Irish home. Mahood returns to an arena-home that resembles a rotunda near Beckett's Paris apartment on rue des Favorites, and a neighboring restaurant displayed a picture of a thief in a jar. *Malone meurt* was written in two notebooks that resemble the one that Malone describes, and the Unnamable complains of narrating, as Beckett does, in "a tongue that is not mine."

This evidence for the personal basis of Beckett's fiction is interesting because it shows how Beckett has filtered his experience so that it evokes our own. The trilogy may be a writer's writing about writing become a writing, but however critics dissect writing, language continues to be the prime mode of apprehending experience, even in this age of other media of communication. The trilogy is written by a feeling thinker who expresses himself in words.

Beckett's trilogy immerses us in four streams of consciousness that flow from his own. Each successive stream gathers momentum from its predecessor. Beckett's French trilogy moves through the pain of personal and cultural memory to involve us in intimate experiences we have darkly known.

4.

PLAYS MANY PARTS

ALTHOUGH Beckett probes most deeply through fiction, he has long been interested in the performing arts. He attended the Abbey Theatre in Dublin, where he remembers seeing the plays of Synge, Yeats, and O'Casey, and in Paris he used to visit big and little theaters. He is still an enthusiast of circus and silent cinema. After the success of *Godot* in 1953, he has numbered theater people among his friends, and he has often seen their work in rehearsal. As early as 1929 he used dialogue form in "Che Sciagura," and twenty years later he criticized modern painting in "Three Dialogues." Actually intended for performance are more Beckett pieces than are usually realized—eighteen.

Performance elicits a more immediate response than print, and I have seen performances of several Beckett plays before I read them. As I tried to analyze the plays for this chapter, I often called a theater to the eye of my mind, and I hope that this chapter will convey some sense of that theater.

FALSE STARTS

Beckett's first play, *Le Kid*, was written in French in 1931. A parody of Corneille's *Cid*, it was staged by the Modern Language Society of Trinity College. Exchange student Georges Pelorson was co-author and director. Twenty-four-year-old Beckett played Don Diègue, father of the Kid, using an umbrella as sword. The manuscript of *Le Kid* is lost, but a review survives in the Trinity College newspaper. Except for two sentences on production, it reads

122

as follows: "And now we come to *Le Kid*. To be truthful, it made us laugh, but with a rather bitter laughter, and it was not at Corneille we were laughing. Really wasn't it rather naïve? It reminded us forciably [sic] of those grand old parodies that used to be shown at the Gaiety some forty years past, 'Carmen Uptodata,' and the like—unless you happened to hate Corneille very, very heartily it was rather a strain on the digestion. The name of the author, or rather adapter, did not appear on the programme, but we have a theory it was the work of Guy de Maupassant—his very last work, if not, indeed, posthumous." The theory is of course incorrect, and the anonymous but decidedly unposthumous author replied to the review in a dialogue entitled "The Possessed." The undergraduate editor evidently thought it necessary to introduce that rebuttal: "We are given to understand that the following is a reply to our reporter's criticism of the M.L.S. Plays; as such we publish it." The following lines appear to refer to the performance: "The Infanta might have cantered/ like a shopwalker/ through the Dämmerung/ but she was not in training./ The Cid (or hero, whose death, we understand, occurred in 1199)/ Could have been transmitted with a seriousness/ more in keeping with the spiritual ancestor of the centreforward./ A production, Professor,/ from every centre of perspective/ vox populi and yet not/ platotudinous/ cannot entertain/ me." In later years Beckett has sometimes been (mis)quoted in comments on his reviewers, but this is his only authentic public reply. Meant to puncture the pompous tone of the student review, the piece is itself pompous but funny.

Beckett took his next venture into drama more seriously, but he was unable to write the play for which he filled three notebooks with material on Dr. Samuel Johnson's relations with Mrs. Thrale. When they met in 1764, Dr. Johnson was 55, Mrs. Thrale 23 and married. During the twenty years of their acquaintance, Mrs. Thrale was almost continually pregnant. Mr. Thrale died in 1781, and after an ambiguous flirtation with Dr. Johnson Mrs. Thrale married Gabriel

Piozzi in July, 1784. Johnson wished never to hear of her again, and he died unforgiving in December, 1784. Beckett intended to call his drama *Human Wishes*, after Johnson's poem "The Vanity of Human Wishes." The play was to contain four acts, one for each year between Thrale's death and his widow's remarriage. But Beckett managed to write only part of the first scene, toward the end of which Dr. Johnson was to make his appearance. Incomplete as it is, this fractional scene of ten typed pages promises the significant rhythms of his plays to come.

Not until Beckett's fertile five-year period, 1946-1950, did he turn again to dramatic form. *Eleuthéria*, Greek for "freedom," was written in French, probably after *Molloy*. *Eleuthéria* is Beckett's longest play—it would probably be about three hours in performance, but it has never been performed. Jean Vilar accepted it for the Théâtre Nationale Populaire if Beckett would cut it to one act, but the author refused. Accepted unconditionally by director Roger Blin at the same time as *En attendant Godot*, announced for publication by Les Editions de Minuit, *Eleuthéria* remains unproduced and unpublished, even after Beckett has lifted his interdiction against *Premier Amour* and *Mercier et Camier*. Intuitively as Beckett seems to grasp different genres, he was more hesitant about dramatic than fictional form. *Le Kid* is lost, but "The Possessed" may indicate the academic stiffness of the parody. Much research prepared *Human Wishes*, and yet Beckett was unable to proceed beyond the first scene. *Eleuthéria* rests on no literary basis; it is complete, and it is clumsy.

If director Roger Blin had found money to produce the three-set, seventeen-character *Eleuthéria* instead of the single set, five-character *Godot*, Beckett's public success might never have happened. A traditional theater audience could have pigeon-holed *Eleuthéria* as another variant on a familiar theme—sensitive young man rebels against bourgeois background. There would have been no striking pronouncement by Jean Anouilh, and it is improbable that the play would have enjoyed a profitable run, so that *Godot* might never have been produced. Beckett would then have struggled on as a novelist, appreciated by the few and ignored by the many. *Eleuthéria* might have freed him from his fascination with the performing arts. And we would have been the poorer for it.

Eleuthéria, or freedom, is the goal of the play's hero, young Victor Krap, but we do not know this until the last of the three acts. We would know from a program note that the action takes place in contemporary Paris, on three successive winter days. In the first two acts the stage is divided between the furniture-filled salon of the Krap house and Victor's miserable hotel room, located near l'Impasse de L'Enfant-Jésus. The main action of Act I is played in the former while Victor moves about his room or reclines on his bed. Conversely, the main action of Act II is played in Victor's room, while the Krap living-room is largely empty, though a manservant enters and exits, and for a few minutes Victor enters to gaze at his father's armchair. By Act III Victor's room usurps the entire stage.

The split stage symbolizes two different ways of life. Act I satirizes the ailing bourgeois Krap family. Their worst affliction is their son Victor who left home two years ago, to live in "sordid inertia." Act II shows us that sordid inertia in Victor's sordid room. After his father dies between the acts, emissaries from the bourgeois world try to lure or threaten Victor back to the maternal bosom. By Act III, as in the well-made play, light dissolves mystery, and obstacles vanish. Victor declares his independence: "Liberty is seeing yourself dead." At the final curtain, having rejected both return and suicide, having looked long and hard at the audience, Victor lies down on his folding bed, *"his thin back turned on humanity."*

The Act I satire is so broad that it borders on farce, as in the obscene overtones of the names Krap, Piouk, Skunk, and Meck (French slang for pimp); in the repeated knocking of the manservant; in the inability of father Krap to

125

urinate; in Dr. Piouk's enthusiasm for birth control to diminish the human race. Act II provides some serious relief
in the character of a glazier who arrives when Victor flings
his shoe through his window; the glazier's exchanges with
his son resemble those of Mercier and Camier, predicting
Gogo and Didi. By Act III Beckett profits from the well-
made play structure that he uses and mocks; he has aroused
curiosity and sympathy about Victor's departure from his
bourgeois home. Victor, having freed himself from that
world, now tries to free himself from himself: "By being as
little as possible. By not moving, not thinking, not dreaming, not speaking, not listening, not perceiving, not knowing, not desiring, not being able and so on." Though Victor
admits that freedom is impossible, he will dedicate his life
to its pursuit: "I will never be free. (Pause.) But I will
ceaselessly feel myself becoming free. (Pause.) I'll tell you
how I'll live my life away: rubbing my chains against one
another. From morning to night, and from night to morning.
That faint vain noise will be my life."

Not only does the familiarly rebellious son rebel in an
unfamiliar language, but the other characters are not cleanly
aligned against him. Even before Victor's predicament is
revealed to us, we are aware that his father dies with some
understanding of his son. The manservant Jacques and the
maid Marie are grateful for Victor's "music." The mysterious
glazier and a planted spectator avidly receive Victor's self-
explanation, which they extort with the help of a Chinese
torturer. And, finally, Dr. André Piouk, who loves humanity
so much that he advocates its destruction by all methods
ranging from abortion to euthanasia, sympathetically offers
poison to Victor. But dead, Victor could not be aware of
his death, and the only death that tempts him includes the
awareness of his death: "You can't see yourself dead. That's
play-acting." Even in the play, however he tries, Victor
cannot attain the freedom of death—complete withdrawal.
And as a play, *Eleuthéria* is very uneven—obvious in the
crucial opening act, tedious in arousing interest in the

second act, and too slow in concluding the third act, after the meaningful moments between Victor, Glazier, and Spectator. Dialogue references to the play as a play bear the stamp of Molière and Pirandello (even to mentioning the author as Beckett, pronounced Becquet). Too diffuse in its broad comedy, the play explains rather than plays its intention.

The experienced Beckett reader can nevertheless discern characteristic Beckett motifs in *Eleuthéria*—the search for self, a man on a bed in a room, obscene and punning names, reflexive comment on the play as a play. But the clumsiness and irrelevance are atypical of Beckett. One might have guessed in 1947 that drama was not his genre—as it was not that of Henry James, Emile Zola, James Joyce, Ernest Hemingway. One would have guessed wrong, but it is nevertheless astonishing that, within about a year of *Eleuthéria*, *Godot* was born.

WAITING

How describe its initial impact to a generation that has grown up with *Godot*? Now that any serious drama seeks a mythic dimension; now that disjunction is the familiar rhetorical pattern of stage speech; now that tragic depth almost always wears clown costume; now that the gestures of drama border on dance; now that expositions are quainter than soliloquies, and stage presence implies neither past nor future—now it may be hard to recall that it was not always so. *En attendant Godot* brought the curtain down on King Ibsen.

After nearly two decades, my bad memory clings to the warmth of that first *Godot* on a damp winter night. I had never heard of Beckett when I first saw *Godot*. I did not know my Bible well enough to recognize the scriptural kernel of the play. I had not read Hegel's *Phenomenology of Mind* well enough to recognize the archetypical Master-Slave relationship. I was not even a devotee of silent comic films. In short, I came to *Godot* with no background; or with too much background of Broadway problem plays, Comédie Française classics, and verse drama wherever I could find it. And yet I knew almost at once that those two French-speaking tramps were me; more miserable, more lovable, more humorous, more desperate. But me.

Laughter did not ring out through the little Théâtre de Babylone, as in performances I saw later. Rather, chuckles faded into smiles or frowns. I must have been too full of feeling to notice the unusual stage silences through which I fidgeted in later productions. The élan of those aboriginal Beckett tramps carried me right over the silences. But Pozzo and Lucky repelled me, recalling a circus-master and his trained animal. Long a coward about physical pain, I could hardly look at Lucky's neck, for fear of seeing his bruises, and I looked with distaste at Pozzo who supposedly caused the bruises I didn't see. Lucky's monologue was so terrible to watch, with Jean Martin's spastic tics, that I thought *that* was the reason I could make no sense of it. I was ashamedly relieved when the other three characters shut Lucky up, and I was not sorry to see what I thought would be the last of him and his master. I can recall none of my intermission questions, but I can still see the Act II leaves on the tree, like shreds of green crêpe-paper. And I caught the point of the dog-song at once. "That's what the play is about." I must have told myself, as I settled back familiarly into the patter of the two tramps. I was surprised by the return of Pozzo and Lucky, no more sympathetic when maimed and subdued. I was even more surprised at the callousness with which the friends treated the unfortunate couple. But I wasn't surprised that Godot didn't come. I was pretty sure that the end of the play *was* the end, but I was pleased to have this confirmed by scattered applause, in which I joined vigorously. I can't remember the number of curtain calls, but there weren't many.

How was *Godot* received by other audiences who did not know that it was to become a classic? It was a running gag in Miami, the American opening city, that taxis could be sure of fares at the end of Act I. Michael Myerberg advertised for (and did not find) an audience of 80,000 intellectuals in New York City. Moving response came from San Quentin prison, but Herbert Blau nearly had a mutiny in his company before he persuaded them to do the play that was so meaningful for prisoners. Several of its first directors returned for another round with *Godot*—Blin, Blau, Schneider. In 1966 Yugoslavian Miodrag Bulatović wrote a sequel, *Godot Came*. Before the death of Bertold Brecht in 1956, he wanted to adapt Beckett's play, and in 1971 Peter Palitsch, once Brecht's student, produced a Brechtian *Godot*, replete with gestus and estrangement. Though the original reception of *Godot* was unexpectedly good, enthusiasm for it is still far from universal. In 1956 Bert Lahr-Gogo received a letter denouncing the play as "communistic, atheistic, and existential." In May, 1971, an American college professor was forced to resign after directing *Godot*, which was declared "detrimental to the moral fibre of the college community."

Beckett would be the last to defend *Godot*. "I began to write *Godot*," he told Colin Duckworth, "as a relaxation, to get away from the awful prose I was writing at that time." I have tried to show that if the prose of the trilogy is awful, it is in the sense of awe-inspiring, and yet I can guess at what Beckett meant. Malone was unable to stick to his spirit of system; doubt eroded each scene he tried to present. The Unnamable was waiting in the wings or the cellarage. In turning to dramatic form, Beckett may have been seeking an order that he could not honestly impose on his fiction. Later he was to tell Michael Haerdter: "That's the value of theater for me. You place on stage a little world with its own laws." But Beckett's little stage worlds are emblematic of our big real world.

The seed of *Godot* is Luke's account of the crucifixion, as summarized by St. Augustine: "Do not despair: one of the thieves was saved. Do not presume: one of the thieves was

129

damned." The two thieves are Didi and Gogo; the two thieves are Pozzo and Lucky; the two thieves are you and me. And the play is shaped to reflect that fearful symmetry. I am not for a moment suggesting that this was a conscious choice on Beckett's part. Embroiled as he was in the murky lyricism of the trilogy, he sought the repose of order—"cawm," as Gogo would say. The *Godot* manuscript bears evidence of Beckett's sure shaping touch; the handwriting, unusually legible rather than cramped with effort, flows along with few changes. The dialogue rhythm, as Colin Duckworth has shown in careful detail, leans on that of *Mercier et Camier*, but the basic form comes from St. Augustine.

Even before the curtain rises, the program informs us that there will be *two* acts, though we do not know how the second will reflect the first. The set pits the horizontal road on the stage board against the vertical tree. The action will balance four characters falling *down* against their looking *up* at the sky. The very names of the four main characters indicate their pairing: Pozzo and Lucky contain two syllables and five letters each; Estragon and Vladimir contain three syllables and eight letters each, but they address one another only by nicknames—Gogo and Didi, childish four-letter words composed of repeated monosyllables. Even the fifth character, the nameless boy, has a brother, and he says that Godot beats the one but not the other. Godot is as arbitrary as the God of *Matthew* 25:32-33: "And before him shall be gathered all nations: and he shall separate them one from another, as a shepherd divideth his sheep from the goats. And he shall set the sheep on his right hand but the goats on the left." Sheep and goat become saved thief and damned thief of St. Augustine's symmetry.

Didi broods about the two thieves early in the play, as we are getting acquainted with what look like two thieves on stage. Though it is not specified in the text, Beckett's two thieves wear similar clothes in production—the black suit and derby of music-hall or silent film, and we laugh at their antics much of the time that they are constantly before us. (For Roger Blin, the ideal cast would have been Chaplin as Didi, Keaton as Gogo, and Laughton as Pozzo.) Pozzo and Lucky have no nicknames, and we view them formally, externally, during their intermittent presence before us. Their clothes are elaborate but dated, their relationship is repulsive, but it is not really our business. Pozzo seems to want to become our business (through the friends), lush as he is with self-revelation (to the friends), but he himself warns that "there wasn't a word of truth in it." Lucky speaks of his civilization rather than himself in his single long monologue, which contains the word "I" only in the mechanical phrase, "I resume." Impersonal Pozzo and Lucky confront personal Gogo and Didi, and for all the many pages that have now been written about the play, *Godot's* theatricality rests very squarely on this confrontation of two couples. To twist what Beckett said about the two-act structure of *Godot*: one couple would have been too few, and three would have been too many. Pozzo and Lucky alone would have been a caricature of human master-slave tendencies, a caricature of human obsession with moving "On." Caricatures summon no sympathy. Without these contrasting caricatures, however, we would respond less immediately to the concreteness of Didi and Gogo. We appreciate their friendship in the contrapuntal context of Pozzo and Lucky. In the shadow of these compulsive wanderers, who wander into obvious deterioration, Didi and Gogo scintillate with variety. Each couple is more meaningful because of the other, replacing the protagonist and antagonist of dramatic tradition.

None of these symmetries is exact, of course. Act II does not repeat Act I precisely. Each member of each couple is distinctive and individual. And looming asymmetrically offstage is Godot. The very first review suggested that Godot might be "happiness, eternal life, the unattainable quest of all men." And Godot has subsequently been explained as God, a diminutive god, Love, Death, Silence, Hope, De

131

Gaulle, Pozzo, a Balzac character, a bicycle racer, Time Future, a Paris street for call-girls, a distasteful image evoked by French words containing the root *god* (*godailler*, to guzzle; *godenot*, runt; *godelureau*, bumpkin; *godichon*, lout). Beckett told Roger Blin that the name Godot derived from French slang words for boot—*godillot*, *godasse*. A decade after *Godot* was produced, I informed Beckett of a San Francisco mortician's firm, Godeau Inc. Beckett's play tells us plainly who Godot is—the promise that is always awaited and not fulfilled, the expectation that brings two men to the board night after night. The play tells us this dramatically and not discursively.

St. Augustine commented on the crucifixions in Luke's gospel: "Do not despair; one of the thieves was saved. Do not presume: one of the thieves was damned." Fifty per cent may be a reasonable chance, but only one of the four gospels argues for that percentage, so that Didi arrives at a dimmer view: "But all four were there. And only one speaks of a thief being saved." It is no wonder then that Didi and Gogo are more tempted to despair than to presume. And yet they do not despair. Instead, they keep their appointment, and they wait. Night after night, they keep their appointment, and they wait. While they wait, they repeat the activities that add up to a life.

From the beginning of the play Didi and Gogo emphasize the repetitive nature of their activities. Were Beckett to direct the play, he would now begin with their attitude of waiting, which would be periodically repeated throughout the play. In the printed text the play begins when Estragon tries *again* to take off his boots. We read the first example of a frequently repeated scenic direction: "*As before*" (in French, even more pointedly, "*Même jeu*," literally "*Same play*"). In Vladimir's first speech he talks about *resuming* the struggle. He notes that Estragon is there *again*—wherever "there" may be. He is glad that Estragon is *back*— wherever "back" may be. Vladimir wants to celebrate his reunion with Estragon.

In the first few minutes of playing time each of the friends asks the significant question: "It hurts?" And the other answers: "Hurts! He wants to know if it hurts!" This first of the many repetitions of the dialogue makes pain general, but also musical. Beckett never sacrifices meaning to sound, but as in his complex fiction he often intensifies meaning through sound.

Immediately after the first utterance of the most frequently repeated line in the play—"We're waiting for Godot"—the friends turn their attention to the stage tree. Estragon says: "Looks to me more like a bush." Vladimir counters: "A shrub." But Estragon insists: "A bush." This exchange sets a pattern of poetic variants and refrains, with Estragon always speaking the refrain lines. Throughout the play, phrasal repetition, most naked in Lucky's manic monologue, is reinforced by gestural repetition: Lucky with his luggage, Pozzo with his possessions, Gogo with his shoes, Didi with his hat, and the music-hall routine in which Gogo and Didi juggle three hats (suggested to Beckett by the Marx Brothers' *Duck Soup*). All the characters repeatedly stumble and fall, but in Act I Didi and Gogo set Lucky on his feet, and in Act II they do the same for Pozzo. Repetition is theme and technique of Didi's round-song which reduces man's life to a dog's life—and cruel death.

In the printed text of *En attendant Godot* the most frequent repetitions are two scenic directions: *Silence* and *Pause*. In the theater repeated stillness can reach a point of no return, but Beckett avoids this danger by adroit deployment of his pauses and silences. They act like theatrical punctuation, a pause often marking hesitation or qualification, whereas silence is a brush with despair before making a fresh start. The play never quite negates a fresh start after stillness claims the stage in sudden night. All stage action has to be wrested from the background stillness, the ever-threatening void. Gogo realizes: "There's no lack of void." And he recalls talking about *nothing* in particular." (The italics are mine; Beckett changes the French "boots" to

133

"nothing" in the English version.) Each of the two acts ends with the stillness after the same lines: "Well? Shall we go?" asks one of the friends, and the other replies: "Yes, let's go." In neither act do they move as the curtain falls.

The opening "Nothing to be done" is repeated three times. What distinguishes drama from fiction is that the Nothing has to be done, acted, performed. The body of Beckett's play therefore contains much doing, constantly threatened by Nothing. To open each act, Gogo and Didi enter separately, each in turn first on stage. At least one of them eats, excretes, sleeps, dreams, remembers, plans, refers to sex or suicide. In both acts they comment on their reunion, they complain of their misery, they seek escape into games, they are frightened by offstage menace, they try to remember a past, they stammer a hope for a future, they utter doubts about time, place, and language, they wait for Godot. Beckett's scenic directions show the range of their emotions: irritably, coldly, admiringly, decisively, gloomily, cheerfully, feebly, angrily, musingly, despairingly, very insidiously, looking wildly about, wheedling, voluptuously, gently, highly excited, grotesquely rigid, violently, meditatively, vacuously, timidly, conciliating, hastily, grudgingly, stutteringly, resolute, vehemently, forcibly, tenderly, blankly, indignantly, attentively, sadly, shocked, joyous, indifferent, vexed, suddenly furious, exasperated, sententious, in anguish, sure of himself, controlling himself, triumphantly, stupefied, softly, recoiling, alarmed, laughing noisily, sagging, painfully, feverishly—with violently and despairingly most frequent.

In each act the two friends are diverted by an interlude— the play within the play of Pozzo and Lucky, who enter and exit tied together. Reciting rhetorically and loaded with props, Pozzo and Lucky are cut down to size when they are "done" by Gogo and Didi in Act II. Alone again in each act, the friends are greeted by Godot's messenger, they hear the monotonous message, and the moon rises swiftly. Refrains, repetitions, and pauses camouflage how *much* is happening on stage. Only in retrospect, after viewing it all, do we realize how much is at stake in these hapless happenings.

V. A. Kolve has compared *Godot* to medieval drama: in the Corpus Christi plays, Holy Saturday, the day between Christ's death and resurrection, is the day when nothing can be known or done, when faith is eroded by doubt. Didi and Gogo are to meet Godot on Saturday, but no Easter dawns with its promise of resurrection. The other medieval form, the morality play, portrays Everyman seeking salvation, the medieval human condition. But conditions have changed since the Middle Ages. Didi ponders salvation, but he has to rack his brain before he can think of the opposite of salvation: the damnation that must have been vividly present in the medieval mind, but that is modern everyday reality. Modern man knows no psychomachia; he waits out a life of Holy Saturdays, closer to the passivity of Zen than to redemption. "Doing the tree" of *Godot* is exercise 52 in the yoga series, standing on one leg to pray, but Gogo cannot keep his balance, and there is no evidence that God sees him.

While waiting for Godot, Didi and Gogo act out their condition, together and alone. Gogo, as his name suggests (English "go"), is the more physical in his needs, complaints, perceptions. Didi, as his name suggests (French "dis"), is more voluble and philosophical. They are interdependent, and yet each is a whole man and not an allegorical abstraction. Simply human, each of them suffers while waiting, but they react against suffering by trying to fill or kill the time of waiting. Their activities have an improvisational quality —dancing, juggling, tumbling, miming, falling, and rising— with Gogo the more active of the two. Their dialogue is varied with questions and exclamations, logic and disjunction, incompleteness and alternatives, erudition and obscenity, synonyms and antonyms, paradox and incongruity, tenderness and imprecation—with Didi the more inventive of the two. Their first discussion of Godot is a music-hall routine, and their duet about dead voices is, in Herbert

135

Blau's phrase, "a superb threnody on desire, mortality, and time." Physically and metaphysically, their words and gestures penetrate our own.

Most of us, however, would be reluctant to see ourselves in the doings of Pozzo and Lucky. Pozzo and Lucky of Act I are ready performers, and their flagrant contrast is part of the performance. They dress according to their social station; Pozzo flourishes his props (whip, pipe, atomizer, watch) whereas Lucky bends under burdens. Lucky can dance and think; actor Jack MacGowran has indicated the three threads of Lucky's monologue: the constancy of the divine, the shrinkage of humanity, the petrifaction of the earth. Lucky's monologue displays Western civilization as shards of religion, philosophy, science, art, sport, and modern industry. In that monologue Lucky utters the word "unfinished" seven times; his sentences do not finish, and his monologue is not permitted to finish. Named with devastating irony, Lucky is modern man with his contradictory unfinished fragments.

The Pozzo of Act I needs all eyes on him to answer a simple question. He recites an elocution piece with studied gestures. But though he may be a dilettante, he has meditated on time and life, theory and practice. Physically, he and Lucky lack the friends' gestural variety, and yet they do move about. Lucky carries, and Pozzo sits; both of them fall and shakily rise. Compulsively, they voyage "on," perhaps to perform at another encounter. Both master and servant deliver set-pieces of dialogue, too thoroughly rehearsed. Pozzo resembles a disc jockey or television announcer, and Lucky a broken record. But by Act II, Lucky is dumb, and blind Pozzo speaks only in passion. No longer able to entertain, they present their misery for the friends' diversion. When Didi questions Pozzo, as a journalist might question yesterday's star actor, Pozzo explodes into the most haunting line of the play: "They give birth astride of a grave, the light gleams an instant, then it's night once more."

136

The night is immeasurably more profound than the twilight of Pozzo's Act I set-piece.

Though less obstreperous than Pozzo and Lucky, Didi and Gogo are also performers. Gogo is a would-be raconteur, and Didi paraphrases the Bible. In Act I Pozzo and perhaps Lucky are aware of being performers, but Didi and perhaps Gogo are aware of being in a play. And they are aware of playing to pass time: "We always find something, eh Didi, to give us the impression we exist?" In giving us that intense impression, the two friends undercut their mockery of their own play. "We are bored to death," complains Didi. Millions of spectators have been entertained by that boredom.

One of the most time-conscious plays ever written, *En attendant Godot* has itself been buffeted by time. In 1971, the same year that it was said to undermine the moral fibre of a college community, *Time* magazine's reporter took a deep breath and pronounced it "no masterpiece" for much the same reason: "*Waiting for Godot* is Beckett's tomb. Need it necessarily be ours?" We seem to have come full circle to some of the early Sunday-supplement reaction to *Godot*. And it is not uncheering that, in spite of the reams that have been written about *Godot*, it can still disturb.

Beyond a very few references, I have said little about these reams. The first book about Beckett focuses largely on *Godot*, and every year brings new interpretations. I have edited a volume that contains theatrical, source, genre, Marxist, Christian, mythic, philosophic, phenomenological, imagistic, linguistic interpretations of *Godot*. Other editors have included other approaches. Many discussions are illuminating, but none is indispensable. It is not even indispensable, or especially helpful, to know Beckett's other works in order to respond to *Godot*. I do not believe that *Godot* is Beckett's greatest work, but it is perhaps his most immediate. As *Malone* presents us with the building-blocks of stories, *Godot* shows us how hard it is to build a play.

137

And since playing is the most direct imitation of living, theater can evoke the most immediate audience response.

I lingered so long on my own first reaction to *Godot* because it is hard today to see *Godot* without ever having heard of it. But if one could, I think one would—as I did—virtually build the play along with the actors. Not in amateur admixtures *à la* "happening," but through absorption in Beckett's scenes. Unlike previous drama that posits a past, *Godot's* *thereness* unrolls before our perceptions, as Alain Robbe-Grillet understood so early. Only the opening lines are gratuitous in *Godot*. After that each line is uttered on cue. Nor does such sequence contradict what I said earlier about the drama's improvisational quality. Improvisation, as today's actors well know, is hard work. Improvisation is not synonymous with spontaneous effervescence. Stage time has to be played through, and each line, each gesture, takes effort. Combining lines and gestures may result from tedious rehearsal, as in Pozzo's set-piece; or word and motion may remain separate. Even words demanding motion may not attain it. Estragon says "Over there" without gesture. When he says, "I'm going," he goes nowhere. Vladimir offers to give Lucky a handkerchief, but he does not approach him. And each act's curtain-line is, "Yes, let's go," but the two actors *"do not move."*

All this serves to focus attention on the very elements of drama—entrances, exits, silence, cues, repartee, blocking, and the offstage unknown. Least subtle in *Godot* are the lines that refer to the play as a play: "This is becoming really insignificant." "I've been better entertained." However, the lines embrace more than the particular situation. And it is this extensibility, rooted in particulars, that ultimately makes a classic of *Godot*, as of *Hamlet*. Hamlet's questions—specific questions in the play's dialogue—probe to a depth undreamed of in our revenge plays. *Godot's* questions—questions, often unanswered, constitute about one quarter of the play's sentences—probe to a metaphysics undreamed of in our physics. The play's opening assertion,

"Nothing to be done" (even more casual in the French cliché "Rien à faire"), is spoken by Estragon about his boots. But Vladimir picks it up as a metaphysical generalization: "I'm beginning to come round to that opinion. All my life I've tried to put it from me. . . ." By the end of the play, Vladimir is still living, so he is still trying to put it from him, still only coming round to that opinion. During the course of the play, he has made such metaphysical observations as: "Where are all these corpses from?" "There's no lack of void." "Time has stopped." "But at this place at this moment of time, all mankind is us, whether we like it or not." (The cross-nationality of the names of the four characters reinforces this assertion.) More humorously, Estragon utters comparably cosmic lines: "People are bloody ignorant apes." "Pah! The wind in the reeds" (on a dusty highway). "Everything oozes." "I'm tired breathing." Near the end, Vladimir paraphrases Pozzo's heartrending line: "Astride of a grave and a difficult birth. Down in the hole, lingeringly, the grave-digger puts on the forceps. We have time to grow old. The air is full of our cries." Like other single speeches in the tragicomedy, *that* is what *Godot* is about. "Our cries" compose its dialogue, orchestrated by Beckett, and understood in many languages.

Ending

Endgame is swathed in pain. Between the writing of *Godot* and the writing of *Fin de partie* Beckett's mother and brother died. After 1950 Beckett felt that *L'Innommable* had brought him to a dead end from which the *Textes pour rien* did not extricate him. In 1954 he began a French play that only slowly became *Fin de partie*. He worked on it during most of 1955, but with distaste set aside a two-act version. *Fin de partie* was not completed in its present form till mid-1956, when Beckett described it in a letter to American director Alan Schneider: "Rather difficult and elliptic, mostly depending on the power of the text to claw, more inhuman than 'Godot.'" For over a year Beckett shied away from translating it into English, where, he felt, "The loss will be much greater than from the French to the English 'Godot.'" Despite the success of the Paris production of *Godot*, director Roger Blin could find no theater willing to help finance *Fin de partie*, which therefore opened at George Devine's Royal Court Theatre in London, in French. Neither *Fin de partie* nor *Endgame* has known a fraction of *Godot*'s success.

The play's pain never deliquesces into pathos. I do not know what Beckett meant by "more inhuman than 'Godot,'" for *Endgame*'s anguish is heartbreakingly human. All living beings die, but only human beings can be aware of themselves dying. And the four human beings of *Fin de partie* are monsters of awareness: "I see my light dying."

When we begin to live, we begin to die. Beckett rarely spares us this knowledge. But *Fin de partie* is a play about the dying of the *last* human beings, and it is appallingly relevant to our split-atom world, whose last inhabitants we may be. The shelter of *Fin de partie* staves off death for a few, but it offers no protection from knowledge of death of the species. The play's attitude toward death is ambiguous since the suffering of living is so acute that death becomes a form of release. That release is painfully approached—all the characters are in pain—but never achieved in *Fin de partie*.

As the action of *Godot* is waiting, the action of *Fin de partie* is ending. The play opens with the word "finished," and it asymptotically approaches its end. The printed text of the play opens with a curiously inaccurate stage direction: "*Bare interior.*" (The French is: "Interior without furniture.") The stage interior is spare but not bare: a picture has its face to the wall (a sign of mourning), one sheet covers a throne-chair on casters, and another covers two touching ashbins (another sign of mourning). *Fin de partie* takes place in a spare interior that is the living—and dying —room of a family. In some ways the family is ordinary,

140

with its attachments and disagreements; in most ways the family is extraordinary, being the last of the human race.

The family of *Fin de partie* has no family name. The program reveals the symmetry of single names: Nagg and Nell, with their vaguely equine suggestion; Hamm and Clov with resonances of a substantial meal. Four-letter words all, all four names mean *nail* (as well as other things): Nell puns on English *nail* as Clov puns on French *clou*. Nagg abbreviates German *Nagel* as Hamm abbreviates Latin *hamus*. The only other person named in the play, an offstage Mother Pegg, is also a four-letter word associated with nail. So that nailhood seems to represent humanity. But Hamm is also hammer that drives the nails on the stage board.

Only a pedantic Becketteer would begin so soon to weave arabesques upon his names. More innocent immersion in *Fin de partie* yields a more general effect—"corpsed," to use Clov's word. In the eleven productions I have seen, audiences were soberly quiet (when they did not walk out in boredom). Only gradually does the humor bleed through.

No work in the Beckett canon is better documented than *Fin de partie*, and no drama deserves it more. Alan Schneider has published the letters that Beckett wrote him while at work on the play. A manuscript and Beckett's type-script of a two-act version are in the library of Ohio State University. The final French version and Beckett's English translation can readily be compared. In 1964 Beckett spent twelve days with actors rehearsing for a London production, and Clancy Sigal has published an article on that period. Then, in 1967, about a decade after finishing the play, Beckett himself directed a German production in the Schiller Theater Werstatt in Berlin, and Michael Haerdter has published a book about that month of rehearsals, which incorporates Beckett's final view of the play he prefers above his others.

The shape of *Fin de partie* is subtler and more relentless than *Godot*'s. The structure is what is often called circular:

141

actors are in the same stage position at beginning and end of *Fin de partie*—Nagg and Nell in their ashbins, Hamm front and center in his armchair, and Clov, the only mobile character, motionless by the door. Hamm's role within the play is also circular: he begins speech after uncurtaining his face, and he concludes by re-covering his face. At and near the play's beginning are monologues by Clov and Hamm, and near and at the play's end are monologues by Clov and Hamm.

The play's dialogue opens with the word "finished" and closes with the word "remain." Between those two words is a surprising economy of words—less in English than in French. When Beckett predicted loss in translation, he probably was not referring to the *number* of words, but they are smaller in number. Beckett cut Clov's song as well as details about the small boy Clov sees through the window. Though the English usually translates the French exactly, it often loses a syllable or two. Thus *comédie* is farce, *autrefois* once, *à vue de nez* roughly. *Il n'y a personne d'autre* sounds longer than There's no one else; *Mais qu'est-ce qui se passe, qu'est-ce qui se passe?* boils down to What's happening, what's happening?

In both French and English, but more in English, the play's dialogue is built on what Beckett later called "the echo principle." Repetition is thematic in *Fin de partie*: the old questions, the old answers keep repeating themselves unto death, or at least unto dying. Although there was little new in the world of *Godot*, things could seem new because memory was so untrustworthy. But in *Fin de partie* almost everything is a memory, and everything has happened before—the echo principle.

My interpretations tend to unravel the strands of a fabric, and I think that the *Endgame* chapter of my last book on Beckett accomplishes this as well as I can do it. Here I propose to recapitulate the main threads: 1) the biblical theme, 2) the ending theme, 3) the grain-of-time theme, 4) the play theme.

142

1) THE BIBLICAL THEME. In the cast of characters Nagg-Hamm recalls Noah-Ham of Genesis. Both father-sons are survivors of world catastrophe, safe in their ark-shelters. But the central parallel underscores the central contrasts. Biblical Noah was beloved of God who made a covenant with him, issuing an injunction to be fruitful and multiply. Beckett's Nagg has fructified the earth with Hamm, who tries religiously not to multiply but to diminish life on earth. Death is the only insurance against another flood or another crucifixion.

Other biblical references erupt sporadically in *Fin de partie*. Biblical Ham was cursed by Noah for seeing him naked. Beckett's Hamm calls his father "accursed" for having engendered him, and Beckett's Nagg curses Hamm for refusing him sugarplums. Hamm mockingly asks Clov what he sees on his kitchen wall—"mene?" The prophet Daniel translated *mene* as "God hath numbered thy kingdom, and finished it." Hamm and Clov use apocalyptic imagery that recalls the Book of Revelations—light and dark, earth and sea, life and death, beginning and end. Into the English text Beckett introduces various "in the name of God"s and "Christ"s, Hamm usually invoking God and Clov Christ. Hamm's chronicle takes place on Christmas Eve; even in fiction he hesitates to foster life on the joyous eve of the birth of Christ. When the three men pray on stage, none of the three feels God's presence. Hamm's final monologue distorts scriptural phrases: "Get out of here and love one another! Lick your neighbor as yourself! . . . The end is in the beginning. . . . Goood . . . Peace to our—arses." The language of excommunication replaces communication.

2) THE ENDING THEME. Clov's first line is: "Finished, it's finished, nearly finished, it must be nearly finished." Clov's four "finished"s are balanced by four "end"s in Hamm's opening monologue. After Nagg tells an old Jewish joke in which a tailor exalts his trousers above God's world, Hamm exclaims: "Have you not finished? Will you never finish?

143

Will this never finish?" In the middle of the play, Hamm pleads with Clov to "finish" them. Just before Hamm tells his story, he almost echoes Clov's opening phrases: "It's finished, we're finished. (*Pause.*) Nearly finished." All these repetitions refer to an end, and in the background is the last phrase of Christ on the cross—"It is finished"—denoting the end of a world. But Beckett's text also uses the verb "finish" for the toy dog, which "isn't finished." In this sense, to finish means to complete, and its application to the dog resonates forward and backward on the other uses of the verb. When this world ends, it will be completed, and that completion is desirable. Yet the endgame does not end.

3) THE GRAIN-OF-TIME THEME. The ending theme is in play-long tension with the inability to end, which I have called the grain-of-time theme. The Eleatic philosophers, of whom Zeno is the best known, "proved" the incommensurability of the finitely measurable with an infinite universe. Grains of sand or millet grains can never quite make a heap; grains of time can never quite make an eternity. Clov's second sentence is: "Grain upon grain, one by one, and one day, suddenly, there's a heap, a little heap, the impossible heap." In *Fin de partie* the heap remains impossible. Toward the end of the play, just before Clov enters with the alarm clock, Hamm says: "Moment upon moment, pattering down, like the millet grains of . . . (*he hesitates*) . . . that old Greek, and all life long you wait for that to mount up to a life." That old Greek, whose name Beckett actually forgot, was Eubulides of Miletus who wrote: "One grain of corn is not a heap. Add a grain and there is yet no heap. When does a heap begin?" Hamm and Clov spend their lives wondering about this question, but the action denies the possibility of change. Each word, each event, is another grain, but the grains never mount up to the impossible heap of infinity.

4) THE PLAY THEME. Hamm's first line is: "Me—(*he yawns*) —to play." Wrenching of normal word order confers emphasis. The line reinforces the chess suggestions of the title; an

endgame is the last phase of a chess game in which the king is endangered. Hamm is both king and player on the board of few remaining pieces. Hamm's self-centered lines and striking costume suggest the residue of a heroic mode. Later Hamm will steal a line from Richard III and another from Prospero (in the English version only). His name abbreviates Hamlet. Hamm is a chess king, a Shakespearian king, and a blind prophet. Above all he is an actor who embraces them all. At times, he is the Hamm-actor of his name, but at other times he is Hamletic in his melancholy, his interrogatives, his holding action, and his use of play to catch both his conscience and his consciousness. Specific references to the play as play are most meaningful in *Fin de partie*, which Beckett designates as "a play" in his English translation. It is an action about actors.

In the numerology of the play, four characters with four-letter names play in an action of four times four, or sixteen scenes. The scenes were Beckett's divisions for rehearsal purposes: 1) Clov's mime and first monologue; 2) Hamm's awakening, his first monologue, and his first dialogue with Clov; 3) The Nagg-Nell dialogue; 4) The excited Hamm-Clov dialogue, with Hamm's first turn around the room, ending on Clov's sigh: "If I could kill him . . ."; 5) Clov's comic business with ladder and telescope; 6) Hamm's troubled questioning of Clov, climaxed by the burlesque flea-scene; 7) the Hamm-Clov dialogue through the mirror-image of the toy-dog episode; 8) Clov's rebellion, aroused in Hamm's story of the madman, and subsiding in the alarm-clock scene; 9) Hamm's story of the beggar; 10) The prayer, ending with Nagg's curse; 11) The play within the play and Hamm's continued story; 12) The second turn around the room; 13) The Hamm-Clov dialogue, leading to 14) Hamm's "role"; 15) Clov's emancipation, closing with his monologue and exit; 16) Hamm's final monologue. Beckett's scenic breakdown highlights the Hamm-Clov centrality in the play. Hamm and Clov are friends like Didi and Gogo; oppressor and oppressed like Pozzo and Lucky.

They are also sitter-stander, professor-pupil, master-dog, passenger-chauffeur, king-knight, prophet-people, mind-limbs, artist-public, action-passion, interlocutor-straightman, father-son, and perhaps lovers. Bound by love-hate and cruelty-compassion, they are interdependent. At the end of play Clov has to summon all his strength *not* to answer Hamm's last call.

1) CLOV'S MIME AND FIRST MONOLOGUE. Compared to *Godot*, the opening of *Fin de partie* is opaque. Clov's gestures unveil his world. His mime is often compared to ritual, but the celebrant is clumsy and absent-minded; he moves awkwardly and handles the sheets sloppily. He exposes the difficulty of coordinating movement with intention. He laughs four times at what we cannot see, and his fifth laugh—at Hamm—is puzzling. His opening mime lasts longer than his opening monologue, as his play-long motions will be more focal than his speech. His opening mime is composed of repetitive gestures, and his opening monologue of repetitive words. His first two sentences are incantatory eschatology; then, abruptly, he introduces himself: "I can't be punished any more." His last two sentences enfold him within the order he desires. The whole scene has sketched the play world as moribund, repetitive, cruel, ambiguously funny.

2) HAMM'S AWAKENING, FIRST MONOLOGUE, AND FIRST DIA-LOGUE WITH CLOV. The world being limned, Hamm proceeds to play. His six yawns outnumber Clov's five laughs. His first word is "Me." Word and gesture focus upon himself. He mentions the other characters in relation to himself: "My father? My mother? My . . . dog?" After these first-person repetitions of me, mine, my, my, my, he repeats the words "suffer," "end," "hesitate." When Hamm whistles for Clov, his first remark is an insult: "You pollute the air." His second is a command: "Get me ready, I'm going to bed." Clov has begun the dialogue with the word "finished"; Hamm wants to begin his day by going to bed. Their

146

subsequent mutual torture pivots on stichomythia, often of monosyllabic lines. They use a rhetorical pattern that I will call *sadistically spurious logic.* Hamm asks Clov if he has not had enough, and when Clov answers that he has, Hamm concludes: "Then there's no reason for it to change." The "then" is a false Q.E.D. If Clov has had enough, there is no reason for it to change, for—sadistically—the punishment must continue unchanged. If Clov had not had enough, that might be a reason for it to change.

The opening dialogue of Hamm and Clov contains the first two comments on the play as play—almost contradictory: "The thing is impossible" and "We're getting on." After a brief intrusion of Nagg from his ashbin, the Hamm-Clov exchange continues. As they feed each other lines, the tension is exacerbated: "Is it not time for my pain-killer?" "I'll leave you." "Forgive me." Their duet ends on Clov's striking line: "Ever since I was whelped." Not only does this support Hamm's reference to him as "My . . . dog," but rhetorically and syntactically it sets up Clov's pronouncement about the exterior world—"corpsed." As Clov's opening scene sets the stage, that of Hamm begins the action.

3) THE NAGG-NELL DIALOGUE. Nagg and Nell function as a subplot. They speak in extremely short lines and extremely simple words, and they speak almost entirely of the past. Nell can even remember being happy, but Nagg challenges the memory. He claims that she used to laugh because he told a good joke, not because she was happy. Their bickering is a pale copy of the sadomasochism of the Hamm-Clov exchange.

4) THE EXCITED HAMM-CLOV DIALOGUE, with Hamm's first turn around the room, ending on Clov's sigh, "If I could kill him. . . ." Hamm's irritation with his parents provides transition to the continual, reciprocal irritation of Hamm and Clov. Hamm does not complete the round of his room, to which the living world is confined. After the anthropocentric routine about Hamm's centrality, the scene ends on

Clov's irritation reaching a murderous climax. The scene moves as swiftly as music-hall routine.

5) CLOV'S COMIC BUSINESS WITH LADDER AND TELESCOPE. During this business, Hamm and Clov make contradictory comments on the play as play. Hamm: "This is deadly." But Clov: "Things are livening up." It is in the middle of this comic scene that Clov invents the word "Corpsed."

6) HAMM'S TROUBLED QUESTIONING OF CLOV, climaxed by the burlesque flea-scene. Hamm is not reassured about the corpsing of the world, and he continues to interrogate Clov about any possible sign of life on earth. But when the sign comes (at this point), it is within the shelter—the flea in Clov's trousers. "*Very perturbed,*" Hamm ejaculates: "But humanity might start from there all over again! Catch him, for the love of God." Love of God for Hamm means that humanity with all its suffering should be unborn, and therefore the flea must be killed, which might reopen the evolutionary line to man. With slapstick verve, Clov drowns the flea in powder, and the dialogue continues. Repetition multiplies, though the play is not half over.

7) THE HAMM-CLOV DIALOGUE THROUGH THE MIRROR-IMAGE OF THE TOY-DOG EPISODE. "*With prophetic relish,*" Hamm forecasts Clov's slow and solitary dying, which may be the image of his own. Soon, however, they return to their stichomythic taunts, with sadistically spurious logic. Upon Clov's seventh threat to leave him, Hamm asks about his toy-dog, leading to the episode that Beckett calls a "mirror-image," since Clov and toy-dog are both lame. The imploring dog mirrors the imploring man of Hamm's chronicle, which mirrors Nagg and Clov imploring Hamm on stage.

8) CLOV'S REBELLION, aroused in Hamm's account of the madman, subsiding in the alarm-clock scene. Clov's rebellion begins, not with the account of the madman, but with Hamm's mention of Mother Pegg. Clov explodes over the word "yesterday," which gives rise to Hamm's lyrical

reminiscence of the madman—painter and engraver—who thought the end of the world had come. Hamm raises his toque to the death implied in Clov's exclamation: "God be with the days [without life]." What Beckett calls a rebellion is a plan to let Hamm know if Clov dies instead of leaving the shelter. Clov will set the alarm. In *Fin de partie* clocks do not tell time but sound an alarm. Swift changes of tone color this scene—Hamm's nostalgia and Clov's accusation about Mother Pegg, the madman's vision of universal death, the clock-consciousness of Clov and Hamm.

9) HAMM'S STORY OF THE BEGGAR. Hamm has to bribe his father to listen to his story of a beggar. On Christmas Eve a man begs for bread for his child. Hamm limits his critical comments to esthetics, which give all the harder edge to the poignant situation in the story.

10) THE PRAYER, ENDING WITH NAGG'S CURSE. It is when Hamm needs new characters for his story that he orders a prayer to God. Nagg, Hamm, and Clov try to communicate with the Almighty, but they break off blasphemously, and the prayer scene closes on Nagg's curse of his son, which resembles Hamm's prophecy about Clov—that he will end in solitude. On stage it is barely noticeable that Nell does not answer when Nagg raps on her ashbin-lid. The scene ends (in the English version) with Prospero's lines at the close of the masque in the *Tempest*: "Our revels now are ended." The Didi-Gogo aspect of *Fin de partie* is finished: repartee, memories, story, prayer. Hamm has exhausted his ingenuity in killing time. He will dissolve his royal role into that of pawn.

11) THE PLAY WITHIN THE PLAY OF HAMM AND CLOV: Hamm's continued story. The play within the play of Hamm and Clov revolves around Hamm's story, which he now calls chronicle for the first time. When Hamm finds nothing more to chronicle, he sends Clov to check whether Nell is dead. Clov replies: "Looks like it," and Hamm raises his

149

toque to death for the second time. If Nell is indeed dead, something new is possible in the stage world, but her death is never verified. Asked about Nagg, Clov replies: "He's crying," and Hamm retorts with the most mordantly spurious logic of the play: "Then he's living."

12) THE SECOND TURN AROUND THE ROOM. After Hamm is back in place, he calls his father twice, and time is mocked when Nagg cannot tell which time he heard.

13) THE HAMM-CLOV DIALOGUE, leading to 14) HAMM'S "ROLE." As the dialogue runs down, Hamm assumes a solitary role—part confessional and part jeremiad. He expresses guilt, quotes from his story, gives orders. His "not even a real dog!" may refer to the toy or Clov. Hamm predicts his own solitary end, as he has predicted that of Clov, and as Nagg has predicted his.

15) CLOV'S EMANCIPATION, closing with his monologue and exit. When Hamm whistles for Clov, the latter arrives with the alarm clock, the emblem of his emancipation. To Hamm's fifth request for pain-killer, Clov replies that there is no more. Clov takes a last look at the earth, and he accuses Hamm of Mother Pegg's death. The mutual Hamm-Clov recriminations explode into violence, when Clov hits Hamm on the head with the toy-dog. Hamm pleads that Clov use an axe or a gaff, those deadly weapons of tragedy. When Clov announces that there are no more coffins, Hamm retorts with the last sadistic piece of spurious logic: "Then let it end!" But the small boy—fact or fantasy—precludes an end. Hamm frees Clov, who utters his last lyrical monologue tonelessly. Unlike Hamm, Clov is not a ham-actor; he assumes no role as he recounts five rumored consolations: friendship, beauty, wisdom, mercy, nature. But all Clov knows is pain. At the last Hamm and Clov address each other with courteous formality—for the first and only time in the play.

16) HAMM'S FINAL MONOLOGUE. Clov re-enters almost immediately. He is incongruously dressed for travel, but he never moves from the door as Hamm resumes his role. Hamm's last lines tie the final knots in the four thematic threads of the play. A) Biblical. Hamm inserts a mistaken reference to prayer in a quotation from Baudelaire, and he uses the word that God used at the world's beginning: "Good." He raises his toque a third time, for his own death. He fulfils his father's curse by calling "Father. Father," and hearing no answer. B) Ending. He asks Clov for a last favor, then resolves to speak no more. C) Grain-of-time. He speaks of "moments for nothing" and a "last million last moments." D) Game. He utters his third "Me to play," refers to the endgame, discards as in a card game. Throwing his whistle to the audience, Hamm becomes an audience for the first time. Instead of receiving plaudits, he gives them in the form of the whistle: "With my compliments." For a moment he is suspicious of Clov's presence, sniffing as at the beginning of the play. His soft call to Clov is followed by the longest pause in the play. But Clov remains still, and Hamm accepts the stillness as absence, bringing the handkerchief-curtain down on his face. This night's playing is over. The world goes asymptotically on toward an end.

Game acting is required for Hamm, who was first played by Roger Blin with large and exigent cruelty. Submerging the text's humor, Blin used the language of Racine and sweeping gestures suitable to Shakespeare, as he annihilated everyone and everything—family, friends, culture, nature, knowledge, instinct. But the annihilation itself had a dying fall—*cascando*—even more moribund when Blin resumed Hamm's part after a decade.

In a London production of 1964 director Michael Blake evidently tried to emphasize the metaphysical meaning of the play, with the remark: "Death has no finality." As an advisor on that production, Beckett was always simple and specific. He warned the actors not to look for symbols, and he dodged a visitor's question with: "I don't know what's in Hamm's head." At first Beckett seemed more attentive to Clov than to Hamm, though he knew both Irish actors, Jack MacGowran and Pat Magee. When Magee asked Beckett what Hamm looked like, the reply was instantaneous: "Like you." Then he added: "A bit of a monster. The remains of a monster. Yes, the remains of a monster." Magee managed Hamm's tragic lines better than the comic ones, and Beckett suggested to him: "Let's get as many laughs as we can out of this horrible mess." But when Magee asked Beckett about Hamm's response to Clov's sighting of the small boy, the playwright replied: "Anxiety, Pat. There should be nothing out there. There *must* be nothing out there. . . . I'm explaining it badly. He wants Clov to see what he's going out into, but if there is something out there alive, it is not as he supposed, and that would be terrible."

This is probably Beckett's second most explicit statement about *Fin de partie*. The most explicit came when Beckett directed his own production in Berlin in 1967. To Hamm played by Ernst Schröder, Beckett explained: "[Hamm] is a king in this chess game lost from the start. From the start he knows he is making loud senseless moves. That he will make no progress at all with the gaff. Now at the last he makes a few senseless moves as only a bad player would. A good one would have given up long ago. He is only trying to delay the inevitable end. Each of his gestures is one of the last useless moves which put off the end. He's a bad player." He is a bad player because he is a good performer; the show must go on. As Beckett admitted during another rehearsal, "Hamm says No to Nothingness."

Hamm expresses that No in the self-conscious meticulousness of his play, and Beckett translated that No into the meticulousness of his direction. He arrived in Berlin with a director's notebook, to which he referred apologetically. He knew the German text by heart. Early in the rehearsal period, he told his cast: "There are no accidents in *Fin de partie*. Everything is based on analogy and repetition." Of the month's rehearsal time, Beckett spent about half the period on individual roles and half on orchestrating the whole; for the latter he used musical terminology: legato, andante, piano, scherzo, and a rare fortissimo (for Hamm's last "What's happening?"). He told Hamm-Schröder and Clov-Bollman: "Your war is the heart of the play." And he explained further: "Clov has only one wish, to return to his kitchen. That must always be evident, as is Hamm's effort to detain him."

As in *Godot*, repetitive gesture reinforces repetitive dialogue. In the opening mime Clov uses the ladder with the same difficulty for each window. He draws the window-curtains identically, from the center toward the wall (like a theater curtain). In his opening and closing monologues Hamm unfolds and folds his handkerchief in four symmetrical movements. Nagg and Nell emerge from their respective ashbins to exactly the same extent. They never turn their heads, and they rarely blink their eyes. Nagg lifts his hand identically to wrap twice on Nell's lid, and Hamm makes a similar gesture when he knocks at the back wall. Hamm's first trip around the room is clockwise, the second counter-clockwise, broken at opposite ends of a chord. In Hamm's recollection of the engraver, he gestures toward the earth-window after speaking of corn, toward the sea-window after mention of the herring fleet. Hamm looks down at the beggar in his story as he looks down at the toy-dog. Hamm, Clov, and Nagg take the same pose to pray, and they drop their hands separately in succession on armrests, thighs, and bin-rims respectively. When Hamm and Clov listen to the alarm, their heads are poised on either side of the clock, so that we see three contiguous circles. When Hamm lifts his toque, Clov lifts first Nell's bin-cover, then Nagg's bin-cover at the same angle, to ascertain whether they are dead.

Easily as precise was the phrasal repetition. Beckett's text creates dramatic tension by different characters speaking the same words, but more often they repeat their own words, and Beckett desired that the words be spoken identically. Elmar Tophoven had translated from Beckett's French into German, but in Berlin Beckett brought the German text closer to the English. He introduced a second "Clov" into Hamm's opening and closing monologues. He changed all Clov's remarks about going to "I'll leave you," so that he finally repeats it ten times (twelve in the English text). Hamm asks for his pain-killer five times. Beckett worked long and hard with Clov-Bollman to achieve a distinctive tone for Clov's repetitions of "There are no more. . . ." In Hamm's story he explodes three times: "Use your head can't you, use your head, you're on earth, there's no cure for that!" Nell sighs lyrically twice, "Ah yesterday." Hamm twice orders Clov to look out of the window, and twice Clov describes both time and weather "As usual." Twice Hamm accuses Clov: "You exaggerate." Twice Hamm orders Clov coldly: "Forgive me. (*Pause. Louder.*) I said, Forgive me." And twice Clov replies: "I heard you." Twice Hamm commands Clov to get his dog. Twice Hamm complains that something is dripping in his head. Twice Hamm asks what is happening, and Clov answers that something is taking its course.

Beckett's favorite line in the play is Hamm's deduction from Clov's observation that Nagg is crying: "Then he's living." But in Berlin he felt that the most *important* sentence is Nell's "Nothing is funnier than unhappiness." And he directed to display the fun of unhappiness. His *Fin de partie* was the quickest of the eleven I have seen—seventy minutes playing time. He asked the actors for disjunction between gesture and dialogue; first they were to assume an attitude and then speak the lines—tired pros all. This was especially demanding for Nagg and Nell, caged in their bins. When Nagg and Nell strained to kiss, they barely moved their heads. Hamm strained at his gaff but could not move his wheelchair. Clov alone was mobile, and Beckett directed his movements to be both painful and funny; bent over, he always stumbled when he passed in front of Hamm, momentarily obscuring all but the toque. On rare occasions of passion, Clov straightened up and flung his left arm out. When Clov spoke to Nagg in his ashbin, his own head disappeared into the bin. In the parallel phrases beginning "Sometimes I wonder if I'm in my right mind," and "Sometimes I wonder if I'm in my right senses," Clov spoke the beginning with verve and the end with sadness. After trying the opposite in rehearsal, Beckett found it funnier that Clov react sadly to being as lucid as before, as intelligent as ever. Partly because Clov alone is mobile, he is the funniest character in the play, but Hamm and Nagg are virtuoso performers, and Beckett insisted that they find three different voices each: Hamm is narrator, protagonist, and beggar of his chronicle, and Nagg is narrator, tailor, and client of his story.

As the process of waiting was filled with activities, the process of ending was filled with energy. Beckett built his moribund stage world on a foundation of repetition. The appropriate color for such sameness is gray—"Light black from pole to pole." In the design of Beckett's friend Matias the ashbins were gray-black, and their color blended into the gray walls of the shelter. Cold light focussed on door, chair, and ashbins—invariant throughout the play. Hamm and Clov wore different shades of gray in their gray shelter. Beckett abandoned the red and white faces of the published text for a gray-white makeup, and he eliminated the bloodstains on Hamm's handkerchief, making it gray-white, a shade whiter than the window-curtains and shroud-sheets.

Though the shelter was rectangular, it did not suggest a chessboard, and Clov's movements did not suggest those of a chess-knight. In *Godot* each of the four performers comes front and center at least once. In *Fin de partie* Hamm is almost always front and center, and he speaks in the idiom of drama—dialogue, soliloquy, aside, underplot, exit. As actor, he is always aware of his role, announcing it three times in the grand manner: "Me to play." In the final monologue Hamm is director and actor; he gives instructions, then performs the actions. As director he superintends his show, even to cues and blocking. He is his own most appreciative audience as well, but he stops short of applause.

After a month of rehearsal in Berlin, Beckett thought about his actors before *their* audience. He addressed his cast timorously: "If I might suggest about curtain-calls. . . ." Hamm-Schröder did not let him finish, insisting that he and Clov-Bollman would simply remain motionless at the end of the play. Nagg and Nell would be represented by their ashbins, and there would be no curtain-calls to spoil the final tableau.

Three years later, at a revival, I saw the same actors taking bows. They are only human, and they succumbed to the only humanness of *Fin de partie*. It would be easier *not* to be human, easier *not* to have been born, easier not to have lived. Logically, Hamm has tried to unpeople the earth, to arrive at the relief of Nothing, but he falters, delaying the end. As Hamm falters, his servant-son falters, his story protagonist falters. To falter is human, to inexist divine. *Fin de partie* is occasionally nostalgic for divinity, but it sinks us deep in the human tragedy of self-conscious mortality.

Falling, Taping, Timing

Acte sans paroles I

When Beckett completed the arduous labor of *Fin de partie*, he swiftly wrote two more works for performance— a mime play and a radio play, *Acte sans paroles I* and *All That Fall*. After writing the stage play *Krapp's Last Tape* in 1958, he repeated that equilibrium with *Embers*, a radio play, and *Acte sans paroles II*, a mime play.

Acte sans paroles I strips the generalized settings of *Godot* and *Fin de partie* to a bare stage. Abruptly, a man is born— "*flung backwards*" on to the stage, in dazzling light. Birth is a pratfall, and man tries to return whence he came, but "Men must endure their going hence, even as their coming hither," and the man is flung back twice more, into his stage-world. Four of his seven pratfalls are caused by offstage forces, but the other three recall the clown tradition of the hostility of intractable objects. Both finite things and infinite spaces conspire toward the downfall of man.

When whistles sound from right and left wings respectively, the lone actor goes exploring into the wings, to be flung back on to the bare stage. When the whistle sounds again, he has learned; he no longer goes exploring. Only later, after misadventures with cubes, carafe, tree, rope, and scissors, does he forget and answer a left-wing whistle, whence his fourth pratfall. This part of the mime is aptly summarized by Jean Anouilh's subtitle for *Godot*: "The Music-Hall Sketch of Pascal's Pensées as Played by the Fratellini Clowns." But this clown spends more time in his struggle against concrete objects than Pascal's infinite silent spaces.

When scissors descend from the flies, he trims his nails with them. When a palm tree descends, he basks in its shade. When a carafe of water descends to just beyond his reach, he clumsily learns to use large cubes and a rope to get closer to the water. But it remains beyond his reach in Beckett's variant of the Tantalus myth.

As in *Godot* and *Fin de partie*, stage business summarizes our lives. The tramps keep waiting, Hamm keeps finishing, the clown learns through movement to reflect, and through reflection to stop moving. When the clown is first flung back from the wings, he turns his attention to the stage to which he is condemned, and he explores its space. He learns to use rope and cubes in space, but he does not reach the water. In frustration, he maintains his self-respect by paring his nails with the huge scissors. When he realizes that the scissors can be used more effectively on his neck than his nails, the offstage forces whisk them out of reach. He reflects for the last time—to no purpose. At the end, all tools disappear. Only carafe and tree remain, but when he refuses to be lured by them, they too vanish. Finally, the

157

actor stares at his useless hands on a bare stage. He has learned the lesson that has haunted Beckett from his early Proust essay: "the wisdom that consists not in the satisfaction but in the ablation of desire."

After the silence of *Acte sans paroles I*, Beckett suddenly found English speech again. While working on *Fin de partie*, he had tried vainly to return to English fiction, but when the BBC asked him to contribute to their series of original radio plays, *All That Fall* emerged. Written in close succession, *Acte sans parole I* and *All That Fall* both use falling as a metaphor for the human condition, which had previously been staged as waiting and finishing. *Acte sans paroles I* offers a series of movements to the eyes, and their limited range implies the limitations of all human activity. *All That Fall* offers a variety of sounds to the ear, but the diapason is scarcely a sample of the traditional harmony of the spheres. Each play adheres to its genre and exploits that genre to make a metaphysical implication.

All That Fall

Donald MacWhinnie, the first director of *All That Fall*, has written a fascinating account of producing this radio play that he describes as "a mixture of realism and poetry, frustration and farce." As Beckett stylized memories of his native Foxrock to create the play's Boghill, MacWhinnie musicalized surface reality to create a radio score. Playwright and director orchestrate rather than imitate, and they accomplish a vivid evocation of suburban Ireland, rooted in the soil but crossed by industrialism. In that milieu Beckett plants his third biblical seed, for his first three distinctive plays germinate from the Bible. Beckett told Colin Duckworth: "Christianity is a mythology with which I am perfectly familiar, so I naturally use it." *Godot* had its two thieves, *Endgame* its flood and anti-apocalypse. The text that provides title and theme for *All That Fall* comes from

158

the *Psalms*: "The Lord upholdeth all that fall and raiseth up all those that be bowed down."

All that fall have to be conveyed through sound in a radio play. Quite literally, *All That Fall* is, as Beckett said, "a text written to come out of the dark." From a pastoral background, one bright Saturday in June, Maddy Rooney sets out to meet her blind husband at the railway station in Boghill. En route she is overtaken by several vehicles: Christy and his cart, Mr. Tyler and his bicycle, Connolly's van, Mr. Slocum and his automobile. With the help of the last of these, she arrives at the station in time to meet the 12:30 train, which is delayed fifteen minutes on its half-hour run. United with her husband on his birthday, she sets out for home. Dan Rooney evades his wife's questions as to why the train was late, but Maddy learns from a boy that there has been an accident; a little child has fallen under the train wheels.

On their homeward journey Maddy informs her husband of the text for Sunday's sermon—a text that they greet with wild laughter because they are bowed down and in perpetual danger of falling. A Miss Fitt has informed Maddy Rooney that she looks "bowed and bent," and Maddy tells her blind husband that he is "bowed down over the ditch." Maddy's journey to the railroad station is a spirited struggle to keep erect and mobile. On the homeward walk the halt leads the blind; Ma and Da Ruin-y skirt various obstacles. Old and ill though they are, they stumble on. It is a young healthy child who has fallen under the train, causing its delay. In Beckett's radio play human beings may hold each other up, but no one raises the child who falls. The Lord, as in *Fin de partie*, is conspicuous by his absence, and as in *Fin de partie*, the biblical theme is a source of mockery: Christy has no head for heights; he walks beside his hinny and his cart of dung, whereas Christ entered Jerusalem high on his hinny. Mr. Slocum "crucifies" his gearbox. Tommy receives no thanks for a Christian act. Miss Fitt fears for

159

her mother's "fresh sole" rather than her soul. On the Rooneys' homeward journey, they hear no Lamb of God but a lamb bleating for suck. And the final news of the fallen child comments mordantly upon the biblical prophecy: "A little child shall lead them."

In addition to the biblical thread, *All That Fall* shares with *Fin de partie* a theme of depopulation. Like Hamm, Dan Rooney confesses to wanting to "Nip some young doom in the bud." The very phrase implies his reason: youth is doom in bud, which should be nipped before it suffers. Dan, like Hamm, is sensitive to suffering. Without mentioning the doomed child, he cries perhaps over its death, which takes place on his birthday. But it is the totality of *All That Fall*, rather than Dan, that conspires to depopulate the world.

Though the play presents catastrophes with comic verve, they add up to the inability of women to replenish the species. Before a word is spoken, we hear the music of *Death and the Maiden*, and we soon learn about afflictions of maiden and matron. Maddy Rooney's first words are "Poor woman." Christy has a sick wife and daughter, Mr. Tyler's daughter has had a hysterectomy, Mr. Slocum's mother is kept out of pain, a hen is run over before our ears, the Rooneys' daughter Minnie is dead, Maddy recalls the sinking of the Lusitania and Titanic, Mrs. Tully's husband beats her unmercifully, Maddy tells Dan of attending a lecture about a dying girl, Dan wants to continue their reading of *Effie Briest*, whose heroine dies young. The news of the death of a child (sex unknown) ends the play. During the play, hinny and vehicles are referred to as "she," and all are impeded in their courses.

The Boghill citizens are in various stages of middle age, and their speech is more virile than their bodies. Christy puns: "Damn the mail," and Maddy links her journey to the "upmail," claiming that all she ever wanted was to be loved twice daily, like the Paris horse-butcher's regular. Named after Mary Magdalene, indomitably carnal at the

160

age of seventy, Maddy challenges ubiquitous depopulation. She rejects the tepid advances of Mr. Tyler (whom she twice calls Mr. Rooney), comparing him to a deer-stalker, and admonishing him: "Heavens, you're not going to ride her flat! . . . You'll tear your tube to ribbons!" But then she calls after him to unlace her behind the hedge. She resents the insinuation that she is as stiff as Mr. Slocum, whose name puns upon his potency, and her entrance to his car is ecstatic with sexual suggestion: "Oh glory! . . . up! Up! . . . Ah! . . . I'm in!" When Mr. Slocum runs over a hen, Maddy exclaims: "Oh mother," and then continues, with extensible resonance: "All the laying and the hatching. (*Pause.*) Just one great squawk and then . . . peace." When Maddy alights from Mr. Slocum's car, it is with suggestions of a breech-birth. While climbing the station steps with the support of spinster Miss Fitt, Maddy subtly taunts her with talk of honeymoon couples on the Matterhorn (Ma for maternity, and horn for cuckoldry—both beyond the reach of Miss Fitt). Maddy shocks her husband by asking that he kiss her publicly. On their homeward walk, she wonders whether hinnies can procreate. In this radio play, where the bowed and fallen are mainly women, Beckett creates his first female protagonist, a descendant of the Wife of Bath.

Maddy Dunne Rooney may proclaim herself a Mad Done Ruin, but her play-long proclamation is indefatigable. Like her successor, Winnie, she is determined to have a "happy day" on this June Saturday, her husband's birthday for which she has given him a tie. Not for her is Gogo's question: "We're not tied?" After a long illness, Maddy sets her two hundred pounds on her feet, while others travel in conveyances. She accomplishes the difficult feat of entrance into and exit from Mr. Slocum's vehicle. She leans on Miss Fitt to negotiate the precipice of the station steps. When the train arrives at 12:45, she misses her husband who has gone to the men's room. Reunited with him, she suffers his ingratitude. On the homeward journey, the weather turns sharply to wind and rain. No vehicle gives them a lift, and

161

children mock them. But she leads gamely on, thirsty for affection, drinking in Dan's narrative. When the boy Jerry overtakes them, she shows concern for his health, then curiosity about the train's delay. Only the shocking news of the child's death can silence her, but it cannot cause her to fall. We hear their dragging feet continuing toward home, until the wind and the rain drown them out.

As Louise O. Cleveland has shown, *All That Fall* divides temporally and sonically into three parts: 1) the hustle and bustle of locomotion, breakdown, and reported pain; 2) the confusion of signals and voices at the station; 3) the couple's weary trudge homeward, each largely in his own thoughts—Dan in his narration and Maddy in her memory. Husband and wife unite to laugh at the biblical text before Jerry arrives with his sobering revelation.

Each of the three sections has its own sound effects in this radio play that creates its world through speech and sound effects. Rural sounds open the play, to be interrupted by the dragging feet of Maddy Rooney. BBC director Donald MacWhinnie used human voices for the animal sounds, and he set the footsteps in an insistent four-beat tempo. It is against this rhythm that Maddy's progress is dramatized.

Outward bound, Maddy listens to music, voices, vehicles. Christy's steps accompany the sound of his manure-laden cart. His hinny whinnies, farts, is beaten. Mr. Tyler on his bicycle rings his bell, squeaks his brakes, and bumps off on his flat tire after Connolly's van thunders by. Mr. Slocum's automobile is announced by its engine, opening and closing of doors, grinding gears, screaming brakes, horn. As we begin to hear of human misery, the sound effects echo the threne—dying music, dying murmur, choked or dead engine, falling signals at the station.

Once the station is reached, the orchestra thins out. But new voices are heard, and the wind begins to rise. Maddy toils up the steps on Miss Fitt's arm, and Mr. Barrell hits Tommy in the stomach. At the railway station, Maddy is snubbed, as Watt was snubbed. But unlike taciturn Watt, Maddy flows into speech. Ironically, Beckett gives her a speech that underlines the limitations of the medium to which she is confined. Maddy describes a distance view of the entire scene—hills, plain, racecourse, station, and the clouding blue over all. "Oh, if you had my eyes," she addresses her listeners, of whom we are part. On radio drama, however, eyes are useless. Finally, the train arrives in a crescendo of *"exaggerated station sounds,"* a thundering climax for the play. Donald MacWhinnie followed the train departure by "remorseless silence." Then blind Dan enters with his thumping stick.

The mechanical age is behind us on the homeward trudge. After the couple manages to descend the station stairs, a donkey brays, then children jeer. The pastoral landscape disappears before our ears, through Maddy's words and generalized sound effects: "The wind—(*brief wind*)—scarcely stirs the leaves and the birds—(*brief chirp*)—are tired singing. The cows—(*brief moo*)—and sheep—(*brief baa*)—ruminate in silence. The dogs—(*brief bark*)—are hushed and the hens—(*brief cackle*)—sprawl torpid in the dust." Maddy and Dan are reduced to their own words, punctuated by pauses and silences. Dan's ostentatious narrative does *not* tell Maddy why the train was late. That information about a child is delivered by a child, before human sounds are drowned in the wind and the rain.

The structural division of *All That Fall*, with its changing auditory textures, shows Beckett's customary mastery of genre, but his major achievement is his control of speech. In this first successful return to his native language since *Watt*, the Anglo-Irish is localized and faintly out-of-date. We find such Irish locutions as "surely to goodness," "destroyed with," "with time and to spare," "stravanging down here," "get on with you now," "nip up to," "will you get along with you." Double entendres abound in Beckett's native English, and Dan is as ratiocinative as the French heroes. But the most vigorous speech belongs to Maddy, who

163

characterizes her language as "bizarre" (probably derived from Spanish *bizarro*, brave.) Mrs. Rooney's outworn phrases ring like crystal on a medium too often burdened with cliché. Though Maddy hopes she uses the simplest words, we find such oddities as "cleg," "pelt," "pismire," "ramdam," and even *"merde."* In the main, however, she is accurate; it is not the individual words that distinguish Maddy's speech, so much as the personal verve. Dan calls attention to such old-fashioned phrases as "never pause," "safe to haven," and Maddy assents that she knows "full well" that her language seems dead. Earlier she has used such literary locutions as "Would I were," "I should not dally," "Oh cursed corset!" "I should not have importuned you." And yet the overall effect of her speech is no more outdated than the speech of the other characters, with their turn-of-the-century surface courtesy. Maddy uses speech more consistently and persistently than anyone in the play, and she does so with indomitable fellowship. But her words serve only to isolate her: "A few simple words . . . from my heart . . . and I am all alone . . . once more." By the time she meets her husband, she characterizes the people she has encountered as "horrid nasty people." Nevertheless, her own concern for others never flags. On their homeward journey, her double entendres no longer linger on sex, but on mind, business, standstill. She still pities the laburnum (labor-numb), she speculates about the procreative power of hinneys, she worries about her neighbor and her husband. She walks and talks past all obstacles. That is her way of saying No to Nothingness—to the Nothingness for which Dan obscurely hopes.

Ma and Da Rooney have one dead child. Ma is "destroyed with . . . childlessness," and she remains incorrigibly carnal—from listening to the Venus-birds to embracing her husband. Dan is weighed down with anguish for the suffering that still lies ahead of the young. His own autobiography of afflictions is what he would wish others to avoid, but the only escape for suffering is death. Ma and Da

Rooney have no living offspring, but they have antithetical attitudes toward generation. Dan is a child of Hamm, but Maddy provides rare comic relief, in the oldest phallic kind of comedy. She may halt, lean, or falter, but she never falls. "Up mail." Pun intended.

Krapp's Last Tape

At first entitled "the Magee Monologue," *Krapp's Last Tape* was written after Beckett heard a radio broadcast of Pat Magee reading from his fiction. Like Beckett's earlier plays, *Krapp's Last Tape* shows awareness of its genre. But there are differences. *Godot* and *Fin de partie* show through word and gesture that they are what they are—stage plays. *All That Fall*, a radio play, presents sounds but not a radio. *Krapp's Last Tape*, a stage play, puts a tape-recorder on stage. The earlier plays play with the techniques of their genre, but *Krapp's Last Tape* plays against its genre by using the techniques of another medium. *Krapp's Last Tape* employs the tape-recorder as a stage metaphor for time past. Unlike Proust's Marcel, Krapp does not have to depend on involuntary memory for lost time. He can find it on spools of tape, methodically numbered, titled, and catalogued.

In *Godot* everything that happens has happened before, but the characters cannot remember. In *Fin de partie* most things that happen have happened before, and the characters remember the past more vividly than they live in the present. In *Krapp's Last Tape* a form of what happens has happened before, but the memory of it has been codified. Krapp calls his tape a "retrospect," and we witness his reaction to retrospects.

After Krapp's initial reading of tape numbers and titles, the dialogue of *Krapp's Last Tape* may be trisected: 1) Krapp listens to a tape made thirty years ago; 2) he records a tape; 3) he listens to part of the first tape. The actions overlap, and from that overlap emerges Beckett's most direct character. By that I mean that Krapp is not estranged from us—not by appearance, setting, or medium. Gogo and

Didi wait on a stage no man's land; shroud-sheets and ash-bins distance us from the characters of *Fin de partie*; invisible Ma and Da Rooney grow to size through sound. But ordinary Krapp is at once spotlighted at his ordinary table. Through the course of the play, he most habitually makes the gesture of listening. Finally he faces us more naked than if he were naked, because he is so utterly alone. He is as familiar as the California bumper sticker: "Dirty old men need love too."

The play-long familiarity is a subtle achievement, where, for once, everything is on the surface. Neither Bible, Descartes, Dante, nor even Proust helps us to know Krapp. A hymn and *Effie Briest* are the only literary references, and the play tells us all we need know about them to understand this old man in whom desire is stronger than memory, as the spotlight is stronger than the nonsuffering of darkness.

We see before us unkempt Krapp at the age of sixty-nine, addicted to bananas that constipate him, to alcohol that he drinks offstage, to desire for women in fact (Fanny) and fantasy (Effie Briest). Sixty-nine-year-old Krapp listens to a tape made on his thirty-ninth birthday, in which he laments his addiction to bananas and alcohol and lingers over his farewell to love. In that tape Krapp speaks of a tape made ten or twelve years earlier, in which he recalls his constipation and his addiction to alcohol and sex. Each age is scornful of those that precede it: in his twenties Krapp sneered at his youth; at thirty-nine Krapp finds it "hard to believe [he] was ever that young whelp" in his twenties; at sixty-nine he begins to record: "Just been listening to that stupid bastard I took myself for thirty years ago, hard to believe I was ever as bad as that." Each age has its ambition: in his twenties Krapp spoke ironically of "the opus . . . magnum"; when he is thirty-nine, we hear fragments of his vision of darkness, impatiently interrupted by Krapp; sixty-nine-year-old Krapp comments sardonically on what may be the magnum opus resulting from his vision; it has sold seventeen copies. Each age has its love: in his twenties Krapp lived off and on with Bianca; at thirty-nine Krapp recalls the eyes of a nursemaid, but he dwells longer on a nameless woman in a boat; at sixty-nine Krapp has to be content with a "Bony old ghost of a whore" whom he perhaps moulds into a fantasy of Effie Briest in Fontane's novel. Each age brings its loss: in his twenties Krapp's father died; at thirty-nine he meticulously describes his surroundings when his mother dies; by the time he is sixty-nine Krapp has no one to lose.

Unlike other Beckett stage characters, Krapp is rooted in a familiar world whose every detail is realistically plausible. Packets of letters or photograph albums are perhaps more usual than tape collections in an effort to retain the past, but the collector's impulse is common to all. A reel on a machine recreates two scenes that move us by the homespun quality of their truth. In a death scene we do not see Krapp's dying mother, but through Krapp's tape we envision how death is surrounded by trivia. In a love scene we have no physical picture of the beloved woman, but Krapp conveys a feeling of belonging to the universe through union with the beloved.

At one level, Krapp is a living emblem of our age of mass media; at another, he converts a machine into a tool for introspection. In the stage present, Beckett makes slapstick comedy of Krapp's weak eyes, but Krapp himself finds eyes seductive. In his twenties Bianca's eyes were "incomparable." At thirty-nine, eyes "like chrysolite," intrude upon his memory of his mother's death. At sixty-nine he can still remember the eyes of his unnamed love: "The eyes she had!"

White-faced and purple-nosed, Krapp vaguely resembles a clown, and his clothes vaguely relate him to the music-hall tramp—rusty-black trousers that are too short, and rusty-black waistcoat with four large pockets; dirty white shirt and dirty white boots. Near-sighted, hard of hearing, he walks laboriously. His stage business is with keys and

167

bananas, providing opportunity for comic mime. Slipping on a banana-skin is one of the oldest slapstick jokes, but Krapp is its victim only once on this day; the second skin he tosses offstage out of his way. Like the actor of *Acte sans paroles I*, he learns.

Krapp's opening mime as written is sexually suggestive—inserting keys in locks, handling the phallic bananas in a masturbatory manner. The gestures predict the dialogue of a dirty old man. When Krapp breaks into speech about his tapes, he speaks of them as animate objects—"the little rascal! . . . the little scoundrel!." But when he begins to read the titles of the tapes, he is puzzled. His past is on tape, not in his head. When the slapstick is over, memories begin. After Krapp listens to the tape within the tape, about the girl in a shabby green coat, he looks at his watch, then disappears backstage, from where we hear three corks pop. In a brief burst of quavering song, he returns to his spotlighted table, to listen again.

During the course of his listening, Krapp stops the machine at the word "viduity." Krapp disappears and reappears with an enormous dictionary, to help him with this word he knew thirty years ago, but knows no longer. His third exit is made after he hears the love scene in the boat; glancing first at an envelope, then at his watch, he disappears backstage. We hear the sound of a bottle against a glass, brief siphon, then *"bottle against glass alone."* The graduation from wine to whiskey is indicated, as in radio drama, by sounds—and not as in radio drama, by the visible effect on Krapp, who comes unsteadily into view, to tape the present.

Krapp is a writer, and yet his speech calls less attention to itself than that of Maddy Rooney, housewife. Krapp singles out for emphasis the words "spooool," "viduity," and "vidua-bird." The first and third give him sensuous pleasure, and we see them as symbols for aspects of Krapp, the spools containing his consciousness and the bird reflecting his virility—"Black plumage of male."

Krapp is not so echoic as Hamm or Clov, but his rare repetitions are also meaningful. Eyes form a leitmotif, and the moment of Krapp's mother's death is marked when the *blind* goes down on her window. On Krapp's thirty-ninth birthday there is "Not a soul" in the winehouse; at his mother's death there is "hardly a soul." Krapp describes the tape recorded in his twenties as ending with a yelp to Providence, and after his mother dies, a dog yelps for a black ball. The dog takes the ball from Krapp "gently, gently," and in the boat of the love scene, "all moved, and moved us, gently." Krapp's relation to Bianca was "Hopeless business," and to his love in the boat Krapp says, "It was hopeless and no good going on." A fire lit Krapp's vision of darkness on the Memorable Equinox, and the play ends on an ironic reference to "the fire in me now." Repetitions emphasize contrasts, as the sixty-nine year old relic before us contrasts with the vigorous voice on tape.

On stage the most telling contrast is played by Krapp against his tape. When listening to thirty-nine year old Krapp denigrate Krapp in his twenties, old Krapp twice joins in the taped laugh, once laughs alone, once listens to the taped laugh, and finally joins in a prolonged laugh at the aspirations of the youngest of the three Krapps. Elsewhere, Krapp switches off to brood, or to wind the tape forward. He is most impatient with the chief item of his thirty-ninth year—the Memorable Equinox—so that we hear mere fragments of a vision that emanates from darkness. Only once before he records does Krapp wind the tape back—to replay the love scene in the punt. Its lyricism fresh in our minds, we hear the sad contrast of Krapp's present tape. Subject and style have faded with the years.

Krapp begins as the younger Krapp began, by jeering at a still younger Krapp. In tough abrupt sentences, Krapp salvages a few details of memory, then gives himself orders. More frequently than in the earlier tape, Krapp refers to himself in the third person. Once we are involved with Krapp, he proclaims his own detachment from himself

169

through his use of the third person. Coming to the meager present, Krapp uses a heat-cold opposition that underlines the poignancy of his situation: "Crawled out once or twice, before the summer was cold. Sat shivering in the park, drowned in dreams and burning to be gone." Krapp completes a hymn that summarizes the play, as Didi's round song summarizes *Godot*, and Hamm's anecdote of the engraver summarizes *Fin de partie*: "Now the day is over,/ Night is drawing nigh,/ Shadows of the evening/ Steal across the sky." But through his imagination that is prodded by tapes, Krapp rebels against the shadows—a rebellion that is climaxed by a self-command, four times repeated: "Be again."

This is Krapp's ultimate order, which he cannot obey. No one can "be *again*," though once is never enough. Significantly, the order to be again is coupled with youthful memories that seem to predate Krapp's involvement with women or writing. His memories are immersed in nature— "in the dingle on a Christmas Eve . . . on Croghan on a Sunday morning." Even as an adult, Krapp recalls love in a scene of natural beauty.

Only in his third playback does Krapp react to the lyrical love scene of his thirty-ninth year. Only this third time does Krapp allow the tape to run to its end, in which he boldly claims that he would not want his best years back. The end of the replay is the end of Beckett's play, and it links the three Krapps: thirty-nine-year-old Krapp has mocked a younger Krapp thanking God that his youth was over, and he has commented: "False ring there." Sixty-nine-year-old Krapp has concluded his recording: "No, I wouldn't want [my best years] back." The pattern of Krapp's life, the pattern of his two tapes, belies the claim. Whatever his best years are, he does want earlier years back, and the tapes cannot bring them. Memory is not life, which is rather a series of successive selves, heard on tapes. Finally, even memory ceases, as the stage recorder tapes the stillness.

In 1969 Beckett directed a German translation of *Krapp's Last Tape* in the Werkstatt of Berlin's Schiller Theater. Working through the large tough frame of actor Martin Held, Beckett amplified his stage directions even while he simplified the stage picture. He pared the opening mime of clown suggestions, stressing the worn rather than the farcical quality of Krapp's clothes. He eliminated clown-business with keys and envelopes, but he added rheumatic fingers for fumbling. Krapp's first gesture was new and moving: Krapp hugs himself and shivers slightly—cold, lonely, lovelorn. Because of the poverty of business, the similarity between the sixty-nine- and the thirty-nine-year-old Krapp is more striking. The man whom we have seen eat two bananas tells us that he just ate three. The man whom we have seen step slowly from his spotlight into darkness tells us that he loves to return from the darkness to himself, Krapp. And yet sixty-nine-year-old Krapp looks in astonishment at the tape-recorder when he hears his voice saying: "Me. (*Pause.*) Krapp."

In building Krapp's role, Beckett gave some attention to triplets: At the beginning Krapp walks three times out of his spotlight into darkness and back. At the beginning Beckett has Krapp disappear backstage three times—for ledger, tapes, and tape-recorder. In the later action Beckett changes the three backstage disappearances for offstage drinking, for a dictionary, for offstage drinking and a microphone. Krapp consults his watch three times during the course of the play. After he records, he looks at the machine three times before he wrenches off his last tape. (He does not throw it away.)

During the course of the play Beckett often separated speech from movement. When Krapp moves about, he says nothing. But when taped speech is heard, Krapp listens with immobile intensity. Beckett made almost no changes in the dialogue, but he did add "That voice!" to Krapp's taped comment on his thirty-nine-year-old tape. "A kick in the crutch" was changed to "between thumb and index." The price of Krapp's book was omitted, and several mocking self-laughs were added.

Most of Beckett's changes made stage movement more precise. Krapp slams objects more frequently, and wordless murmurs accompany his discontent. His slouching walk is unbalanced. Before assuming the listening posture, Krapp looks over his right shoulder into the darkness. At the mention of Bianca, the girl in green, the nursemaid, the nameless love (three times), Krapp bends his head to the machine in the same intent way. In the most extended playing of the love scene—the second—Krapp's head sinks down upon the table. When he switches off, he hugs himself and shivers, as at the beginning. In his own recording, each "Be again" rises in intensity, but not in volume. Then Krapp strikes his head as he explodes: "Once wasn't enough for you." But he subsides into his final listening position, the same as at the start. Finally, the lights go out, and it is dark except for the tape-recorder light, the machine turning in silence.

Most of Beckett's memorable characters are old, but Krapp alone conveys the weight of his years. The play was inspired by Pat Magee's distinctive whispering voice with its evocation of unrelieved weariness. Roger Blin, who was to have taken the role in the original French production, bowed out because it made him feel too old. Martin Held, who was physically wrong for the part, seemed to shrink visibly by the end of his forty-five-minute performance. Jean Martin bordered on senility, with red eyes, twitching cheek, and drooling mouth. Old age assaults them all.

Embers

Who but Beckett would give the title *Embers* to a radio play whose central image is the sea? Embers and sea are protagonist and antagonist in this play that ventures into a new domain of drama. *Godot* and *Fin de partie* function best on a small proscenium stage, where precision and sim-

Pat McGee and Jack MacGowran rehearsing Hamm and Clov in the RSC
Endgame. (PHOTO COURTESY SAMUEL BECKETT)

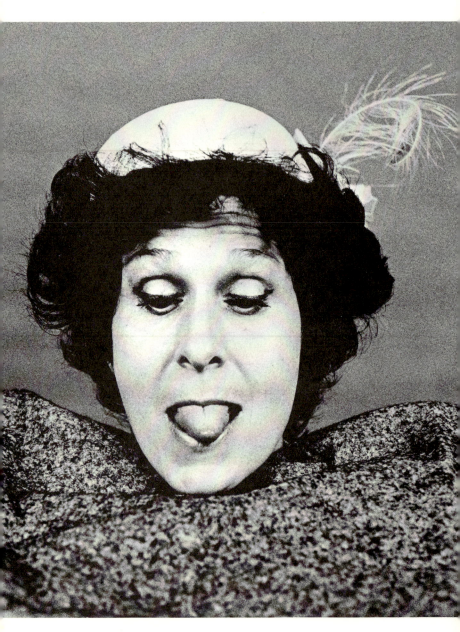

Beatrice Manley as Winnie in Act II of *Happy Days*. (PHOTO SCHMID

plicity seem to compel words and gestures into a meta-physical dimension. Similarly, the few objects and pratfalls of *Acte sans paroles I* insist upon metaphysical interpreta-tion. In contrast, there is self-sufficiency in the everyday ordinariness of sounds and Irish voices in *All That Fall*, of tapes and memories in *Krapp's Last Tape*. And yet both plays are unmistakably part of the Beckett canon, drama-tizing distress with extensible humor. All these plays are characterized by the "mortal liveliness" of the protagonists, as the Unnamable said of Malone. But *Embers* is the first step into dramatic limbo, with characters at once alive and dead, realistic and symbolic.

Life's fire flickers against the sounds of the sea of infinity. The play's protagonist, Henry, describes the reduction of life to embers: "burning down," "no flames . . . embers," "sound of dying, dying glow," "fire dying," "fire out." Even as Henry observes the dying embers, and listens to the sea of death, he asserts life with hard and definite sounds to oppose the liquid timelessness of the sea. That is *his* way of saying No to Nothingness.

Written in English within a year of *Krapp's Last Tape*, *Embers* is essentially a monologue, since the other charac-ters are products of the protagonist's imagination. Henry alone has footsteps that we can hear over the radio. His silent father is signalled by no sound; the voices of his wife and daughter are preceded by no footsteps; Bolton and Holloway, the characters in Henry's story, are possibly his creations. As Krapp peoples his world through tapes, Henry peoples his world through his mind, and in a radio play we can know his mind only through what he says.

What is distinctive about this radio play set at the edge of the sea of infinity is the progressive realization of Henry's world, his refusal to be sucked up by the timeless sea. Henry summons his blind drowned father to be with him, but he cannot put words into his father's mouth. Neverthe-less, we obtain a picture of the sea-possessed man, seeking sunlight in his blindness, scorning his son who is afraid to swim, sitting pensive on a rock like a Rodinesque thinker. To his blind father, or to us, the blind audience of radio drama, Henry says: "the sound is so strange, so unlike the sound of the sea, that if you didn't see what it was you wouldn't know what it was." And of course we cannot see the sea in radio drama.

Like Hamm and Krapp, Henry gives himself orders, barked in doublets. His opening words are: "On. On! Stop. Stop! Down. Down!" Each time he is obeyed. After he sees the sea for us, he commands: "Hooves! Hooves!" And we hear the answering hooves probably created by his imagination—a timed steady rhythm to combat the soft sucking sound of the sea. Success goes to Henry's head, and he fantasizes about a ten-ton mammoth, shod with steel, rhythmically tramping the world down. After telling his unresponsive father that he keeps talking to drown out the sea, after nostalgically mentioning his stories about Bolton, Henry muses or commands: "Bolton. Bolton!" And hesitantly, Henry weaves him into a story which he corrects as he composes: "shutters . . . no, hangings," "the light, no light," "sitting there in the . . . no, standing," "conversation then on the step, no, in the room." But Henry cannot sustain the story. The phrase "not a sound" begins to intrude—Henry's hope for silence from the sea. He breaks the story off, after evoking the play's title: "Not a sound, only the embers, sound of dying, dying glow, Holloway, Bolton, Bolton, Holloway, old men, great trouble, white world, not a sound."

Henry asks his blind father—or us—to close eyes and listen to the sea: "A drip! A drip!" But the dripping sound is different from the sea, and when the timed beats of the drips are cut off at his command, the shifting sea resumes. Henry tries to continue his story, then gives up. He tries to return to memories of his father, imitating his father's scorn of him: "A washout, that's all you are, a washout!" For a moment, Henry finds relief in the hard firm noise of a door slamming in his imagination. Then, by cruel association, his father's word "washout" leads him to think of his wife, Ada: "Wish to Christ she had." More explicitly, he wishes "to God we'd never had [the child]." (The French is plainer: Henry's father calls him "avortement"—abortion.)

In spite of Henry's unflattering reminiscences about Ada, she answers his summons: "Ada. Ada!" During the conversation with Ada, Henry again succeeds in evoking the sound of hooves. In a memory within a memory, Henry hears his daughter Addie taking music lessons, riding lessons. But she is no more successful than he in sustaining hard timed sounds to combat the soft timeless sea. In both lessons, her wail rises to paroxysm before it is cut off—reflecting Henry's pain. Infinity sucks up the hard efforts within time.

In another memory within a memory, occasioned by Ada's repetitions of the word "don't," the sea's roughness is heard as Henry makes love to Ada, over her protests. Back in the imaginary present, Ada suggests reasonably that something is wrong with Henry's brain, that he ought to see Holloway. Instead of answering her, or commanding a noise, Henry "*catches up two big stones and starts dashing them together.*" On the radio, we hear the *sound* of the clashing stones. Throwing a stone away, Henry exclaims: "That's life!" and throws the other stone away. It is not the stones that are life, but their sounds. Life is timed movement: in Addie's music lesson, the notes are "hammered," and in her riding lesson the hooves gallop. Henry refers to his love-making with Ada as "hammering away at it." *That's* life, as opposed to the infinite impersonal sea.

Ada tries to calm Henry, suggesting that he see Holloway, and informing him that sea-sounds are only on the surface: "Underneath all is quiet as the grave. Not a sound." But top and bottom, that is what Henry fears—the timeless quiet of the grave. He implores Ada to keep talking: "Every syllable is a second gained." But Ada leaves Henry after a few more words, and he can no longer command her to return. He tries to summon others: "Christ! Hooves! Hooves! Christ!" But we hear no sound of hooves, and we hear no indication of relief from Christ.

Henry creates a scene of Ada for his father, but soon she is out of reach of his imagination. Again Henry calls on Christ, and then tries to continue his story. But this time there are no embers; the fire is out. Bolton pleads with Holloway: "Please! Please! Please, Holloway!" And soon Henry is pleading: "Ada! Father! Christ!" Another sentence of his story, another call to Christ, and Henry walks to what the sound directions tell us is the water's edge. From his appointment book, Henry reads: "Plumber at nine." In Henry's story it was at nine that Hollow-way was to perform a "panhysterectomy." Nine, the hour of Christ's crucifixion, is the hour of the death of a world. Those who live in time must die in time, as opposed to the eternal sea.

Henry is puzzled by his note on the plumber, and then comments: "Ah yes, the waste." Life will have been a waste; Sunday will bring no Easter resurrection. There will be nothing and silence at last: "Not a sound." The three words are Henry's last sound, echoing his words about embers, Ada's words about the depths of the sea, and his own words about the white world of his story. The silence of nonbeing finally drowns all being. The radio play's last sound is "*Sea,*" which drowns all embers of life.

Acte sans paroles II

If we might make a proportion out of plays, it is possible to view *Acte sans paroles II* with relation to *Acte sans paroles I* as *All That Fall* to *Embers.* In the first term of the proportion, we have a familiar world with men behaving in familiar ways, but in the second term we have representative men behaving symbolically. The divisions are not absolute, however, and all four plays are distinguished by Beckett's humor. In the first two plays living is marked by falling; in the second two plays living is marked by rhythmic timing— of sounds on radio, of gestures in mime.

In *Acte sans paroles II*, two men perform a series of actions, one after the other. The two men are behavioral opposites: "A is slow, awkward . . . , absent. B brisk, rapid, precise." A is goaded into his day's activities, which consist of prayers, pill-taking, clothes-donning, carrot-eating, whose result is to change the position of his sack with respect to B. A's most characteristic action is to brood. B is goaded into his day's activities of checking the time, exercising, brushing teeth, combing and brushing hair, brushing clothes and dressing, eating carrots, using map and compass, whose result is to change the position of his sack with respect to A. B's most characteristic action is to check the time on his watch. A's slow motions and B's rapid movements last approximately the same time and achieve precisely the same end or non-end. The comedy depends on the timing—A versus B.

When the goad again prods A into prayer, we have come full circle. The sum total of human endeavor is on the surface of the mime play. As opposed to *Acte sans paroles I*, however, where mysterious offstage forces controlled the action, the goads of *Acte sans paroles II* are visible to us and palpable to the actors. And they become increasingly mechanized, like the goads of our world; the first goad is "strictly horizontal," the second goad is supported by one wheel, and the third goad by two. But A still needs two pokes from the goad to face his day, and presumably a three-wheeled goad will need to poke B only once. Activities will remain the same for each actor. Life in time accomplishes nothing, however one responds to time, but movements through time can be delectable play.

TIMELESS

Happy Days

Each Beckett play opens on different terrain. But though the "scorched grass" of *Happy Days* is new on Beckett's

177

stage, other aspects of the play are familiar. Its "blazing light" looks like the "dazzling light" of *Acte sans paroles I*. Winnie, a female protagonist, was preceded by Maddy Dunne of *All That Fall*. Her fixed centrality was approximated by Hamm in *Fin de partie*. A quasi-monologue was already spoken by Krapp in *Krapp's Last Tape*. *Happy Days*, like *Godot*, is divided into two acts. *Happy Days* contains invisible sounds of radio drama (bell ringing, nose-blowing) and exaggerated gestures of mime (Winnie's business with the contents of her bag, Willie's business with his hat, handkerchief, postcard, and newspaper). Props seem to be familiar—hat, sack, and parasol as in other Beckett works; revolver as in melodrama, and music-box suggesting musical comedy; implements of personal hygiene as in *Acte sans paroles II*, or in our own daily lives.

Happy Days repeats details of earlier Beckett plays, but *Happy Days* can be appreciated without reference to any other Beckett work. As Beckett would explain when he came to direct it, he wanted to write a play that would live through its text alone. The text is largely spoken by a partly buried woman, under a blazing sun. The image is immediately arresting, but its cruelty only slowly etches itself upon our consciousness, as our eyes begin to ache in the unrelieved brightness, as we learn that this sun never sets, as we watch it victimize Winnie, sinking into her grave. In spite of the mounting irony against the play's title, we are hardly prepared for the appalling bareness of the second act—a talking head, that motif of folklore. Winnie's head sustains a discourse, which is finally punctuated by the climactic arrival of Willie in full dress. Like previous Beckett's plays, *Happy Days* ends in stillness, but the last scene reflects obliquely on one of the oldest images of Western culture—Oedipus facing the Sphinx. Beckett's Sphinx asks a different question—Kiss or kill?—and Willie's answer is visual—man is the animal who crawls on all fours though middle-aged. Upright man in his prime is only a memory or a legend, as is Willie's single syllable, "Win."

In Act I of *Happy Days*, half-buried Winnie is the upper half of an hourglass. More literally than Shakespeare's Chorus in *Henry V*, she turns "the accomplishment of many years/ Into an hour-glass." Living in an endless present, she doubts "the accomplishment of many years," as we have all doubted the passing of time while it passes. Though Winnie's opening line seems to acknowledge that time passes— "*Another* heavenly day" (my italics)—she comes to refer apologetically to "day," "night," and "die" as "old style." In Act II she states explicitly that time itself is "old style." Since the sun never sets, there are no more days or nights, and there is no more death. It is through a bell that Winnie is invaded by consciousness. In Act I she begins her bell-bound day with an automatic prayer, but soon she invokes deity as a mere expletive. Though she begins with prayer, and plans to end with song and prayer, Winnie marshalls other resources for living through her day: the stage props, her husband Willie, composition of stories, and almost inadvertent recollection of lines of verse. An emmet appears momentarily, her parasol bursts into flame, but Winnie can scarcely depend on such distractions in a world even more "corpsed" than that of *Fin de partie*. She tries to endure through the happy day with careful deployment of props and Willie, and, to a lesser extent, with fictional invention. She tries to endure by talking her way through each bell-bound day.

Winnie herself sees her bag as her main prop: "There is of course the bag. . . . There will always be the bag. . . . Even when you are gone, Willie." In her bag Winnie finds toothbrush, toothpaste, mirror, spectacles, medicine-bottle, lipstick, hat, magnifying glass, comb and brush, music-box, nail file, revolver. Except perhaps for the last of these, the props are those of any middle-class, middle-aged woman. Winnie uses them to endure until the bell for sleep. And so do we. Thus we camouflage our dying, but Winnie cannot die, and she lives in her present, noting its several facets, of which the most vital is Willie.

He alone—and not the props, however she personalizes them—can rescue Winnie from the solitude she calls her wilderness. He can and does. Throughout Act I Willie gives evidence of his presence, and responds as witness to Winnie's presence, though he speaks only fifty-two words. He returns Winnie's parasol when she drops it; he lends her his treasured obscene postcard; he solves her grammatical problem as to whether hair is singular or plural; he tells her five times that he hears her; he charges her to "Fear no more"; he identifies the burden and motion of the emmet, he laughs more or less together with her; he puzzles over her phrase "*Sucked* up?"; he shows five fingers when she asks for a mere one; he bursts into song in accompaniment to her music-box; and, in his most extended speech, he defines "hog" for her. Presumably, he even follows her nagging instructions for crawling into his hole. In Act II we learn that he has given Winnie the bag, parasol, and revolver—the only objects still within Winnie's field of vision. If we can overlook Willie's taciturnity, it would be hard to imagine a more cooperative husband—at least until Act II, when he appears "dressed to kill" in "morning coat," full of unfathomable intention.

Before that final tableau of an endless end, Winnie has punctuated her discourse with quotations from English poetry. Inserted into a late draft of the play, these quotations at once enrich and undercut Winnie's own language. If we judge by quantity, Shakespeare is Winnie's favorite poet, since she draws upon *Hamlet* (twice), *Romeo and Juliet*, *Cymbeline*, and in Act II on *Twelfth Night*. Milton's *Paradise Lost* is recalled once in Act I and once in Act II. Other poems cited in Act I are the Khayyam-Fitzgerald *Rubaiyat*, Gray's *Ode on a Distant Prospect of Eton College*, and a Browning poem that neither Beckett nor I can identify. In Act II Winnie mumbles niggardly phrases from Keats's *Ode to a Nightingale*, Yeats's *At the Hawk's Well*, and Herrick's *To the Virgins to Make Much of Time*. She has a more extensive recollection of Charles Wolfe's "Go forget me." Winnie tends to quote inexactly or incompletely, and she uses the description "exquisite" and "classics" only for the maudlin verse of Charles Wolfe. In Act II she calls for "unforgettable" and "immortal" lines, but none pour forth. Winnie's taste is nearly as uncertain as her memory. She opens her quasi-monologue on a prayer and closes it on a musical comedy libretto, but through her quotations Beckett reveals the ironic resonance of her repetitions of "happy days." The better we know the poems, the more ironic the resonance.

Of the play's fourteen quotations, six comment on the cruel landscape in which Winnie spends her happy days. Ironic are 1) Winnie's reference to *Hamlet*'s "bird of dawning" that sings at Christmas, whereas she knows neither dawn nor Christmas; 2) her Miltonic greeting of the merciless sun as a holy light; 3) her recollection of the "beechen green" and numberless shadows in which Keats's nightingale sang; 4) her evocation of Omar Khayyam's "Paradise enow," which consists of a jug of wine, a loaf of bread, and above all "Thou/ Beside me singing in the Wilderness." More reflective of Winnie's actual situation is the line she does not quote (following the one she does) from Yeats's *At the Hawk's Well*: "A well long choked up and dry."

Three other quotations on Winnie's happy day speak of woe, and one implies grief:

woe woe is me . . . to see what I see
O, woe is me,/ To have seen what I have seen, see what I see! (*Hamlet*)

Oh fleeting joys—(*Lips.*)—oh something lasting woe.
O fleeting joys/ Of Paradise, dear bought with lasting woes! (*Paradise Lost*)

something something laughing wild amid severest woe
And moody Madness laughing wild/ Amid severest woe. (*Ode on a Distant Prospect of Eton College*)

181

cheek . . . no . . . (*Eyes right.*) . . . no . . . (*Distends cheeks.*) . . . (*Eyes left, distends cheeks again.*) . . . no . . . no damask.

She never told her love,/ But let concealment, like a worm i' the bud,/ Feed on her damask cheek. She pined in thought,/ and with a green and yellow melancholy/ She sat like Patience on a monument,/ Smiling at grief. (*Twelfth Night*)

Three other quotations are spoken in the face of death. In making up her lips in the mirror, Winnie exclaims: "Ensign crimson" and "Pale flag." When Romeo thinks Juliet is dead, he speaks to her: "Beauty's ensign yet/ Is crimson in thy lips and in thy cheeks,/ And death's pale flag is not advanced there." Later, Winnie tests Willie's hearing with a line from *Cymbeline*: "Fear no more the heat o' the sun." Imogen's brothers sing this as the opening line of a dirge when they believe Imogen is dead. In Act II of *Happy Days*, when Winnie is at last face to face with Willie, she asks him: "Where are the flowers? (*Pause.*) That smile today." Willie sinks his head in answer; perhaps he too knows Herrick's lines: "And this same flower that smiles today/ Tomorrow will be dying."

Winnie does not often seem to be conscious of the ironic resonance of her quotations, but she herself uses her stories to cast ironic reflection upon the happy days we witness. More inventive than Hamm in *Fin de partie*, she works at *two* different stories, though she labels only one a story. The other, sustained through both acts, records the observations of the Cooker or Shower couple (both words are German for "look") when they are faced with the phenomenon of Winnie. Mr. Cooker or Shower gives voice to the very questions and exclamations that are passing through the minds of many of the theater audience: "What's she doing? he says—What's the idea? he says—stuck up to her diddies in the bleeding ground?"

Only in Act II does Winnie start what she herself calls a

story: "There is my story of course when all else fails." Mildred (Winnie's own name in an earlier draft of *Happy Days*) will begin in the womb and have a long life. Four or five years old, she has a new doll with full set of clothes. Announced as fiction, Mildred nevertheless reflects Winnie, with whom she shares a taste for clothes and props. Winnie endows Mildred with Willie's mobility, and her dolly with his china-blue eyes. Like Winnie, Mildred is frightened, but Winnie does not allow her to give vent to terror until she herself finishes her account of the Cooker couple, concluding as in Act I: "Last human kind—to stray this way." Then Winnie imagines a mouse running up Mildred's thigh, and Winnie screams three times in the fear that she shares with her character.

The word "reflexive" is often applied to Beckett's work; his novels refer to his other novels, his stories contain other stories, his plays converge upon inner plays. But *Happy Days* is extraordinary in the range of both its reflection and its extension. The set is at once heaven, hell, and scorched earth. Most of the props indicate the daily routines of Western woman or man, but the revolver introduces a note of melodrama and a dark hint of death. A more ordinary prop, the toothbrush, slowly leads toward a kind of damnation; when it is first seen, Winnie uses it to brush her teeth; then she tries to read what is printed on its handle; with the help of spectacles and magnifying glass, Winnie finally makes out: "Fully guaranteed genuine pure hog's setae." Instead of querying the meaning of "setae," as most of us would, Winnie asks for a definition of "hog," which Willie renders as: "Castrated male swine. Reared for slaughter." But Beckett's Malone wrote: "For all pigs are alike, when you get to know their little ways, struggle, squeal, bleed, squeal, struggle, bleed, squeal and faint away, in more or less the same way exactly." Willie's summary is more theatrically pointed, but the sentiment is identical.

Occasionally, Willie himself is no more than a prop for Winnie, and yet Beckett creates a play-long tension between

Winnie and her largely invisible husband. Both given to hats, handkerchiefs, and reading print, they resemble other Beckett couples in their suggestive oppositions: man-woman, motion-speech, pragmatism-esthetics, animal-bird, earth-air, philology-philosophy. Willie's newspaper excerpts comment on the condition of human beings condemned to an earth that does not accommodate their aging and death. Winnie's quasi-monologue implies more: literally sinking into her grave, she is irresistibly drawn to the heavens. Old-fashioned in her vocabulary ("naught," "would I had," "tis," "beseech," "bid," "amiss," "God grant," "dire need"), she clings to the comfort of half-remembered classics. Unlovely and perhaps unlovable, she ritualistically and volubly performs her toilette.

In Act I, her first happy day, she predicts the happy day to come: that she will sink farther into the earth, that the parasol will renew itself like a phoenix, and that Willie will come around to her side of the mound. Act II repeats the motifs of Act I, but it is more stringent. Buried to her throat, Winnie still refers to three visible props, she still talks to an invisible Willie, she still tries to remember verse, and she still composes stories. She still can speak of "great mercies" and "that is what I find so wonderful," but she does not claim that these swift days are happy, until the arrival of Willie. In a striking audio-visual effect, Willie appears in full dress just after Winnie evokes their wedding day. Presence recalls and punctures the past in a play that apparently denies time, but nevertheless yields to "old style" in its title, *Happy Days*.

Written in English, depending so intimately upon English poetry, *Happy Days* had its world première in New York's Cherry Lane Theatre, directed by Alan Schneider and starring the late Ruth White. Schneider was at some pains to remove the labels of "pessimistic" and "obscure" that had been attached to Beckett, and Ruth White evidently succeeded in voicing cheer and clarity for her Winnie. After Beckett translated the play into French, Roger Blin directed

Madeleine Renaud in a production that toured several countries. Even more gregarious than the American Winnie, the Frenchwoman flirted with her audience, and the Winnie-Willie smile did not fade at the end. Many actresses are moving in Act I of *Happy Days*, if they can convey the life inherent in things, but Act II is too deeply internal for most actresses.

In 1971 Beckett directed *Happy Days* at the Werkstatt of the Schiller Theater—his third production there. He began rehearsing *Glückliche Tage* in West Berlin on August 10, 1971, and his production opened at the Werkstatt on September 17. Some weeks before rehearsals, Beckett had begun a careful study of Elmar Tophoven's German translation. Beckett underlined and numbered the text's many repetitions, and he noted some forty minor changes for the dialogue. He introduced a few changes into Act II so that the lines would echo those of Act I. These are difficult to convey in English, but an example may illustrate the principle. In the English Act I Winnie remarks to Willie after their laughter at God's poor joke: "I think *you would back me up there*, Willie." In Act II, commenting on sadness after sexual intercourse, Winnie says: "*You would concur* with Aristotle there, Willie, I fancy." In German, both italicized phrases were brought closer to "You would agree."

Before the rehearsal period, Beckett had memorized the entire German text (with gestures), and he had composed his *Regiebuch*. Eighty-five pages, handwritten in English, testify to the care with which he examined *Glückliche Tage*. After marking the German text, Beckett apparently noted directorial matters as they occurred to him. On the flyleaf of the *Regiebuch*, probably penned last, is a neatly printed table of contents; on the facing page is Beckett's division of the play into rehearsal scenes, eight in Act I, when Winnie is buried to her waist, and four in Act II, when Winnie is buried to her neck. In Act I the divisions are: (1) opening to "Old eyes"; (2) to the point where Willie fans himself visibly and Winnie takes up her magnifying glass; (3)

185

Winnie's "Fully guaranteed" to Willie's "It"; (4) to end of laugh; (5) to Winnie's "No one. (*Smile off. Looks at parasol.*)"; (6) to Winnie's ". . . (*Voice breaks, head down.*) . . . things . . . so wonderful"; (7) to end of Mr. Shower-Cooker story and end of nail filing; (8) to end of Act I. And the Act II divisions are: (1) to Winnie's "And now?"; (2) from Winnie's "The face" to "Gently, Winnie"; (3) to Winnie's "Sing your old song, Winnie"; (4) to end. These divisions are in no sense structural, but a matter of mechanical convenience for rehearsal purposes only.

The *Regiebuch* reveals that Beckett reconsidered every word and gesture of the text, as well as all props and sound effects. He enumerated the contents of Winnie's bag and specified that they be worn-looking, conspicuous, and non-realistic. He drew sketches of her parasol and spectacles, and he noted that she should handle glass props with her left hand, setting them down on her left. Furthermore, Beckett wrote specific directions regarding sound. For each of the eight times a bell rings, he indicated pitch, volume, and duration (shorter than in the printed text); when Winnie strikes Willie with the parasol, the second blow was to be louder than the first.

Early in the *Regiebuch*, Beckett focused on Willie, who is invisible and inaudible through most of the play. Beckett nevertheless knew Willie's every word, motion, and breath. A diagram traced Willie's invisible crawl into his hole, and another diagram traced his visible crawl up the mound. Beckett listed Willie's three Act I positions: sitting against the mound (partly visible), lying behind the mound (invisible), lying in his hole (invisible). Willie's voice was to sound different from his different positions, but he was to read the same newspaper advertisements in the same way each time. Beckett counted Willie's words and described his actions during the dozen scenes of the two acts, and he added breathing noises to indicate Willie's exertions. A page and a half of minute description detailed Willie's final crawl up the mound.

It is mainly Winnie whose role fills the pages of Beckett's *Regiebuch*. He listed her repeated refrains and her repeated gestures, and he separately listed variations upon those repetitions, or the varying possibilities for her phrase "happy day." When she is buried to her waist in Act I, Winnie has three main series of movements: she turns back and right to look at Willie, she turns forward and left to explore her bag, and she looks closely at her toothbrush trying to read the inscription. Each of these three main movements contains three variants: (1) she simply turns to Willie, or turns and then leans back, or turns, leans, and cranes as far as she can; (2) when she begins to explore her bag, she is sometimes prevented, sometimes interrupted, and she sometimes plunges her hand in; (3) to read the print on her toothbrush, she tries with naked eyes, with glasses, then with glasses and magnifying glass before she deciphers: "Fully guaranteed genuine pure hog's setae." Beckett was equally concerned with the precision of Winnie's emotions, listing her thirty-one smiles, five happy expressions, and eight hints of gloom. Opposite the English of Winnie's fourteen quotations, Beckett noted standard German translations of these texts, other than Tophoven's published versions.

The *Regiebuch* is primarily a record of stage details, but one note in the eighty-five pages suggests the philosophic basis of the drama: "Relate frequency of broken speech and action to discontinuity of time. [Winnie's] time experience incomprehensible transport from one inextricable present to the next, those past unremembered, those to come inconceivable." Since Winnie's experience of time is apparent in the dialogue of the drama, the note reveals how the play's technique mirrors its metaphysics: interrupted gesture and fragmented speech convey the subtly discontinuous groundwork of lived time. In spite of Beckett's note, however, Winnie does have memories, and in Act I she tries to conceive of a future. By the reviving of memories, her past is converted to a present, and her future becomes a mere prolongation of the immediate moment. Drama has long

187

been defined as the art of the present, and Beckett builds that definition into *Happy Days*.

In successive plays Beckett has imposed increasing restrictions upon his actors. His *Regiebuch* meticulously, almost maniacally, delineates such restrictions. Beckett's hope is that severely imposed limits will demand more of the actor, intensifying his emotional expression, rather than inhibiting it. Though he does not use Grotowski's word "score" for his texts, he is a musician who appreciates his instrumentalists. He once told Charles Marowitz: "Producers don't seem to have any sense of form in movement, the kind of form one finds in music, for instance, where themes keep recurring. When, in a text, actions are repeated, they ought to be made unusual the first time, so that when they happen again—in exactly the same way—an audience will recognize them from before." When Beckett came to direct, he orchestrated his score.

Before rehearsals began in Berlin, Beckett studied sketches with his scene designer Matias, who had also designed the French set of *Happy Days*, eight years earlier. Beckett no longer wished Winnie to be *"in exact centre of mound,"* but slightly to stage left, so as to give more importance to Willie. Matias' earlier set had substituted a baked desert for the scorched grass of the text, and on the shallow Werkstatt stage depth was gained by adding mounds and hillocks. The set was thus to look more realistic, in contrast to the decidedly unrealistic image of a partly buried Winnie.

Rehearsals were complicated in that Eva Katherina Schultz, Winnie, was playing in repertory throughout the rehearsal period, and Willie had to be replaced three times before Rudi Schmitt stayed with the part. On the first days of rehearsals Beckett did not read the whole play aloud, nor did he ask his actors to do so. And he offered no explanations or interpretations. Rather, he focused at once upon Winnie's lines and gestures. Instead of the symmetrical, head-down sleeping position of Madeleine Renaud (the only Winnie Beckett had seen), he suggested a pose that he proceeded to demonstrate—left hand protecting the bag and right hand folded back to protect the nape of the neck. When Winnie is summoned to consciousness by the bell (rung by Beckett), there was to be a separation of words from gestures.

Even before Frau Schultz learned her lines, Beckett indicated the vocal variety he expected. Winnie was to speak in three main voices—normal, intimately to herself, and with pronounced articulation to Willie. In Act I she imitates Willie's voice as he implores her to take the revolver away from him; in Act II she imitates his proposal of marriage. Winnie's sustained story necessitates another three voices in each act: ordinary narrative, a gruffly energetic Mr. Shower-Cooker, his lady companion filled with terror and hatred. Moreover, in Act II Mr. Shower-Cooker's voice was to have an erotic tone as he asked about Winnie's legs. In the story about Mildred and the doll Winnie was to contrive a doll-like voice. Further, Beckett wanted a special tone for reading the print on the toothbrush, and he wanted something close to a chant for the literary quotations, which are not readily recognizable in German. At one point during rehearsals, Beckett compared Winnie to a bird, and said that her voice should convey her weightlessness. What he called "the many colors" of Winnie's Act I voice had to be a richly contrasting background for her "white voice" of Act II.

During the course of rehearsals, Beckett worked long on coordinating gestures and words. Thus, the *sound* of Winnie's verbal flight opposes the *sight* of Willie studying his dirty postcard. When Winnie looks at the pornographic postcard, her devouring eyes oppose her disapproving words. Later in the rehearsal period, Beckett gave attention to pacing; after Willie repeats Winnie's "Fear no more," for instance, Winnie was directed to speak very quickly.

Though Beckett made few general remarks about his text, some of his laconic observations are informative. He early told Winnie that the bag was her friend, the bell her enemy, and that she had to convey this throughout the play. In Act I Winnie turns to Willie twenty times, and seventeen times to the bag. In Act II the bell rings five times (one fewer than in the printed text), forcing Winnie to open her eyes; she looks more often (eight times) in Willie's direction (right) than in that of the bag (left). About Winnie's quotation from *Romeo and Juliet* Beckett remarked that "Ensign crimson" is life, and "Pale flag" death. When Winnie is able to talk without prompting from props, she should be both surprised and pleased. Beckett wished the phrase "old style" to be pronounced very slowly and distinctly the first time, but with increasing casualness afterward. Similarly, Winnie should linger over her first mention of a "happy day," but then should take the phrase for granted. In their shared laugh Willie was to begin alone, then be joined by Winnie, but he was to end alone again. Beckett described the laugh in French as *"rire jaune,"* which might be translated as bitter laughter. When Winnie remarks, "Ah earth you old extinguisher," Beckett wished her to suggest that she, as well as the parasol fire, was being extinguished by the earth, and he added: "Winnie's fate is all the more pathetic because this weightless being is devoured by the earth."

After ten days of rehearsal of Act I, Beckett recited Act II for Frau Schultz, complete with eye movements. By Act II Winnie can no longer speak full sentences or remember whole lines of verse. Volume and duration of speech are both reduced in the new present, far bleaker than the second act of *Godot*. Beckett stressed the importance of Winnie's line: "Then . . . now . . . what difficulties here, for the mind." Accordingly, she was to emphasize the difficulties of "then." Beginning with the auxiliary verb of a continuous past, Winnie breaks off unbelievingly; she then resumes her recollection as a recitation rather than an account of past experience.

Only midway during the rehearsal period was the final

190

Willie cast, and Beckett rehearsed him alone for two days, playing Winnie himself. He compared Willie to an old turtle, very much of the earth. Even though the audience cannot see Willie, Beckett wanted him to mime the actions Winnie described. Details of Willie's part, like those of Winnie, were built on triplets. Willie has three periods of visibility. He puts a hat on three times (twice the boater, and once the stovepipe) with the same flick of the finger against the hat. He blows his nose resoundingly three times. Beckett changed his text to have Willie turn the pages of the yellowed newspaper three times at first reading, then another three at the second. Beckett added to his text three cries from invisible Willie—the first two when Willie is struck by Winnie's parasol, and the third when Winnie's medicine bottle hits his skull, causing it to bleed.

At the end of Act II Willie crawls into sight. As soon as the set was built, Beckett crawled through Willie's stage path, and he corrected Willie's movements right up to the dress rehearsal, always insisting upon the dramatic quality of silence during that climactic crawl. In the final tableau Beckett carefully positioned Willie's hand to sustain the ambiguity as to whether Willie reaches for Winnie or the revolver.

Just before the opening, there were inevitable technical difficulties: since Beckett wanted absolutely no shadows on stage, the lighting had to be reworked. The harsh bell-sounds rose twice in pitch, but they had to be more precisely timed. The long toothbrush handle was balanced by the long revolver muzzle, but the parasol handle, without the sheath of the text, was of shining chrome that had to be darkened. Music box and burning parasol were not perfected till the technical rehearsal, when the parasol continued to burn backstage. For the technical rehearsal Beckett reduced the size of Willie's handkerchief so that, perched unprotectively on his bald head, it looked comically dainty. Even after the dress rehearsal, Matias wanted

191

Willie's morning clothes to look older, his newspaper to be less yellow, and Winnie's bag to hover more indeterminately between black and gray.

As Beckett is shy, he suffers in an audience-filled room, and he has never attended his opening nights. At the dress rehearsal of *Glückliche Tage*, when the house is traditionally half full in West Berlin, Beckett was as tense as any other director on a first night. He sat in the tiny side balcony of the Werkstatt and frowned through much of the performance, but he gave the actors no notes afterward. On opening night he came to the theater about half an hour before curtain-time. He patiently received the traditional gesture of good luck: three breaths blown over his shoulder. In Frau Schultz's dressing room he spoke privately to his Winnie. Leaving the theater before curtain-time, he autographed programs for a few people who waylaid him at the stage door.

After the performance Beckett met theater workers and friends at a post-opening party in his favorite café. Though he asked no questions, he listened courteously when others discussed the production. As though he had not lived with it for thirty-seven obsessive days in Berlin. As though the production had no relationship to him.

After his months of concentrated work for production of *Happy Days*, Beckett took a dislike to the play, but for me, perhaps because I am a woman, it remains intensely stirring. *Godot* is more beguiling, *Fin de partie* more greatly tragic, and *Krapp's Last Tape* more simply human, but *Happy Days* haunts me as the quintessential drama of modern humanity. Literally a consumer of goods, Winnie uses those goods to protect herself against her wilderness. Already in her grave, Winnie begins by looking to heaven, but she voices faith only hesitantly: "Prayers perhaps not for naught." Even as her flesh is baked and buried, Winnie counts her blessings. Dubious about past and future, she embraces the presence of her present. Her kisses and wedding-toasts have inexplicably been replaced by the bar-

192

ren stage, but she will not admit that she was born merely to die.

Winnie's temperament and background have taught her to keep a stiff upper lip. She never despairs, her eyes only once well up with tears, her voice breaks eight times, but she smiles thirty-one times. She determinedly reiterates "happy day," "great mercies," "That is what I find so wonderful." Lacking the imagery of Vladimir, Hamm, or Krapp, Winnie resorts to quotation for short poetic flights. Her own speech accumulates banalities, and yet it is harrowing in its rhythmic force. When Winnie does utter an imaged sentence, she implies a wish for annihilation: "And if for some strange reason no further pains are possible, why then just close the eyes—(*she does so*)—and wait for the day to come—(*opens eyes*)—the happy day to come when flesh melts at so many degrees and the night of the moon has so many hundred hours." But even that wish is couched in terms of dissolution in a long present rather than nonbeing in eternity.

For Winnie feels that time has no meaning, even though she must endure it. And the basis of that feeling is human mortality, of which she rarely speaks. Less terrifyingly lucid than Hamm, Winnie is not the Pollyanna whose role she plays. Or not only that. It is because she knows where she is—under a hellish light, returning to the dust—that she *assumes* the role of Pollyanna rather than of Cassandra. Because man's fate can drive him mad, Winnie maintains her equilibrium as we all do—living in a minor key. It is a gallant part, played with discipline if not splendor, with style if not panache, and with gentle lovable grace.

Play

Happy Days gave birth to the triplet of *Play*. Winnie, buried to her neck under a scorching sun, is replaced by three urned figures under a spotlight. A marriage play is followed by a play about a lovers' triangle. (*Words and Music* may have preceded the first draft of *Play*, whose fourth of ten typescripts in Washington University Library is dated August, 1962, whereas *Words and Music* was completed in December, 1961.)

The first typescript of *Play* suggests that Beckett heard the play in his mind's ear before he saw the details in his mind's eye. That first typescript is almost all dialogue, except for two handwritten scenic directions. At the beginning Beckett noted: "Full light and voices"; at the beginning of the second part "Diminished light and voices." The play's central division is already apparent in this draft: the first part presents recollections of a lovers' triangle, and the second part more lengthily presents the trio's reactions to their immediate situation, in which a spotlight plays a large role. Only in the second typescript did Beckett see the members of the triangle immured in white boxes. By the fourth typescript the boxes have turned into white urns a yard high, and Beckett's handwritten scenic directions set the basic acting pattern: "All spots on faces alone. Transfer of light from one face to another immediate. No blackout except where indicated. Extortion of speech by light not immediate. At every solicitation a silence of 4 or 5 seconds before voice begins. Except on 5 occasions where longer delay indicated." Thus the story—play—came to Beckett before the method of soliciting its narration. After whistle and goad of the mime plays; after the bell of *Happy Days*, a spotlight prompts the action of *Play*. This technique suggests the traditional metaphor of God as light, but Beckett's light is capricious and unfathomable. It controls our view of the play.

Play is composed of intercalated monologues, each speech elicited by a spotlight, and through ten typescripts Beckett honed those monologues to precision and interaction. In all ten versions the three characters are denied any stage business, any entrances or exits. Immobile in three identical gray urns, they even look alike. Through all ten versions, each of the actors believes he is alone, even though both halves of the two-part play start with their collective (and therefore

194

incomprehensible) words. Through all ten versions, the first movement of *Play* intercuts individual memories of their earthly relationship, whereas the longer second movement, played in half-light and at half-volume, dwells upon individual responses to the situation we see. The whole of *Play* is *da capo* in structure, but the actors never learn this. They do not know that they are in a purgatory, condemned to repeat and repeat and repeat both the earthly triangle and self-discovery in an elsewhere. Unable to communicate with one another, ignorant of the fate of the other two, each of the three people reviews and re-views the triangle. Time dissolves in repetition.

Play runs some forty minutes in the theater, played through twice. The first part takes about ten minutes to introduce us to the lovers' triangle, which is as old as monogamy. It does so in bits, snatches, and half-echoes that elicit a nervous suspense. The situation of *Play* is usually labelled a marital triangle, but Beckett is more laconic; his characters are designated as M, W1, W2—a man and two women, legal status of no interest. They assert their relationship with no need of proper names, and we seize that relationship in the first intelligible sentence of dialogue: "W1: I said to him, Give her up."

The jigsaw puzzle of facts cannot be solved in any single viewing, but the printed text yields the details. M-W1 is the original relationship. When W1 grows suspicious that M is having an affair with W2, W1 accuses him and threatens to commit suicide. In spite of his denial, W1 confronts W2 and threatens to kill her. W2 also denies guilt, and W1 hires a detective, whom M bribes to tell no tales. Suddenly, M confesses to W1, who forgives him. W1 visits W2 to gloat, so that W2 threatens M with the termination of their affair, but then she relents. Each woman thinks that her rival attracts the man with money. Each woman wishes to go away with M, but he pleads professional obligations. All continues as before, the man devoted to each of the women, to both of them. Suddenly, the man disappears. W2, thinking that he has returned to W1, burns his things. W1, thinking that he has returned to W2, falls ill but later drives to her rival's house, to find it deserted. As Barbara Bray wrote in her review of the original production: "The story itself is superficially the most banal tale imaginable: a triangle—man, wife and mistress—which comes to grief." Familiarly banal. Who of us has not figured in some triangle? Who of us has not cringed at our own melodramatic clichés? And who, if we are old enough, cannot look back in compassion at our own passion and its victims?

However hazy we may be about the details of interplay, the play situation is all too familiar. But Beckett's staging is so unfamiliar that it undercuts the banality. These passion-charged figures have impassive faces and toneless voices. Their ardent physicality is buried in the separate urns; only the urns can touch. Even memories have to be prompted. We absorb their singular situation along with their cliché triangularity, so that the total effect is unfamiliar and disturbing.

As well as ironic. The play's very first word—the choral "Yes" before the words diverge—is ironically inapplicable to the situation that faces us on stage, affirmative of nothing. Carefully modulated choral phrasing allows no sense through its rhythm, so that the play opens with a devaluation of words. In the first comprehensible speeches, each character locked in himself, the word "give" links the three —exactly what none of them can do:

W1: I said to him, Give her up.
W2: Give him up, she screamed, he's mine.
M: Give up that whore, she said, or I'll cut my throat— (*hiccup*) pardon—so help me God.

Each memory of a demand is different. Each of the additions to the word "give" shades into melodrama. M's hiccup and pardon—three times repeated during the course of the play—is Beckett's inspired device for undercutting the melodrama with a hint of purgatory.

196

In the opening speeches, too, there are echoes of what
Alec Reid has called "verbal telepathy." M's speech closes:
"I told her I did not know what she was talking about."
And W2 begins: "What are you talking about? I said." The
words "bitch," "dogged," and "bloodhound" are divided
between the three characters. Each of them uses, or is said
to use, the verb "smell." The grand passion begins to tremble
whenever they quote one another—a comic technique that
Beckett carries over from his fiction:

> M: I can't have her crashing in here, she said, threaten-
> ing to take my life. I must have looked incredulous.
> Ask Erskine, she said, if you don't believe me. But she
> threatens to take her own, I said. Not yours? she said.
> No, I said, hers. We had fun trying to work this out.

Such fun is unimaginable in true melodrama. Even funnier
is M's commentary on the dialogue he quotes:

> M: I ran into your ex-doxy, she said one night, on the
> pillow, you're well out of that. Rather uncalled for, I
> thought. I am indeed, sweetheart, I said, I am indeed.
> God what vermin women. Thanks to you, angel, I
> said.

The juxtaposition of sweetheart-angel against vermin-
women is comic, as is the hovering pillow-phrase. The very
technique of undercutting is later inserted into the text:

> W2: He has told me all about it, she said. Who he, I
> said *filing away*, and what it? (my italics)

The filed language mocks the melodrama it presents, and
stage presence suggests that there is more—or less—to language than meets the ear. (Beckett's French translation
plays with sound to undercut the triangle: "je le fis filer,"
"Tu pues la pute," "une machine à machin.")
    Beckett achieves tonal contrast from his rare repetitions
in *Play*. When M cannot deny the affair to W1, he recalls:
"So I took her in my arms and swore I could not live without

her. I meant it, what is more." And when he cannot deny to
W2 that he has resumed intimacy with W1, he recalls: "So
I took her in my arms and said I could not go on living
without her. I don't believe I could have." Needing them
both, M cannot cope with the situation, and he says twice,
at brief intervals: "I simply could no longer—." The first
repetition of inability is comic in a hackneyed situation, but
the second becomes serious by its brevity and incompletion.

We never know how the three of them arrive in their urns,
each believing that the other two are still alive. In the
second part of *Play* each responds directly to the prompting
light-beam, each aware that the response is inadequate.
Their language loses the clichés of melodrama, and it is
musicalized by increased repetition. The word "all" begins
to reverberate through their speech. Though their dialogue
no longer builds a plot, it does build a pattern: the three
begin with conscious reaction to their limbo, the two
women addressing the spotlight as an undesirable lover.
All three find the present confusing but preferable to
a past on earth. All three pity the two whom they believe
to be still on earth. All three turn from the earth to a preoccupation with the here-and-now. All three are unable to
keep from questions, and all three are aware that there may
be no sense in trying to make sense of their situation. At
the last W1 personalizes the light; M tries to impersonalize
it as mindless; W2 hopes for and perhaps attains the mind-
lessness of madness. It is she who utters the most striking
metaphysical image of life in time: "Like dragging a great
roller, on a scorching day. The strain to get it moving,
momentum coming—." Then, after a three-second blackout:
"Kill it and strain again." The steps of the pattern are
skewed—not sequentially as clear as I have made them.
In the final choral speeches, the word "dark" is repeated
by W1, "shade" by W2, and "peace" by M. In the theater
we feel their yearning for these states, rather than hear
their attainment.

198

Banal as love triangles are, they permit Beckett to intersect infinity with a virtually timeless cliché. Like Murphy's Belacqua bliss, preferring to *re*live rather than live, *Play*'s three characters prefer their roles of audience to those of actors. Detached from the passion of their lives—"all that was just . . . play"—all three acquire compassion in limbo, imagining peaceful scenes for the other two. Only the man has a fantasy of the *three* of them together. His final line of the play, after the repetition, becomes inclusive: "We were not long together—." Its first utterance refers specifically to his love affair, but by the end it has acquired a metaphysical dimension, for human beings are never long together before the urns claim them, and beyond the urns, what?

Beckett names none of his three characters, but the servant of W2 is called Erskine, a name that Beckett changed from Arsene in the seventh typescript of *Play*. W2 describes Erskine as "coming and going on earth, letting people in, showing people out." Erskine and Arsene were Watt's predecessors in Mr. Knott's establishment, and Beckett's return to these names indicates, I think, that, for all the surface differences, this limbo of urns resembles Mr. Knott's inscrutable premises. Its denizens serve time, ask questions, seek knowledge, but finally learn nothing of the heart of mystery. The characters of *Play* learn nothing about their surroundings, though they deliver information to the prompting spotlight, which Beckett calls "soliciting" in an early draft, "a unique inquisitor" in the published version. Toward the last, they question whether anybody sees them. Of course, it is we who see and hear them—at play in the theater. We are part of their inscrutable surroundings. We know that "all that was just . . . play," but the thrust of Beckett's *Play* leaves us wondering about our own lives, about all life: "All this, when will all this have been . . . just play?"

Beckett was never sole director of *Play*, but he advised on German, French, and English productions, as well as on a French movie version. The French experience prompted a letter from Beckett to George Devine, first English director: "According to the text [the repetition] is rigorously identical with the first statement. We now think it would be dramatically more effective to have it express a slight weakening, both of question and of response, by means of less and perhaps slower light and correspondingly less volume and speed of voice. . . . The impression of falling off which this would give, with suggestion of conceivable dark and silence in the end, or of an indefinite approximating towards it, would be reinforced if we obtained also, in the repeat, a quality of hesitancy, of both question and answer, perhaps not so much in a slowing down of actual débit as in a less confident movement of spot from one face to another and less immediate reaction of the voices. The whole idea involves a spot mechanism of greater flexibility than has seemed necessary so far. The inquirer (light) begins to emerge as no less a victim of his inquiry than they and as needing to be free, within narrow limits, literally to act the part, i.e. to vary if only slightly his speeds and intensities."

After the London production, Beckett permitted still greater freedom in the repetition, and his notes to this effect are published in England at the end of the paperback edition of *Play*. Those notes focus on the intensity of the light and the volume of the voices, but his final note affects the text itself: "Changed order of speeches in first repeat in so far as this compatible with unchanged continuity for actors. For example, the order of interrogation W1, W2, M, W2, W1, M at opening of I becomes W2, W1, M, W2, M, W1 at opening of II, and so on if and as desired." This radical change is in harmony with the play's timeless setting. Chronology was vitally important in earthly affairs, but chronology is already transcended in the replay of what was "just play." There can be no earthly reason to insist upon it or upon any temporal order. The speeches come to us in time, but it does not matter what time.

200

Words and Music

In 1961 and 1962 Beckett wrote two parallel radio plays in his two languages of composition—English *Words and Music* and French *Cascando*. Both plays step out from *Embers*, in which a man tries to blend the voices of his past and his imagination into a defense against nonbeing. But in the radio plays of the 1960's, the blend is distilled. Bearing a superficial resemblance to *Play*, each radio play has three personae: a master of ceremonies, a narrative voice, and music. (A jettisoned radio play of November, 1961, also has three characters—Homme, Femme, and Musique.) In each play the Master of Ceremonies attempts to control the Narrative and Music, but in each play they elude him. Both plays are closer to Beckett's French fiction than are his other works in dramatic form, and they are the least popular of his works in dramatic form. In both plays, a being struggles with language to convey his state of being, but language betrays him.

Words and Music begins where George Herbert's *Collar* ends: "Methought I heard one calling, 'Child!'/ And I replied, 'My Lord!'" Beckett's Croak calls his Joe soon after the beginning of *Words and Music*, and Joe-Words replies: "My Lord." Herbert's persona finally accepts his collar of subservient mortality, but Beckett's Lord Croak, as his name implies, is himself mortal.

Music and Words in that order ("the natural order," as Pozzo might say) open the radio play in humble service to a club-carrying Croak, but they are in conflict with one another. Music is a small orchestra tuning up, to which Words reacts with the words of Henry in *Embers*: "Please! Please!" Words prevails upon Music to subside into silence, while he proceeds to deliver a scholastic composition on the passion of Sloth. His rhythms, and even some of his phrases, recall Lucky's monologue, but he is more subtly interrupted—by the shuffling arrival of Croak, and by the resumption of Music's tuning.

Calling Words and Music, Joe and Bob, his balms and

his comforts, Croak successively announces three themes for their combined effort—Love, Age, Face. For Love, Words can do no better than repeat his dry scholastic pronouncements on Sloth (once even mistaking the word "sloth" for "love"), and Music plays without expression. Croak calls for Music as Words protests. Then Words continues, questioning the meaning of "love" and "soul," and again Music plays as Words protests. They do better with the second theme, Age, during whose composition Croak calls them "Dogs!" Hesitantly, feeling their way, Words and Music arrive at a song that summarizes several Beckett old men, tended by hags but haunted by a face in the ashes. That face becomes the theme of their third joint effort, Music beginning warmly and Words coldly. Words catalogues the features of a face, until Croak cries out in anguish: "Lily!" Words tries to continue, but Music interrupts, and Words protests as earlier. Almost in spite of Words, the features of the face begin to move, and Music accompanies softly. The final song, with the accompaniment of Music, makes no mention of a face, as Words gropes on in this blind medium, toward primal being: "Toward where/ All dark no begging/ No giving no words/ No sense no need/ Through the scum/ Down a little way/ To whence one glimpse/ Of that wellhead." At the end of the song, a distinctively Beckettian poem, Croak drops his club and shuffles into silence. Joe-Words replaces him, no longer protesting but pleading with Bob for Music. After a recapitulation of *elements already used or wellhead alone,* the last sound is the sigh of Words, finally wordless. Does the sigh mean contentment? Or despair? In either case, Words and Music *have* blended for two songs, Age and minimal Being, before Croak shuffles away and Words expires into a sigh.

Cascando

"Cascando" is itself a musical term, describing the dying away of sound—slowing down of tempo, diminishing of

202

volume. In this second radio play, the Master of Ceremonies, the Opener, opens with words, and a Voice pants immediately into a story. Rhythmically, the Voice resembles that of *Comment c'est*, written two years before. Like all the French narrative voices, this one yearns to finish. So the basic tension is no longer words against music on a given theme, but opening against closing any story at all.

In Voice's first speech, we recognize the story's protagonist as an avatar of Molloy, Malone, and their fictions. This time he is called Woburn (in the original French, Maunu, naked miseries). This time the Opener arbitrarily summons the music to interrupt Voice. But gradually, as in *Words and Music*, Music and Voice come together. In *Words and Music*, the play-long tension was between Words and Music, then secondarily between Croak and their combination. But *Cascando* is more complex and more word-centered.

Of the three roles—Opener, Voice, Music—the last presents no difficulties, since he meekly obeys the orders of Opener. Voice, however, tries to tell the story of Woburn, and at the same time he tries to hit on the combination of words that will enable him to go silent. Opener is trying to avoid stories or even images, and he is trying to confine his activity to opening.

The broken phrases of Voice project a throwback to Beckett's epic figures in greatcoat and jammed-down hat, crucified in mud, sand, stones, or bilge. Moving from hill to sea, persistently, "he clings on." When Music joins Voice, the latter airs his own difficulties in locating Woburn, in recounting his adventures. Voice's last words are a pleading command, ambiguously addressed to either himself or Woburn: "Come on . . . come on—."

Opener begins with Beckett's spirit of method. In May, the month of reawakening, Opener shows how he opens and closes Voice; how he opens and closes Music. When either of them weakens, Opener commands "Full strength." He demonstrates how he opens them both together. But as

Opener lapses into speech about himself, opening and closing begin to take place without him—"Good God." And he has no choice but to accept their playing together: "Good." In subtle counterpoint against Opener's effort at method is the intrusion of his own existence.

Opener reports that "they" accuse him of opening nothing, of living in his head. "They" say that the voice is in his head, and he counters with the question as to whether the music is in his head too. Lapsing into a reminiscence in verse form, Opener offers a brief picture of two outings—"An image, like any other." However, it is not like *any* other, but an image that has haunted Beckett from the meeting of A and C in *Molloy*. Now the meeters take the form of two outings; it may be to these two outings, or it may be to Voice and Music that Opener refers: "As though they had joined arms." Opener's final two "Good"s, recalling God's pronouncement at the creation, praise the marriage of Voice and Music. With Woburn clinging in some void, Voice calls "Come on . . . come on—" and Music accompanies him into silence.

Cascando is Beckett's only play since *Fin de partie* to be written in French, and it absorbs the narrative problems with which he wrestled in the French fiction: How tell a story? And why? Or, conversely, how be silent as long as the mind churns words? *Cascando*, buried as it is in the creative imagination, seems irrelevant to any world at large. As in the case of Beckett's French fiction, however, the imagination has had to live *through* the world in order to retire into what it hopes to find as itself. There has to be a melody before cascando.

Film

"I told Sam he should publish [*Film*], but he doesn't feel it's a piece of literature at all—it wasn't intended to be a piece of literature," said the film's director Alan Schneider in 1965. *Film* has been published, of course, and it is probable that more people have read it than have seen

204

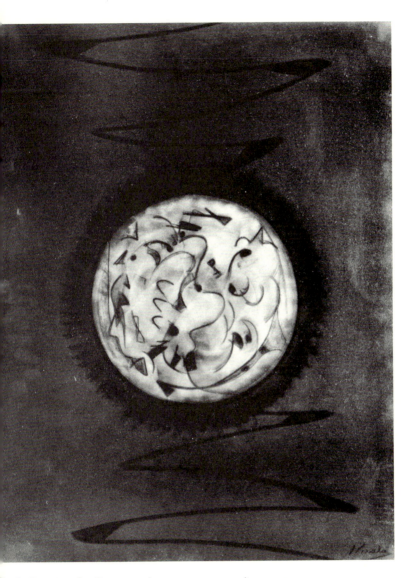

Nuala Painting for *Lessness*. (PHOTO POLLITZER)

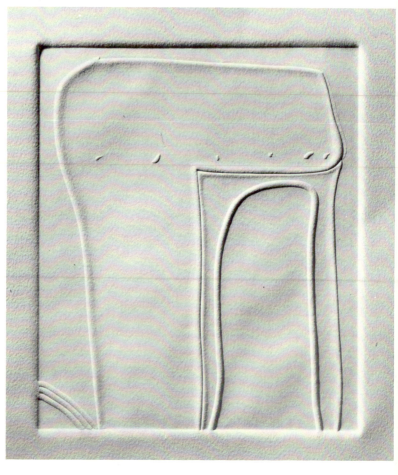

HM Erhardt Graphic for *Bing*. (PHOTO MANUS PRESSE)

Beckett's one movie. Nevertheless, *Film* is not literature; it does not marry the meaning to the music of language. Instead, it resembles Beckett's mime plays in tracing a series of actions, and as in the mime plays, a "message" emerges almost too clearly in actions freed from the ambiguities of words.

The script of *Film*, which was published as written and not as filmed, uses Berkeley as a springboard: *Esse est percipi*. (To be is to be perceived.) Beckett's next sentence summarizes the movie's action: "All extraneous perception suppressed, animal, human, divine, self-perception maintains in being." The movie's protagonist will suppress, successively, his perception by humans, by animals, by a divine image. He will try also to suppress self-perception, but finally the movie camera coincides with his imagination to maintain him in being—a state for which Beckett uses the word "investment." More single-mindedly than Beckett's fictional heroes, then, his movie protagonist seeks to attain an approximation of nonbeing. In the script Beckett designates the protagonist as O (object) and the perceiving eye as E. His basic convention is: "O enters *percipi*=experiences anguish of perceivedness" only when E observes O from behind, at an angle greater than 45°.

But between physics and metaphysics, Beckett intended the movie to be comic, since it is comic for a human being to seek nonbeing—or it can be. The script specifies: "Climate of film comic and unreal. O should invite laughter throughout by his way of moving." On the street "[O] storms along in comic foundered precipitancy." Beckett does not again use the word "comic" in his text, but his comic intention is clear in such details as a seventeen-step process for ejecting from a room both a large cat and a small dog. It was Beckett who suggested for the main role Buster Keaton, the deadpan comedian, whose face would be hidden through most of the film. And it was Beckett who consented to Keaton's appearance in his traditional flattened pork-pie Stetson rather than the hat originally intended.

205

The first title of *Film* was *The Eye,* and eyes are as plentiful in *Film* as in *Krapp's Last Tape.* In the first shot human beings move in couples down a street, all in the same direction. If they are not quite "eyeball to eyeball," like Sam and Watt, they are "all contentedly in *percipere* and *percipi*"—perceiving and being perceived. Except O. In long coat and hat on this summer day, he hugs a wall as he makes his furtive way against the general direction of movement. In blind haste, he jostles an elderly couple, who stop to look at him, she raising her *lorgnon,* he lowering his *pince-nez.* They look after O, but they are looked at by E, so that they experience "an agony of perceivedness." O enters a dark doorway. Hiding from footsteps, O is not perceived by a little old flower-woman, who also experiences an "agony of perceivedness" when E has her in sight. O hastens upstairs to unlock a door into a "small barely furnished room," in which are a large cat and a small dog, a parrot in a cage and a goldfish in a bowl. All the animals have eyes. The room's single window and mirror present a threat of eyes, and O hastens to cover them, as in a house of mourning. With meticulous patience, he eventually manages to eject both dog and cat, he tears a print of God in four, and he covers the cage and bowl, escaping from assorted eyes. Seated in a rocking chair, he inspects seven ages of his life, committed to photographs. In all but the last someone's eyes inspect his face—his mother in the first two, then a dog, the college rector, his fiancée, a little girl. In the last picture O is thirty, looking over forty; hat and overcoat designate him as the man we have been sleuthing. In the photograph he is not only unperceived but only part perceiver; he wears a patch over his left eye. Moving backward through his seven ages, O tears each of his photographs in four—no preferential treatment over God's image. When O dozes off, semi-secure in his rocking chair, the camera finally catches him full-face, but with head bowed. O seems to sense E's gaze even though asleep, and E withdraws to circle the room but returns to focus full on O. The latter starts up, opening his eye; the other eye is covered by a patch. We cut to E, a blurred image but clearly the same face—one eye and one patch, a nail at the temple above the patch, and on the face an expression of "acute *intentness*." We cut back to O, who closes his eye, covers his face with his hands, begins to rock in his chair. After a cut back to E "as before," we cut again to O, who bows his head, face buried in his hands, till the rocking dies down and the movie ends. The perceiving eye has trapped its object.

Like Hamlet, Krapp bends his eye on vacancy, but O seeks to offer vacancy to various eyes. Triplets structure his efforts, as they do those of Krapp. O moves through three locales—street, hallway, room. He encounters three elderly people—woman with *lorgnon*, man with *pince-nez*, and flower-woman—who experience their own agonies of perceivedness. O is perceived three times by E—when he is first sighted, when he enters the vestibule, and in the final "investment." In the room O's actions form a three-part sequence: Preparation of the room, period in the rocking-chair, final investment. Three kinds of eyes threaten O—human, animal, and imaginary (photographs, print of God, formal possibilities). Three pairs of eyes are described as "severe"—God the Father, and both photographs of O's mother. Unlike *Play*, however, *Film* is not a triangle but a duo; man is his own quarry.

In an unusual remark to a reporter Beckett himself summarized *Film*: "It's a movie about the perceiving eye, about the perceived and the perceiver—two aspects of the same man. The perceiver desires like mad to perceive, and the perceived tries desperately to hide. Then, in the end, one wins." The perceiver wins in a movie, because the camera eye is the *sine qua non* of film, and yet what we finally see as E is not a camera but the blurred face of O. The invisible camera is a metaphor for inescapable self-perception.

The patched eye indicates the rapprochement between O and E; each has only partial vision, but together they add up to the whole self. The movement of Beckett's film is a

207

steady zeroing in on the self. First O is in a light and popu-lated street, then he is in a dark and narrow hallway with only one other person. Finally he is boxed in a deserted room, where eyes assault him all the more sharply. At the last he is face to face with his camera-eye-I—the investment.

The investment is a prepared climax because the comic images have been in play-long tension with the disturbing camera angle—our own angle of vision. That tension is heightened, as Raymond Federman has pointed out, by the film's near silence. And yet the one sound of *Film*—"sssh"— is largely inclusive. The woman with the *lorgnon* utters the sibilant to her companion with the *pince-nez*, but it is the signal of silence for the rest of the film. It is also a com-ment on the medium of film, which is visual in spite of "talking" pictures. "Sssh" may even signal silence for real-istic questions: Why is O in hat and coat on this summer day? Why is it only E who can arouse anguish at perceived-ness? Why is O going to his mother's room? What has hap-pened to O between the age of twenty-five, smiling in uniform, holding a child who may be his, and the age of thirty, when he looks over forty, and wears a patch on his eye? Sssh. The questions cannot be answered realistically, but only metaphysically.

Bishop Berkeley was delighted that *Esse est percipi*. Man's being was witnessed by God's perception. But Beckett's O has experienced a trauma that makes him yearn for nonperceivedness and nonbeing. Shivering and seeking concealment, he cannot escape his consciousness, which is blurred because consciousness of consciousness cannot be clear.

Film's director Alan Schneider has written a disarming account of its filming. When the opening scene of strolling couples filmed badly, the movie was introduced instead by a close-up of Keaton's wrinkled bloodshot eye. The rocking-chair's back seemed to have eyes of its own, as did the portfolio in which the photographs were kept, and these eyes were incorporated into the film. Throughout the filming, the camera's versatility was rigorously restrained, to preserve what Beckett called the angle of immunity or nonperceivedness. As compared with the clear image of O, that of E is blurred, but we see E so briefly that I think I would not have appreciated the distinction, had I not read in the script: "It will not be clear until the end of film that pursuing perceiver is not extraneous, but self."

Film, like Beckett's literary works, compels attention to each detail in order for us to savor its tragicomic specificity. And like other Beckett works, *Film* comments on its medium. In fiction words veil while they reveal. In drama activities make up an action. Radio plays are composed of a sequence of sounds. Film casts a film over what it seems to reveal. Into all genres pierces a gimlet consciousness.

Eh Joe

After two years, Beckett followed *Film* by *Eh Joe,* a television play which also presented the impossibility of avoiding self-perception. Written for the late Jack MacGowran, the man was first called J, then Jack, and finally Joe. Unlike *Film, Eh Joe* uses voice, but voice—what is heard—is strictly separated from figure—what is seen. *Eh Joe* begins with the visible—Joe. What Joe does at the beginning of the television play resembles what O does in the room: draws curtain over window, draws hangings before locked door, draws hangings before locked cupboard. Having then checked to see that there are no eyes under the bed, Joe begins to relax. After the camera "pursues" Joe, it zooms in on him in nine distinct moves toward his face. However, the camera never moves while the voice speaks.

The voice is that of a woman, *"low, distinct, remote, little colour, absolutely steady rhythm, slightly slower than normal."* But since the voice is unattached to a body, it seems to emanate from Joe himself, who always looks as though he is listening to an inner voice. The woman's voice taunts

209

Joe with his fears, and through her taunts she builds a portrait of Joe, which somewhat resembles that of Henry of *Embers* in his inability to love. Unlike Henry, however, Joe wants to strangle other voices in his head; "mental thuggee" is the arresting phrase for the murder of those who loved him. The woman reviews her relationship with Joe. Then she sketches Joe's relationship to his God. After the sixth camera move, she indicates tersely that though she once loved Joe, she "found a better." Beginning with the seventh camera move, however, she talks about another woman. Joe evidently loved this woman briefly, routinely, with the same gesture and phrase he had used for the speaking woman. Joe left his brief love, knowing no more of her fate than an obituary notice in the newspaper. After the ninth and last camera move, Joe remains transfixed at the harrowing description by one former mistress of the suicide of another.

First came the effort to drown herself, and the inability; then the effort to slit her wrists at the seaside, but the inability through fear of pain; at last she succeeds with "tablets," which she swallows on the way to the sea, "Finishes the tube . . . There's love for you . . . Eh Joe? . . . Scoops a little cup for her face in the stones." Finally, the woman's voice is almost inaudible except for the words in italics as she etches the girl's last passion into Joe's mind: "*There's love for you* . . . Isn't it, Joe? . . . Wasn't it, Joe? . . . *Eh Joe?* . . . Wouldn't you say? . . . Compared to us . . . Compared to Him . . . *Eh Joe?*" Joe, like "us" and "Him," are cruel lovers, victimizing those who love us.

In the radio play, *Words and Music*, Joe as Words recited a set-piece on the theme of Love, but in *Eh Joe*, Joe is wordless about the nameless woman who killed herself for love of him. The self-perception he flees haunts him insidiously through the voice of a woman who has found a better love than he, telling him of one who did not look. Compared to love unto death, other love scarcely deserves the word.

210

Come and Go

Ever since the appearance of *Fin de partie*, people have predicted that Beckett was so boxed in the self-imposed limitations of his drama that there was no way for him to continue. But only a decade after *Fin de partie* did he apparently justify the predictions, writing a three-minute play, *Come and Go*, in 1965, and a thirty-second play, *Breath*, in 1966. (Though *Breath* is usually dated later, Beckett narrated it to me in May, 1966.)

Come and Go, for which Beckett has coined the word "dramaticule," has three women characters, each of whom has nine short speeches, one exit, and one re-entrance. The equilibrium is exquisite. As each woman in turn departs into stage darkness, one of the remaining women whispers into the other's ear. The recipient of the secret, *"appalled,"* exclaims: "Oh!" Then she asks whether the absent one is aware of her fate. The teller of the secret invokes God in a fervent hope for ignorance. The absent one returns, and the three women face front.

The three women of *Come and Go* are dressed in turn-of-the-century coats and hats, which recall Chekhov's *Three Sisters*. The first full line of dialogue—Vi's "When did we three last meet?"—echoes the three witches of *Macbeth*. A few lines later, as Hugh Kenner has noticed, they are three little maids from school. Even the three daughters of Lear appear when two seem to conspire against the third. During their few minutes on stage, we may wonder whether they are the three fates. Ringed with these shadowy suggestions, the three women are faintly illuminated by their monosyllabic names—Vi, Ru, Flo. They *vie* for arcane information; they express *rue*—"Oh!"; life *flows* on. Holding hands *"in the old way,"* they face front for Flo's final line: "I can feel the rings." "No rings apparent," notes Beckett's text, but in the theater we cannot be sure.

As the three women have come from and gone into stage

211

darkness, they have come from and will go into eternal darkness. Without the memories of *Play*, they can only imagine the marriages they never made. Their common "Oh!" (differently spoken by each of them) punctuates their several resonances: they will never go to Moscow, they will never be consulted by a hero, they will never outgrow their schooldays, and each pair of them will not quite scissor the other's life. Like us all, they "come and go" on earth—briefly.

In Beckett's own production of *Come and Go* in Paris, he first dressed the women in bright colors and feathers that suggested birds. Subsequently, however, he removed adornments, muted the colors, and slowed the playing time to seven minutes.

Breath is briefer. From the miscellaneous rubbish of the stage-earth (without the naked bodies of *Oh! Calcutta!*), a faint cry is heard. Light and breath reach maximum in about ten seconds, hold for five seconds, and fade to the cry "*as before.*" Vagitus and death-rattle are identical. And then there is silence; a lifetime has left no trace in eternity. The mortality that has haunted Beckett from his earliest work has at last received its most pointed expression in what Beckett has called "a farce in five acts." It would be—I'll risk the word—*impossible* for Beckett to carry dramatic concentration further.

Not I

Though a thirty-second, characterless play might seem an ideal terminus for Beckett's drama, he shapes each individual work rather than a corpus. In 1972 *Not I* was produced—a mouth speaking at a silent figure in djellaba.

Beckett's stage plays are visualized for the box stage, which serves the playwright as a basic metaphor: life in a box, a cell, a prison. *Godot* and *Endgame* occasionally tease the audience beyond the imaginary fourth wall, but the convention of the wall is never violated. The actors appear to be playing not for an audience, but for one another;

Beckett insists on the performance quality of the performance on stage. Pirandello had already theatricalized the
artifice of theater; Brecht had incorporated stage machinery
into his sets; Beckett's actors undertake roles for one another, so that the real audience is almost always watching a
stage audience. This is obvious in *Godot* and *Endgame*,
where the characters are self-conscious performers. Krapp
is an audience for his own tapes, Winnie needs Willie as
audience, the three characters of *Play* play to the spotlight,
each of the three women of *Come and Go* sings her inaudible aria for another, even *Breath* may be inspired by
light. *Not I* is the culmination of these actor-audiences on
stage.

The audience-figure in black djellaba (Beckett's seed-
image for the play) is constantly visible to us, whereas the
performer is reduced to her mouth. Resembling a throbbing
wound in the dark, the Mouth discharges words that musically shape a Beckettian life. Beginning with birth—"out . . .
into this world"—a female voice tells of a sudden April
onslaught of words, undergone by a woman nearing the age
of seventy. And Beckett's text is at once that onslaught and
the objective account of it, as Dante's text is an address to
the reader and an account of a journey. In some fifteen
minutes of rushed monologue the Mouth evokes a nearly
silent life, and that life is counterpointed against the April
torrent of speech accompanied by buzzing within the skull
and flickering light without. On stage a highlighted Mouth
palpitates against a still background figure, and the words
arrive so swiftly that the effect is sensual rather than sen-
sible. Behind the stage picture lies an old legend that at the
moment of death, one re-views one's life. But the Beckettian
Mouth contains a brain rather than an eye, and the words
probe the meaning of the autobiography they deny. Five
times the voice is interrupted, or interrupts itself: "who? . . .
what? . . . no! . . . she!" At the fifth interruption the voice
adds: "SHE!" To each "*vehement refusal to relinquish third
person*"—Not I—the audience-figure responds with a slow

213

shrug "*of helpless compassion.*" Or, more accurately, he responds four times, with diminishing movements, and on the fifth refusal he remains still. (At the New York première he bowed his head.)

Beginning with *Play*, Beckett's stage characters live in limbo; their containers, visible or invisible, are a metaphoric shelter from the darkness of non-being. The light is where they are, and in *Not I* life is an illuminated mouth. Looking larger than life, it seems to float and turn in black space. From that bright spot pours a tumult of words, patterned through melodic repetition.

All Beckett's dramas play uniqueness against repetition, but *Not I* does so with syntactical daring that is matched only in *Comment c'est*. Incomplete sentences reflect the incomplete stage presence—a mouth—and the story of a still incomplete life, "coming up to seventy," almost over, and yet continuing. During the discourse the mouth is interrupted or interrupts itself twenty-one times for correction or elucidation of the discourse. Five of the interruptions reject the pronoun "I"; seven interruptions remind the voice of the constant buzzing or dull omnipresent roar in the invisible skull. The other interruptions try to render the discourse more accurate, from the first that designates the sex of the newborn infant, to the last that finally and conclusively refuses to relinquish the third person—she, not I.

Beckett's fiction has been preoccupied with the identity of the self, but this is the first time he has dramatized it so nakedly. Some ten years earlier he had already refused identity beyond a face to Winnie of Act II. *Play* denies expression to faces, and *Come and Go* denies faces to bodies. They are all avoiding the self-betrayal of emotion. *Not I* highlights a mouth, as *L'Innommable* and *Textes pour rien* eliminate all but a voice, owner unknown. The female stage mouth knows as little as the fictional voices about the provenance of words, and it denies knowing what they mean, intermittently refusing to acknowledge that they mean anything.

214

The refrain is familiar in Beckettland, but *we* know that the words have prismatic meanings. So in *Not I*. They create five scenes that summarize human experience: 1) a loveless premature birth, 2) survival through silent list-shopping at the supermarket, 3) the presence of tears in the palm of the hand and the awareness of owning those tears, 4) the silence under court-room questioning, and 5) five times evoked, the April morning when this late spring speech erupted. Economically, Beckett has sketched images for a life whose resonance is extensible to us all—born too soon, surviving mechanically, feeling and watching ourselves feel, wondering about the meaning of the living as we live.

The Mouth frames a quiet life which has occasionally burst into winter speech, but nearing life's end, the Mouth suddenly finds itself full of the very April speech it describes. Being on the verge of non-being froths into discourse—as punishment, since "God is love?" With meaning, since "God is love?" But there is no telling in the telling by the telling. The telling falsifies the experience. "Spared that," the Mouth says of love, of screams, of feeling itself. Once the feelings are translated into words, the subject becomes an object, and there can be no "I."

The words of the Mouth end in the birth-death of spring, with senses raw and words of little sense. And yet Beckett has conveyed a sensual sense—a buzz, a ray, an evanescent hint—through the music of his Mouth.

Beckett's successive plays reduce plot, character, speech, or gesture, and yet all of them present us with man playing. I play therefore I am. Beckett himself is skillful at games, from cricket and rugby at Portora Royal School to today's chess matches against computers. In his plays of the 1950's he has gradually hardened the rules so that each move becomes a triumph over the immense inertia of Nothing. Beckett's plays after the 1950's, however, are less like games than like discourses in the spirit of gamesmanship. In them Beckett gives the impression of pushing Being to the edge of Nothing, and yet the gamesmanship is not gratuitous, or no more gratuitous than life itself.

Beckett has been candid that theater plays only a supporting role in his creative life: "Theater for me is a relaxation from work on the novel. You have a definite space and people in this space. That's relaxing." But Beckett is rigorous even about relaxation. It is he who defines his space and beckons its inhabitants. Beckett has penetrated stage space with a dusty road and scorched grass; he has bounded it by walls or darkness. And he has peopled stage space with characters who suffer and who reflect intermittently upon their suffering. Their gestures and phrases are wrested from the darkness on the face of the deep, so that they are comically clumsy in the sudden light of their stage lives, but the clumsiness demands precise acting.

From his first distinctive drama, *En attendant Godot*, to his most recent *Not I*, Beckett offers us concentrated imitations of the actions of our lives. Pozzo's celebrated line becomes the scenario for *Breath*, written nearly two decades later: "They give birth astride of a grave, the light gleams an instant, then it's night once more." The instant's light of life is always threatened by darkness, silence, nonbeing. But life is lived deeply only through facing darkness, silence, nonbeing.

In *Godot* the light is already twilight, but the actors fill it with a series of inventive activities, which are what they appear to be on stage, but which are also indicative of the kind of activity that keeps *us* busy most of our lives. In *Fin de partie* the light is gray—"Light black from pole to pole." Activities are slowing down, and yet they do not stop or reach an end. While there's life, there's endlessness. This is true, too, in the ambiguous title, *Krapp's Last Tape*, for "last" may be most recent or final. Krapp has dared to play with darkness, but he records and listens in the light, which becomes his life. In *Happy Days* we find ourselves in the light with a vengeance, for Winnie's blazing sun never sets. She lives out the happy days of her life while

216

she returns to dust, like the rest of us. The three characters of *Play* live only in spotlighted instants; in the unlit silence they know no repose—dark, shade, peace—for nonbeing can have no knowledge of itself. *Come and Go* shows the three human fates subject to mortality; each has only to step into darkness for her doom to be whispered, though she will then look bravely back into the light. *Breath* in thirty seconds conveys the instant's gleam of light-life. *Not I* illuminates a mouth-wound that exudes four scenes of felt life. Live theater is the most ephemeral of arts, and in his eight stage plays Beckett hews close to man's mortal center, for which each performance is a metaphor.

The corpus of Beckett's theater recalls the long theater tradition of the West. All his plays mix genres, but *Eleuthéria* leans on the well-made play, *Godot* on the medieval morality, *Fin de partie* on Shakespearean tragedy, *Play* on the problem play. Several Beckett plays contain *commedia lazzi*, clown tricks, silent comic scenes, but his most telling gift is for dialogue. Formal or colloquial, witty or meditative, the words mean more than they seem to say. Pauses, emphases, hesitations, repetitions point to wider meanings. Definite people in a definite place may be relaxing for Beckett, but his stage speech prohibits relaxation either for actor or for audience.

Beckett's pair of mime plays dispense with speech, condensing myth into gesture. The first play draws props from biblical tradition, the second from contemporary habits, but all props prove to be pointless—like the actions they inspire.

The four radio plays, like the mime plays, stimulate doubt in their genre. Does all that sound (and fury) signify any more than nothing? Sound and something like fury are more evident in *All That Fall* and *Embers* than in *Words and Music* and *Cascando*. The earlier two plays orchestrate sounds and voices to build a world—the Irish town of Boghill in the first, seaside memory-fantasies in the second. The one peoples a world to show the aloneness of life, and the other peoples a mind to show the aloneness of living. Both plays fade into silence through inhuman noises—wind and rain in the first play, and the sea in the second. The later two radio plays, in contrast, center on the problem of combining meaning and music. They do what they say, but they also suggest metaphoric extension to the difficulty of making any sense of the music of the spheres in the language of men.

Images are dubious too, Beckett suggests in his movie and his television play, where the protagonists seek to avoid perception, showing us the partiality of our perceptions. *Film* illustrates this in what Beckett himself describes as an "unreal" context; that of *Eh Joe* seems more real. Intended for a more intimate screen, *Eh Joe* plays an accusing voice against its visible victim, the human face—one of the set themes of *Cascando*. A woman makes a cup of stones for her face; death occurs when flesh joins stone, but death also lies in the insidious voice in Joe's head.

Beckett's plays are serious games, imposing their own rules. Conflict is condensed to basic opposition: Didi and Gogo cannot leave the Board, and Pozzo and Lucky cannot linger on it. Hamm cannot stand, and Clov cannot sit. Winnie talks while Willie crawls. The mouth recounts to a silent figure. The radio plays cannot be seen, and the mime plays cannot be heard. *Play* lacks gesture, and *Come and Go* is almost all gesture. *Words and Music* and *Cascando* oppose words to music; *Film* opposes perceiver to perceived; *Eh Joe* opposes image to voice. Human beings rarely touch each other in Beckett's drama, but urns and ashbins touch, as Nothing re-forms around them and us.

Each of Beckett's plays is best played literally. Beckett conceives his plays concretely, even when the concrete is no heavier than a breath. So precise are his scenic directions that there are few options for director and actor. It is through a rigorous context that the actor must strain his unique mystery. Though Beckett's plays have been performed widely, few directors are capable of the disciplined fidelity he requires, and few actors are capable of the selfless concentration that alone can elicit the self he limns. Fanatical exactitude has to be second nature before the full deep nature of the roles can materialize concretely. It is only a seeming paradox that Beckett's plays are most symbolic when most concrete.

Beckett says that his drama has been relaxation for him, and that relaxation has attracted a larger public than his fiction. Beckett's plays through *Happy Days*, like the fiction through the trilogy, embrace a broad range of human experience, offered up in concentrates, but theatrical concentrates are mirrors. Paralleling the fictional trilogy is a theater trilogy—*En attendant Godot, Fin de partie, Happy Days*—that spirals slowly through human relationships toward bare Being. The post-Winnie drama, like the post-trilogy fiction, drills more pointedly within the brain. All Beckett's plays reach down to the root of drama: *dran,* to do, to perform. By radicalization of the elements of performance, Beckett contrives that less means more, but meaning means only in performance. The human actor acts.

5.

LYRICS OF FICTION

I HAVE interrupted chronology to follow Beckett's drama in its sequential development, but Beckett never confined himself to a single genre for as long as a decade. In the 1930's he wrote fiction and poetry; in the 1940's he wrote fiction, poetry, and drama. We find the same themes orchestrated for the special genre, but fiction has been his most abiding loyalty, and in the 1950's he found himself unable to complete any fiction. *L'Innommable* seemed to him a dead end: "In the last book, 'L'Innommable,' there's complete disintegration. No 'I,' no 'have,' no 'being.' No nominative, no accusative, no verb. There's no way to go on." And yet, as the voice says at the end of *L'Innommable*: "you must go on, I can't go on, I'll go on." And on Beckett goes, into a fourth dimension of prose, where a fusion of words sometimes borders on confusion, and where the meaning seems buried in the melody.

Textes pour rien

"Nothing to be done," says Gogo to open *Godot*. And though he does many things on stage, they add up to nothing because Godot does not come. His actions accumulate into a nothing to be done, a nothing to be played while waiting for Godot. Comparably, Beckett designates his thirteen *Textes*, written a year or two after *Godot*, as being "for nothing." He thus sends his fictional voice through the looking-glass, in search of nothing. John Fletcher informs us that Beckett thought of the title (in French) in a musical context; *mesure pour rien* is a rest bar, and Beckett's texts give his stories a rest while continuing his words. *L'Innom-*

220

mable, nominally a novel, devotes less than one-fifth of its words to stories; the rest of its words worry a self that the narrator cannot define but zeros in on. In contrast, the nameless, unnamable narrator of the *Textes* more or less accepts himself as undefinable but nevertheless continues to utter words—toward nothing, for nothing. His rest bar seems to be Heidegger's question: "Why is there being at all and not rather nothingness?" He does not try to answer that question; no, not so foolish as the Unnamable in his "wordy gurdy." By the timeless time of the *Textes*, the "wordy gurdy" is "wordshit," and the speaker or speakers sink into the shit, reaching toward Nothing rather than Being. A being seeking non-being entails inversion of life-death, womb-tomb, light-dark, energy-entropy. The self moves toward birth into Nothing, and at the same time it cannot control its tropisms of Being.

Published in a different order from their final form, the individual texts were clearly labelled *for nothing*: 3, 6, 10 were first published in May, 1953; 11 in July, 1953; 1 and 12 in May, 1955, six months before the thirteen appeared in book form—all and always for nothing. The thirteen texts parallel the thirteen poems of *Echo's Bones* in their movement toward lifelessness, but the text forms are not derivative, and all thirteen—the unlucky number that lures Beckett—seem to be spoken by the same disembodied voice. The unparagraphed pages recall Molloy or the Unnamable, but the texts are more difficult to read. Molloy offers us a soulscape, the Unnamable tries to focus his anguish, but in the eternal present of the space-time continuum of the *Textes*, sense seems to slip through the words, strained between interstices and abstractions. The narrator struggles through a cloud of unknowing, a veil of words uttered by "the head and its anus the mouth." In the *Textes*, more than in *L'Innommable*, stories dissolve into lyrical phrases, as the voice stabs at definition, causation, induction, deduction. Questions arise through assertions, as in *L'Innommable*, but in the *Textes* the answers are more

221

consistently negative; the word "No" becomes an interjection, beating a resonant time through the jungle of syntax.

The word "text" suggests poetry as much as fiction, and Beckett earlier used the word for both genres (a 69-line poem of 1931, and a prose excerpt from the 1932 *Dream*). The thirteen texts for nothing, like lyric poems, are short and rhythmic. The thirteen texts for nothing, like fiction, try to tell the narrator's story, his nihilotropism. In these undramatic lyrical monologues the residue of fiction is spare—few characters, landscapes, images, or objects, as the texts move toward the dark silence of Nothing.

The *Textes* begin with an abruptness that is swiftly modified: "Suddenly, no, at last, long last, I couldn't any more, couldn't go on." A landscape follows, quickly blotted out. In a kind of exposition, the "I" situates himself at the bottom of a trough at evening, having left his den, his home. The "I" refuses to grapple with the old body-mind conflict. Only a voice or voices is certain, shaping old words into old questions: How can I go on? What possessed me to come? Who are the people attached to the voice? The familiar world is up above in the light, but from this hole rises a jumble of phrases recalling the end of the trilogy: "I'm up there and I'm down here, under my gaze, foundered, eyes closed, ear cupped against the sucking peat."

From the very first *Texte*, place, time, and condition are indistinguishable; memory is rarely distinguishable from fiction; first and third persons are interchangeable. Like the narrator of *Le Calmant*, the "I" hears the voice evoke his father reading him the story of Joe Breem or Breen, who heroically swam through the storm, a knife between his teeth. In *Le Calmant* the narrator becomes Joe, then diverges from him; in the first text the narrator becomes his father *and* his son; he is both, and he is neither, "tired out with so much talking, so much listening, so much toil and play."

The second text looks back and up—"Above is the light" —dredging a small population of memories or fictions: a

Mother Calvet with dog, baby buggy, and a kind of trident. Then, after immense pain—"you a living mustard-plaster" —Mr. Joly on Sunday as in the Moran half of *Molloy*, the farm of the Graves brothers one of whom we may have met in *Watt* or *Mercier et Camier*, Piers a cowherd or a plowman as at the beginning of English literature. *Texte* 4 names "vulgar Molloy" and "common Malone," those mere mortals. *Texte* 5 mentions wealthy Pozzo of *Godot*. But their time is past. Characters have thinned down to mere names.

In contrast, four characters grow before our eyes, impeding the progress toward Nothing. In *Texte* 3 the voice succumbs to an old habit: "I'll say I'm in a body." After some hesitation, the body has a companion, a maimed war veteran so that it, too, companionably assumes the body of a maimed war veteran. Irrepressibly and with comic economy, the voice situates the pair in familiar Beckettian scenes of misery and tenderness. "Nothing human is foreign to us," Beckett parodies the Terence line as he depicts the happy hours of his dying derelicts. And yet the parody is serious too, for the pair *is* endearingly human in this most localized of the thirteen texts—in the heart of Dublin. The couple recalls Didi and Gogo "besotted with brotherliness." But no sooner is a name born—Vincent—than the voice cuts off the fiction: "No, that's all memories, last shifts older than the flood." This minimal hold on flesh and life must be relinquished to arrive at Nothing.

Toward the end of the eighth text objects demand a body: white stick, ear-trumpet, bowler hat, and a pair of brown boots require connection "by the traditional human excipient." The aggregate almost succeeds in becoming a beggar, but again the voice is ruthless with denial: "No, the answer is no. For even as I moved, or when the moment came, affecting beyond all others, to hold out my hand, or hat, without previous song, or any other form of concession to self-respect, at the terrace of a café, or in the mouth of the underground, I would know it was not me, I would know I was here, begging in another dark, another silence, for another alm, that of being or of ceasing, better still, before having been." Begging, in short, for Nothing.

Texte 11, after the usual hesitancies, presents us with a last concrete character, first young "having terminated my humanities," then old "having terminated his humanities," and finally in fragments "having terminated their humanities"—a complete biography in a page-long sentence. Old young, the fictional being spends his verbal life wetting his trousers in a urinal on rue d'Assas. Mutilated, he bristles with humanity in spite of the triple repetition of termination of humanities. The life sentence ends "rent with ejaculations, Jesus, Jesus." The nameless fictional being ends on this repeated name—at once a cry of anguish and a god made man. Then the voice reclaims its negative terrain, moving from evening to night, toward Nothing.

With few characters and images, the texts contain two specific settings that echo and predict other Beckett works. In the fifth text the scene is a court, reminiscent of Kafka's *Trial* and prophetic of *Comment c'est*. The voice is at once "judge and party, witness and advocate," and above all court scribe. But this court is emblematic of another court, "where to be is to be guilty." The text exhibits an arid legalism, through whose prose falls the burden: "it's noted."

In the seventh text the voice is seated (!) in the third-class waiting-room of the South-Eastern Railway Terminus, ready with his ticket—"my ticket is valid for life." A journey is one of the oldest metaphors for life, but there is no train departure and no journey; the station is soon in ruins.

Elsewhere in the texts there are bare hints of Dublin, Paris, London, but these cities are recalled through an inferno suggested by the damp and the dark. Dante's ninth circle is specifically evoked in the sixth text: "Plunged in ice up to the nostrils, the eyelids caked with frozen tears, to fight all your battles o'er again, what tranquillity, and know there are no more emotions in store, no, I can't have heard aright." Dante and Wordsworth blend in rhymes in this melodic sentence—o'er, more, store; fight, aright.

In some half-dozen texts mind opposes body, in spite of the voice's early determination not to be trapped in their conflict. Through some half-dozen texts course tears, whatever their source. In several texts particular words are pinpointed and virtually drained of meaning: here, me, being, hear, tell, story, now, then. All the texts are set at evening, projecting a dark night of the soul. All the texts claim their origin in a voice, and all the texts are written in the words of the voice, irregularly but constantly interrupted by a rain of "no"s. In the eighth text the voice wishes: "Ah if no were content to cut yes's throat and never cut its own"; because of persistent negation, being can neither begin nor end. By the last text, the voice wonders "whose the screaming silence of no's knife in yes's wound." A difficult image of no's jabbing at, cutting into the affirmation of being as suffering. Beckett chose this image as the title of the English edition of Stories, Texts, and Residua— No's Knife.

Varying in length between about seven hundred and seventeen hundred words, the thirteen texts can be read as a short sonnet sequence. But instead of moving toward a final couplet in the Shakespearean way, the texts tend to circle back upon themselves. Seven of the texts open and close on similar words, and the last sentence of the sequence is an intricate arabesque upon the first few sentences: "Suddenly, no, at last, long last, I couldn't any more, I couldn't go on. Someone said, You can't stay here. I couldn't stay there and I couldn't go on." This is being at the edge of nowhere. By the end being is still at the edge of nowhere: "And were there one day to be here, where there are no days, which is no place, born of the impossible voice the unmakable being, and a gleam of light, still all would be silent and empty and dark, as now, as soon now, when all will be ended, all said, it says, it murmurs." The opening "long last . . . here . . . there" has become a spacetime "where there are no days." In spite of the inability to "go on," an "impossible voice" has made lyrical fiction out of the very urge toward insentient Nothing, the self-denial of an "unmakable being."

In May, 1956, Beckett said to Israel Shenker: "The very last thing I wrote—'Textes pour rien'—was an attempt to get out of the attitude of disintegration, but it failed." Apparently the Nothing of nonbeing could not serve Beckett's fiction, and Beckett's remarks to Shenker close with a forlorn reference to the suicide of painter Nicolas de Staël. But Beckett himself struggled to achieve an attitude of reintegration. He worked dissatisfied at *Fin de partie*, having abandoned attempts at a novel in English. *From an Abandoned Work*, a scrap from that abandoned work, was first published in the Trinity College newspaper on June 7, 1956, some six years after the completion of the *Textes*. For book publication, Beckett grouped it with later works that he called *Têtes-Mortes*, and it is in this context that it is best considered.

Comment c'est

During the 1950's Beckett completed no sustained fiction. About a decade separates *Textes pour rien* from *Comment c'est*, and Beckett occupied that decade with plays and translations, but his fertile five-year period had closed in 1950, never to reopen. Though he published *Textes pour rien* in 1955, he viewed it as a failure because it did not extricate him from "the attitude of disintegration." Almost by accident he salvaged part of a novel in English, which he found it impossibe to continue: "There was just no more to be said." In that novel he tried to reintegrate elements of fiction—events in a plot, a character with body and mind, recognizable landscapes, and comprehensible syntax. *From an Abandoned Work* is not divided into paragraphs, and many of its sentences are not constructed on grammatical principles. However, periods separate one thought or feeling from the next, and within pseudo-sentences,

226

syntax is clarified by liberal use of commas. The story's first three sentences cannot be parsed, and yet their meaning is clear. "Awful English this," the narrator comments in his last sentence, and in terms of conventional grammar that is true. But by frequent abandonment of conventional sentence structure, Beckett endows the piece with a powerful oral quality. *Textes pour rien* turns in the main from the explicit writing of the trilogy to a speaking voice, and *From an Abandoned Work* appeals even more directly to the ear.

This oral quality is even more strongly heard in *Comment c'est*. Before the whole book was published (in French) in 1961, an excerpt was printed in 1959 as *L'Image*. It is instructive to compare part of this piece with the finished form. The narrator, lying face down in the mud, sees his most extended image—a Beckettian parody of love. This time the lovers are in their teens, but as grotesquely ugly as Moll and Macmann. With their dog, the couple climbs a mountain for a picnic lunch:

> suddenly we are eating sandwiches alternate bites I mine she hers and exchanging endearments my dear I bite she swallows my dear she bites I swallow we don't yet coo with our bills full my love I bite she swallows my treasure she bites I swallow brief mist and there we are again dwindling again across the pastures hand in hand arms swinging heads high towards the heights smaller and smaller I no longer see the dog I no longer see us the scene is cleared some animals still the sheep like granite outcrops a horse I hadn't seen standing motionless back bent head sun animals know blue and white of sky it goes out on an April morning in the mud it's over it's done the scene is empty a few animals still then goes out no more blue I stay there way off on the right in the mud the hand opens and closes that helps me it's going let it go I realize I'm still smiling it's no use now none for a long time now my tongue comes out again lolls in the

mud I stay there no more thirst the tongue goes in the mouth closes it must be a straight line now it's done end of image (my translation, based on Beckett's *How It Is*).

L'Image is difficult even for the experienced Beckett reader, and it must have been all but impenetrable for the newcomer. The sense unit is no longer the sentence but the phrase, and in order to make the block of prose intelligible, we are forced to read slowly in separate phrases. The sense is pictorial, as suggested by the title *L'Image*, and yet we see a scene rather than a mere image. Though Beckett has created several fictional scenes that are pictorial and almost palpable—Murphy in his rocking-chair, Watt on the station floor, Molloy in Lousse's house, hatted Malone in bed—none is so scrupulously exact as *L'Image*. Possibly Beckett's stage work sharpened his visual precision. In the lines before those quoted, he deploys figures and objects like a theater director, stipulating the narrator's position in the mud, the couple's position on the earth, the directions in which they turn, even to the number of degrees in the angle. From the narrator's tongue reaching down into the mud to the tongue re-entering his mouth and retiring behind closed lips, the scene is highly visual. But there is also dialogue in the image—the more striking because it is so rare. Before the couple's picnic, the narrator is tempted to cry out to his teen-age self: "Plant her there and run cut your throat." We may recall Dan Rooney's "Nip some young doom in the bud." Die at the summit of love and loveliness, before doom descends. It is against that resonance that we listen to the cliché endearments of the young lovers, hilariously mixed with their mastication, heartbreakingly evanescent. No wonder the mist falls soon after, destroying the image of young love.

When I first read *L'Image* in the short-lived English periodical *X*, I guessed that it was a companion-piece to *From an Abandoned Work*. I thought that *Textes pour rien* marked Beckett's turn to short lyrical fiction, in which a voice would perform acrobatic feats with rhythm and syntax. *From an Abandoned Work* looked backward to a reintegration of traditional fictional components, but *L'Image* seemed a Beckettian step forward in its syntactical disintegration that presented young love through a muddied distance. Beckett's return to English was thus a return to richer reference whereas the re-return to French entailed resumption of voluntary impoverishment.

That contrast still seems to me valid, but what I did not know was that *L'Image* was not a self-contained work but a small part of an extended work that, for lack of a better word, we may call a novel. My first glimmer of that novel came in September, 1960, when *Evergreen Review* published Beckett's *From an Unabandoned Work*, and noted laconically: "Samuel Beckett has been working on his 'unabandoned' novel." The unabandoned novel was *Comment c'est*, but I never thought to connect the French *Image* with the English free verses of the first eight pages of that novel, as yet unpublished in French. "Découverte de Pim," another excerpt of *Comment c'est*, also appeared in 1961, still retaining paragraphs. *L'Image* appeared in block prose. At some point in composition, Beckett shifted to free verse: he began translation into English even before finalizing the French, and there is great discrepancy between the two languages. Though the first eight pages of *How It Is* embody numerous revisions over the *Evergreen Review* version, the radical newness is already there. Without capitalization or punctuation, the print appears in irregular verses. This is not only a matter of typography, though Beckett's work shares that aspect with concrete literature. Through the visual typography, paradoxically, Beckett emphasizes the oral lyricism of his fiction. Though most of the verses of *Comment c'est* endure for longer than a breath, the reader is forced to breathe as guided by the verses. The technique of reading resembles the technique for reading the block prose of *L'Image*, but the process has a different feeling in that rest-breaths correspond to the blank spaces on the page. And within the verses, only the reader's voice can determine how the phrases are grouped. The reader's voice has to echo the voice of the narrator of *Comment c'est*, even if both are mute.

Translated by Beckett himself, the English *How It Is* seems like another work from *Comment c'est*. English accentual rhythm reads differently from French tonic rhythm. English loses the repeated pun on the title: *Comment c'est* sounds exactly like *commencer* (to begin) in a book that speaks continually of its end. *Quaqua* of the "without" means "shit" in French. Sack and cord trail a host of associations in French—most notably *homme de sac et de corde* (a criminal who is stuffed into a sack, which is tied with a cord and thrown into a river to sink). Denuded of these suggestions, the English text is more condensed and formal, but Beckett introduces new sound play and repetition.

The English title *How It Is* is at once interrogatory and affirmative; the individual words are indefinite, and yet the trio seems to insist on fact. Comparably, the individual verses seem capricious, but the whole book has an appearance of order, a large Arabic numeral announcing each of the three parts. Again and again, this trisection is emphasized. In the very first verse of *Comment c'est* we read: "how it was I quote before Pim with Pim after Pim how it is three parts I say it as I hear it." These three parts are soon named as the journey, the couple, the abandon. How it was and how it is—past and present—fragment into these fictional events, which will prove to be cyclical.

Literally and metaphorically, the central event of the book is the couple, the meeting of two beings, which has haunted Beckett at least since A and C of *Molloy*. Through their various avatars in his fiction and drama, these two beings join most climactically when the narrator meets Pim in *Comment c'est*, the "with Pim" repeated and repeated, then reflected in the narrator's meeting with Bom, as in the countless meetings that supply momentary identity to

230

countless characters. For by dint of repetition, Beckett endows the meeting with the resonances of self-cognition we have all experienced in rare moments of merging with another human being.

We do not know the name of the narrator of *Comment c'est*, but the name of Pim is hammered at us from the first page on. Only in Part 2 do we learn of a meeting between the narrator and Bom, and it seems at first that Beckett sets Bom in opposition to Pim, his tormentor against his victim, but soon we grasp the four stages to life in the mud: journey toward one's victim, union with the victim Pim, journey toward one's tormentor, union with the tormentor Bom. The small naked males are virtually indistinguishable, though the narrator is a little larger than Pim.

Bim and Pim are voiced and voiceless variants of the same simple name that has appeared in several Beckett works. In the story of Belacqua's death in *More Pricks Than Kicks* Bim and Bom are grouped with Grock, the clown whose humor rested on failure, and with Democritus, the philosopher who laughed at metaphysics. In *Murphy* Bim and Bom Clinch are the sadistic attendants of the Magdalen Mental Mercyseat. In the first published version of *En attendant Godot*, in a passage that Beckett deleted from subsequent editions, he compares Pozzo and Lucky to Bim and Bom:

Estragon—You'd think it was the circus.
Vladimir—The music-hall.
Estragon—With Bim.
Vladimir—And Bom.
Estragon—The stalinist comedians. (My translation.)

"The stalinist comedians" also suggest Lucky and Pozzo, slave and master, oppositions in human society. In *Comment c'est* Bim and Bom as Pim and Bom are victim-tormentor oppositions in human society, turn and turn about. In a passage composed only for the English version of *How It Is*, Beckett delineates the relationship that is at

231

once one of love-hate and of opposing aspects of a single person: "and that linked thus bodily together each one of us is at the same time Bom and Pim tormentor and tormented pedant and dunce wooer and wooed speechless and reafflicted with speech in the dark the mud nothing to emend there."

Though the couple's meeting is the main event of *Comment c'est*, and Pim its main character, lesser characters enter the narrator's memory or imagination. Pam Prim is the wife of Pim, Kram is Pim's witness and Krim his scribe; a dog is Skom Skum. Rhyme and slant-rhyme conspire to suggest the interchangeability of these creatures, reduced to a residue of being. Any one-syllable name ending in *m* will do, as earlier Beckett names began with *m*, thirteenth letter of the alphabet.

Rather than plot, characters, or objects, setting sustains the lyrical fiction of *Comment c'est*. The nebulous nowheres of *L'Innommable* and the *Textes* are engulfed by ubiquitous mud. Dante first set the scene in the fifth circle of his *Inferno*, but Beckett's mud, in spite of its absorption of shit and vomit, lacks the disgusting detail of the *Inferno*. In Beckett's early essay on Proust, he used as epigraph Leopardi's *E fango è il mondo*, and in *Comment c'est*, mud *is* the world—warm, thirst-quenching, and not uncomfortable. In the first of the texts the narrator lies face downward in a dank trough; in *Comment c'est* all mankind comes to lie face downward in the mud. As in the texts, memories, dreams, fantasies, or fictions belong to "life in the light" above. And as in the texts, images do not linger long. Curtains open on a scene, as in the theater, and images vanish through "brief void" or "brief black," like cinematic blackout. The here-and-now of *Comment c'est* is darkness, silence, and loneliness in the mud. Each creature crawls along toward a fellow, tortures that fellow until he crawls away, and then the creature crawls toward his own torturer. Half of his life the creature spends with fellows, and half alone. Thus, long sentences of solitary confinement are paradoxically imposed on millions of beings, each speaking his own idiom.

It is the idiom—the narrator's speech—that embodies the major innovation of *Comment c'est*. In a letter to Hugh Kenner, Beckett wrote not of his narrator but "the narrator/ narrated" who claims to be narrated, always quoting. The Scribe of the fifth text already uttered the refrain of *Comment c'est*: "I say it as I hear it." The narrator/narrated combines some twenty phrases, many times repeated, with other phrases, less often repeated, or used only once, to yield a mesmerizing verbal melody. On the page the phrases are gathered into irregular unpunctuated verses that visually emphasize the repetition that is also rhythmed by the recurrent word "again." The verse arrangement is restful to the eye, but it is also restful to the mind. Concentration is needed to pierce to meaning, as one's own voice echoes that of the narrator/narrated.

Repetition is central to both structure and texture of *Comment c'est*. The narrated phrases are repetitive, and the narrated lives are repetitive. Originality is disclaimed by the narrator/narrated: "I quote" and "I say it as I hear it." The most frequent burden of the book is "vast stretch of time" (varied by "vast tracts of time"). Like time, the narrator/narrated stretches as he crawls through the mud. Ironically, Beckett insists most strongly upon the endless length of time in the middle of the book, which focuses on a couple, a human intercourse that should shorten time. Since Part 3 brings the end, we can understand the increased frequency of "when the panting stops." In order to listen to the interior voice, the panting has to stop, and this is equivalent to a temporary death. As Dan Rooney of *All That Fall* could not simultaneously speak and move, the narrator/narrated of *Comment c'est* cannot simultaneously listen and breathe.

Of the many refrains when the panting stops, several are used over a dozen times: "I say it as I hear it" underlines the fact that the narrator/narrated is always quoting; "brief movements of the lower face" describes the narrator's soundless speech; "present formulation" indicates that this is only one version of the narrator's life; "we're talking of . . ." focuses whatever needs emphasis; "question of . . ." or "no question of . . ." designates the miscellaneous subjects that pique the narrator's curiosity; "all that" lumps and dismisses whatever is under discussion; "good moments" comments ironically on a cruel experience; and "something wrong there" criticizes word, phrase, verse, or accumulation of verses. The last refrain is varied in Part 3 by "something wrong something quite wrong" and "something very wrong there."

As always in Beckett's work, the verbal music is inseparable from the meaning, but never before has his music been so hypnotic. We have to interrupt the melody to probe to meaning, but there always *is* meaning, even in so imageless a verse as "a little less of no matter what no matter how no matter when a little less of to be present past future and conditional of to be and not to be come come enough of that on and end part one before Pim."

Buoyed up in the mud, murmuring soundlessly, Beckett's primeval crawler somehow converts his words into the print we read. Though his phrases are childishly simple, they bear traces of considerable education. He himself informs us of his study of anatomy, geometry, geography, mathematics, astronomy, physics, humanities, and natural history, also mentioning his loss of Latin. Given as he is to monosyllables, he still uses an astonishing vocabulary: acervation, speluncar, dextrogyre, introrse, euphoria, peripeteia, procumbency, thenar, flageolet, osmosis, buccinator, piriform, lubricious, meatus, serotine, scissiparous, oakum, capillarity. And he sprinkles learned references through his phrases: Apostle's Creed, Belacqua, Malebranche, Erebus, Heraclitus, Thalia, Haeckel, Klopstock. In spite of the oral quality of his discourse, he is sensitive to written form, making three references to parentheses, two to commas, and one to paragraphs in his unpunctuated continuum of verses.

Invocation, apposition, and labials receive passing mention, but above all it is verbs that interest the narrator, who worries about tenses in his account that cuts verbs to a minimum, accumulating skepticism about the ability of time to pass.

In spite of the three-part division of *Comment c'est*, comparable to Malone's effort to divide the time of his dying, categories overlap. What the narrator calls "images" are supposed to disappear after Part 1, before Pim, and certainly the first part *is* richest in images. The very first image is called "life in the light," and yet that life is not nearly so vivid as later images—scissoring a butterfly's wings, a child praying at his mother's knees, a little old man or boy crying into his hands, a hand pulling a crocus on a string, a foot caught in an elevator shaft, a dream of Christ in an alb, and above all the extended scene of adolescent love announced as the last image. Other images are not specifically labelled as images—"Belacqua fallen over on his side," "towering between its great black still spread wings the snowy body of I know not what frigate-bird." Toward the end of Part 1, images give way to numbers—"I always loved arithmetic" and "dear figures when all fails a few figures to wind up with." The narrator/narrated uses numbers to mock his snail-crawl, and yet the crawl arrives at the image of the book's climactic event: "instead of the familiar slime an arse two cries one mute end of part one before Pim that's how it was before Pim."

In Part 2 images are not mentioned, and numbers are ruled out—"no more figures"—yet both are present. Vivid are an Eastern sage whose nails grow through his palms, Pim's watch ticking through eternity, the sex life and hospitalization of Pam Prim, a man on his knees before a door, and above all the narrator's education of Pim. One image recurs three times in Part 2—St. Andrew's cross, an X, and it is always evoked in connection with Pim. The symbolic crucifix becomes a symbolic X; the crucifixion endures, but its meaning is now unknown. In spite of the visual repetition of the cross-X, the most haunting repetition of Part 2 is auditory—the "paroxysm of communication with Pim."

By Part 3 images thin out in a muddy present: "a few old images always the same no more blue the blue is done never was the sack the arms the body the mud the dark living hair and nails all that." The Bom-narrator couple replaces the narrator-Pim couple, each involved in a discontinuous journey eastward. As the images diminish, numbers proliferate. The trisection of infinity is mirrored in the trisection of the book, in which the numbers eight (octosyllable, eight planes, May 8, octogenarian, eight thousand years), ten, and fifteen (yards, seconds, blows, words, others) recur. Whatever the substantive, numbers return to the mud in Part 3, where millions of creatures undergo the four stages of the human condition, present formulation: voyage toward another, torment of the other, awaiting still another, torment by the other. The basic human condition involves three people in two roles—"millions millions there are millions of us and there are three." Bom tortures the narrator, who crawls away to torture Pim, who crawls away to be tortured by Bom, and so on ad infinitum.

Since numbers run wild in the middle of Part 3, the tenuous personality of the narrator/narrated is further eroded. Though he does not, like the Unnamable, seek to find himself, he does express the trauma of dissolving into Pim, into Bom, into numbers—"no one here knows himself it's the place without knowledge whence no doubt its peerlessness." He expresses this trauma of "being this voice these scraps nothing more" by broken phrases, difficult syntax, introduction of "ill" before past participles, and increased echolalia at the end of the book. By the end of Part 3 images and numbers are rejected, to return to Pim's tormented utterances, now extorted from the narrator/narrated himself. But the immediacy of the pain is such that we feel it directly, forgetting that the narrator is narrated.

The arbitrary trisection of experience is and is not accurate; it is accurate in bounding a brief sadomasochistic

236

coupling between two long stretches of loneliness—"divide into three a single eternity for the sake of clarity"; it is inaccurate because all life of all time is threatened by ubiquitous dirt and dark.

Accurate or inaccurate, the tripartite division stresses the meeting of the narrator with Pim, and Pim's lessons in language are the most cruelly vivid verses of the book. Pim cries out when he is discovered by the narrator; ergo he has a voice. The narrator listens to Pim's instinctive song, then hears the ticking of Pim's watch. The narrator attaches the name Pim to this fellow-creature, which he also claims as his own. Only then does the narrator-trainer focus his relentless attention on language. First a theme song, then a few words to the tune. Jabbing the can-opener into Pim's buttocks, the narrator teaches Pim to speak: "table of basic stimuli one sing nails in armpit two speak blade in arse three stop thump on skull four louder pestle on kidney five softer index in anus six bravo clap athwart arse seven lousy same as three eight encore same as one or two as may be."

Lessons in speech are followed by lessons in script, which resembles what we read: "unbroken no paragraphs no commas." Speech and script are forced to reveal the life of Pim in the light—"real or imaginary no knowing." Pam Prim is at once the unhappy wife of both Pim and the narrator. Their life above recalls the events of Beckett's trilogy, before the narrator denies the whole narration. In order to end, the narrator invents a witness Kram and a scribe Krim (punning on German *krimkram*, junk); and the scribe keeps three notebooks—one for movement, one for speech, and one for his own commentary. The narrator/narrated is the object of generations of witness-scribe teams, but soon he wipes them all out, returning to Pim and his life in the light, which is indistinguishable from that of the narrator/narrated. Soulscapes of Beckett's earlier fiction return with economical familiarity: "sea beneath the moon harbour-mouth after the sun the moon always light day and night little heap in the stern it's me all those I see are me all ages the current carries me out the awaited ebb I'm looking for an isle home at last drop never move again a little turn at evening to the sea-shore seawards then back drop sleep wake in the silence eyes that dare open stay open live old dream on crabs kelp."

After denying Pim, the narrator imagines both of them dead, Krim and Kram engaging in an incredulous dialogue at their expense. The narrator returns to Pim to end Part 2. The narrator's torture-training of Pim is of unparalleled intensity, whose agony speaks for all men living in unknowing: "but he can't affirm anything no deny anything no things may have been different yes his life here pause YOUR LIFE HERE good and deep in the furrows howls thump face in the mud nose mouth howls good he wins he can't."

In afflicting Pim with language, the narrator uses nails, fists, and can-opener, and an odd combination they appear. Nails and fist are weapons of primitive combat, suitable to this primeval slime, but the can-opener belongs to modern industrialization. Pim, a fellow-creature, is the can opened by this instrument, and his words are the sustenance that is disgorged.

The can-opener is the vital object in the relationship of Pim and the narrator, but the sack is the vital object while the narrator is alone. He synonymizes it with his life. Specifically designated as a coal-sack, the jute bag is a pun on the galactic coalsack. The latter is a dark void in the starry heavens, but the former embodies all that is tender and nourishing in the solitude of the narrator. Not only is the sack a container for the cans of fish (which suggest contemporary vacuum-packing of Christ), but it serves as a pet, a pillow, a fetus, a friend, a lover: "I take [the sack] in my arms talk to it put my head in it rub my cheek on it lay my lips on it turn my back on it turn to it clasp it to me again say to it thou thou." In *Comment c'est* man offers tenderness to a thing but cruelty to his fellow-man.

Beckett's first notes for *Happy Days* overlap his final revision of *How It Is*, and some carryover is apparent. Both protagonists have to live through an eternal present, so that they almost gag at the word "day." Both are attached to their sacks, but both are ultimately more dependent on their fellow-men. The one in the damp dark and the other in the dry light, both focus on enduring through time— Winnie till the bell for sleep, the narrator till the end of Part 3. Winnie tries to tick off time by acting with her limited means. The narrator measures time in the phrases breathed between his breaths, quotations though he claims them to be.

The brief final verse of *Comment c'est* circles back to the book's first verse: "good good end at last of part three and last that's how it was end of quotation after Pim how it is." Almost every word of the last verse has been implicitly denied: "good" punctuates a series of "ill"s. Part 3 is identical with Part 7, 11, etc., for the last can never be the last, and how it was merges with how it is. Pim has had no effect. Though Beckett sustains the fiction of quotation, the narrator's unique idiom rests on the basis of our common language. Last verse loops around to first verse, immersing us in our own muddy uncertainty.

Overtly, the world of *Comment c'est* does not resemble ours, except for swift images in the light. But having reached a certain age, or certain moods, most of us have known the curtains across the light. In our loneliness, we victimize loved ones or lend ourselves to victimization. And sometimes we are the wiser, or the better, for the relationship.

Comment c'est continues the Beckett narrator-protagonist's effort to know himself, which is to know ourselves, since the self he seeks is the lowest common denominator of conscious, word-using being. To find himself, he isolates himself, generalizes himself, transfers himself into another observable being, Pim. The three parts of the novel are illusory, since its only event is the meeting with Pim, an effort at examining the self as simultaneous subject and

239

object. Part 1 whets our appetite for this investigation, Part 2 shows it in all its precise cruelty, and Part 3 suggests that it is painful self-investigation. The closing pages of Part 2 purport to quote Pim's extorted speech, and the closing pages of Part 3 shift to the narrator's first-person speech. But the rhythms and words are similar. Striking are the capitalized phrases engraved five times on Pim's back— "YOUR LIFE HERE"—and the narrator's self-questioning sequence beginning "HOW WAS IT" and ending "I SHALL DIE." Pim's "yes"s and "no"s lead to the "no answer"s of the narrator at the end of Part 3.

Finally, how it is is not. Our being remains a mystery, but Beckett has musicalized the mystery into an extraordinary fiction. Rhythm lulls us in the warm dark mud—a repetitive rhythm that seems to imitate the body's movements through the mud and the mind's movements through *its* mud. Then, with Pim, we are abruptly startled into questions and pain, the pain of questions. Only one voice rises from the mud, whatever *quaqua* may surround it. Only one person is attached to these miscellaneous sacks, cords, cans, can-openers. The suffering of the narrator/narrated-protagonist-Pim-Bom is the epitome of our own, if we happen to be tormented by questions about love, loneliness, or human destiny.

Têtes-Mortes

Comment c'est is Beckett's last extended nondramatic work. For a few years after writing it he confined himself to drama and translation, but then he tried his French hand at fiction again. *Imagination morte imaginez*, *Assez*, and *Bing* were written in that order in 1965-1966. Then Beckett grouped the three pieces (setting *Assez* before *Imagination*) with his translation of *From an Abandoned Work* written a decade earlier. In French the four pieces were published in a slim volume entitled *Têtes-Mortes*, a rare French word that Littré defines as a chemical residue, for which the more usual term is *caput mortuum*. In English translation Beckett

240

used the word Residua, with resonances in law (the residue of an estate), chemistry (the residue of filtering, combustion, or evaporation), and mathematics (deviation from the mean of a set). Though the pieces bear on these matters, they are above all residua of fiction, reduced in length, reference, and continuity, but not in a stringent lyrical quality. Two of the four pieces—*Assez* and *Imagination*—do not appear to be literal remains of efforts at longer works.

From an Abandoned Work

From an Abandoned Work backtracks from the nudity of *Textes pour rien* since it contains events, characters, images. The nameless narrator is the first Beckett protagonist to tell his own story in English, but his voice bears the burden of the uncertainties of his French predecessors. Arbitrarily, he decides to focus on three days of his youth—his passion. Like Beckett's first narrators in French, he makes his fictional selection without apparent cause or purpose. Like the first French *nouvelles, From an Abandoned Work* counterpoints a journey against a shelter, and like the first walk-talkers, their English-speaking descendant is responsive to animals.

The protagonist of *From an Abandoned Work* begins with his departure from home—"bright and early," setting out on his way "though I have never in my life been on my way anywhere, but simply on my way." Turning his back on his weeping, waving, white mother, the wanderer soon sees a white horse, for which he knows the German word *Schimmel,* which also means mildew. He makes no connection with a verse from *Revelations,* but we may recall: "A pale horse and his name that sat on him was Death." The narrator merely remarks: "White I must say has always affected me strongly." The next day he is attacked by stoats and considers himself lucky not to be bled white. On the third day he meets a terrifying roadman named Balfe. By the end of the story the narrator's three-day journey has become an eternal journey toward an endless end: "Then

241

it will not be as now, day after day, out, on, round, back, in, like leaves turning or torn out and thrown crumpled away, but a long unbroken time without before or after, light or dark, from or towards or at, the old half knowledge of when and where gone, and of what, but kinds of things still, all at once, all going, until nothing, there was never anything, never can be, life and death all nothing, that kind of thing, only a voice dreaming and droning all around, that is something, the voice that once was in your mouth." In this long lyrical sentence that recalls parts of *L'Innommable*, the only actual things that emerge from the repetition of the word "thing" are the *leaves* of the past and the *voice* of the present—both implicitly filled with words, the only stubborn residue of life in the encroaching void. Unlike the voice-writing of *L'Innommable*, however, this voice is "all around"; the narrator has a sore throat, perhaps the result of the "voice that was in your mouth."

From an Abandoned Work shows us a world outside the narrator's mind. In that world the narrator moves actively, even though in recollection. A compulsive walk-talker, the protagonist makes his way by means of the steps he describes and the words we read. No longer, like his Unnamable ancestor, does he seek a self; he simply allows his momentum to carry him. His pace is a metaphor of his style—a lingering walk and a rapid run; similarly, the narration lingers over details but skips swiftly over connectives. Proportion is flouted as the first of the three days occupies some two-thirds of the tale, and there is no hint of what happened between the third day and the indefinite time of narration. The narrator narrates by voice, and yet his voice somehow becomes print, since the narrator addresses his reader directly: "Please read again. . . ."

Like other Beckett characters, the protagonist of *From an Abandoned Work* wishes for the end. Though he cannot end, he fantasizes about his death. His love for the anagrammatic words "over" and "vero" implies that truth lies in overness—the end. But since he cannot end, he describes

242

the three days in the long tedium of his life. About ten times, he strays from that chronology into meditation, association, interrogation; then sternly recalls himself to these three days, punctuating them with sporadic "now"s. As he describes them, he relives them. He fills a world with persons, animals (even dream animals), landscapes, stars, rocks, flowers, ferns, colors, a house, a room, a clock, a stick, and two unnamed books. Though he describes many moving things, he hates things that move. Though he once delineated Milton's ordered cosmology to his father, his own cosmos is disordered. Though his parents and Balfe are dead, he re-views them vividly. Raging, he declares his love for three kinds of phenomena—still and rooted things, white animals of dreams, and words above all. Through his love, then, the narrator connects words to immobility and whiteness, suggestive of the static purity of nonbeing. And yet his own words are moving and colorful. His unparagraphed rush of prose is full of sounds and passion, crackling with syntactical variety—rhyme and alliteration, interjections and interrogations, nouns and adjectives, adverbs and adverbial phrases, prepositions and conjunctions, and especially verbs and collectives, "to the general from the particular." Though the protagonist claims that he is old and weak, his active words belie the claim. But the syntactical fragmentation seems to reflect a fragmentation of his personality. Though he states that he never loved anyone, he is half in love with nonbeing—white rather than dark as in earlier works—and yet his energetic language adulterates that love. Nothingness is held at bay by the active abandon of this abandoned work.

Assez

Of the three French pieces written during 1965-1966, *Assez* is most obviously linked to the preceding fiction. A first-person narrator speaks of adventures in the past, but for the first time that narrator is an androgynous creature with feminine sensibility. Beckett carefully leaves no clue

243

as to her "real" sex. Like Molloy, the narrator of *Assez* spends her life journeying. Like Malone, the narrator attempts to impose some order on the narration. Like the Unnamable, the narrator is nameless and perhaps unnamable. As in *Textes pour rien*, a voice discourses, but the opening paragraph mentions a background pen, whose words we read in print. Like *Comment c'est*, *Assez* focuses on a couple; as the center of *Comment c'est* is "with Pim," the center of *Assez* is "with him." Alone in a timeless present, the narrator of *Assez* looks back on and virtually relives her activities "with him"—listening to his words, walking as they hold hands, together cubing ternary numbers, watching him mirror the constellations, bending her body to the needs of her mentor-lover-companion.

But resemblances to earlier Beckett works serve to highlight the uniqueness of *Assez*, which is Beckett's *Paradiso*. The couple of *Assez* lives through an eternal spring, without wind, darkness, or extremes of temperature. Far from agglomerations, they walk through vacation-lands near sea or mounds. Always together, their relationship is harmonious (though the pupil's hand does not feel at home in that of the mentor); the pupil fulfills every desire of the mentor. They perfectly exemplify the biblical verse: "Can two walk together, except they be agreed?" And the couple's agreement is prelapsarian: "The same needs and the same satisfactions," recalling the old Latin proverb: *Satis est quod sufficit*. (Enough is what satisfies.)

At the unspecified time of narration, however, their paradise is a paradise lost. The narrator is alone, and she begins her tale: "All that goes before forget." Paradoxically, however, the tale consists of what she cannot forget—the past made present. The first three paragraphs of *Assez* announce the story's three themes: 1) its means of transmission (the last Beckett mention of this theme), 2) the conditions of paradise for two, pivoting on the word "desire" (the most intense Beckett treatment of this theme), and 3)

244

the entrance into solitude and old age (the most oblique arabesque on this obsessive Beckett theme).

The narrator arbitrarily bounds her life by two specific days—the day her mentor alluded to his infirmity and the day her mentor told her to leave him. Her life thus begins and ends on the caprice of another. As the story unfolds, however, her life becomes a fiction since she tells four versions of their separation, unaccountably designated as her disgrace, and the fourth version contradicts the first three. Moreover, the narrator calculates that her life lasted one decade of the nearly three decades that the couple spent together, and yet their wandering in this "endless equinox" has a timeless quality.

Though the narrator is "brought up short by all [she] knows," her knowledge and experience are limited, in typical Beckett fashion. She remarks of the cotton gloves worn on their clasped hands: "Far from blunting the shapes [these gloves] sharpened them by simplifying." Similarly, the gloved prose acts to sharpen by simplifying. Nothing happens to the couple, except that they meet and part. By day they walk on flowers, and at night they lie on their sides, mentor enfolding pupil. Though the mentor likes to climb slopes, they do not stop to admire the view. Occasionally, the mentor, bent as he is, looks at stars through a mirror. Our world is thus reduced to simple, general, harmonious components, often repetitively viewed. When, toward the end of the story, the narrator declares that she could name a radish if she saw one, that root becomes a scarlet climax after the simplified sharpening of objects.

The narrator portrays her mentor as a primordial walk-talker with imperious demands. His resonances are sexual, esthetic, and religious. During their life together, the mentor utters "ejaculations and broken paternosters," and his fragmented language mirrors a world composed of fragments. As the couple explores its repetitious sameness, the mentor resorts less and less to language, and the narrator speaks (or writes) in simple declarative sentences, combined into short paragraphs: "The art of combining is not my fault. It's a curse from above." Sometimes, ellipses occur. Bare of the commas that figured so prominently in the trilogy, and even in *From an Abandoned Work*, the prose is punctuated by periods. Though questions are frequently and resolutely disclaimed, there are two question marks, and, symmetrically, two exclamation points. The first exclamation mark punctuates their calculations, and the first question mark punctuates their geodesy. The second exclamation mark punctuates the single direct quotation from the mentor: "I have it!" The "it" is no less than a constellation. The second question mark appears near the end of the story, abruptly, after a terse summary of the mentor's words: "What do I know of man's destiny?"

The most pervasive refrain of the story (less frequent in English than in the original French) treats of the questions that were not asked, with three iterations of "I never asked myself the question." But the very suppression of questions raises them for us: Who are these mythical creatures? Is their separation permanent? What is a human life? Is there a limit to suffering? What *do* we know of man's destiny? The unasked questions are a throwback to fiction, but this is short fiction that maintains itself by the narrator's *unquestioning* statements. Midway through the piece, the past becomes the present: "I see the flowers at my feet and it's the others I see. Those we trod down with equal step. It is true they are the same." The same because all objects and actions are repetitively similar. The same, too, because both flowers are made of words.

The mentor's cramped, idiosyncratic manner of walking is reflected in the narrator's cramped, idiosyncratic method of recounting. But the narrator's words also seem to echo those of her mentor—few in number, sometimes fumbling, sometimes repeated. After an interval of calculation, the narrator returns to the inevitability of words, which the nar-

rator consciously brings to an end. She emphasizes the
calming effect of the flowers that sustained them, and the
very idea of calm came from the mentor. The narrator then
decides to wipe out everything but the calm-giving flowers.
With rare success, the final sentence achieves a heavenly
calm: "Enough my old breasts feel his old hand." "Enough"
because the words have fulfilled their purpose, evoking at
once the paradise of idyllic companionship and its staleness
in the repetition of "old."

The opening paragraph of *Assez* contained four repetitions of the phrase "too much," ambiguously referring to
both words and silence. But the last sentence begins with
the word "enough." The cumulation of words has brought
an image into being, and the narrator has therefore spoken-
written "enough." The narrator's final sentence contains
Beckett's last use of the first person singular in his fiction—
too singular to be written with impunity.

Imagination morte imaginez

A central couple links *Assez* to *Imagination morte imaginez* (written a few months earlier), but the narrating voice
differs radically. With an effort at scientific exactitude, a
third-person observer describes a white world and at times
addresses an unspecified second person. The title typifies
the syntax. And sets the stage: "No trace anywhere of life."
The imagination, dead, commands itself—or us—to probe
toward life. Beckett brings back a third-person, ostensibly
omniscient, narrator only to deprive him of all knowledge
but that which is immediately observable in an imagined
scene. Based at an indefinite vantage-point in infinity, the
narrator alternates objective description with clipped imperatives—"no way in, go in"—to himself? to the reader? to
the would-be witness of being? The titular imperative,
"imagine," yields the image of a still white world. No longer, as in *From an Abandoned Work*, is white a pure reflector
of all colors that clothe the living; as in the white world of

Embers, rather, white engulfs living and nonliving alike—"ground, wall, vault, bodies."

Beckett's earlier works stripped his characters of background, biography, or even parts of the body, but now he has enough of these human agonies. Empirical, declarative, elliptical, his new narrative voice diminishes the very possibility of life in an imagined void. Banishing landscape and color, the resolutely objective voice sees within ubiquitous whiteness a white rotunda, three feet in diameter, three feet in height. In the first *Tête-Morte, From an Abandoned Work*, the walk-talker had voiced a desire: "Oh but for those awful fidgets I have always had I would have lived my life in a big empty echoing room with a big old pendulum clock. . . ." In *Imagination* the figdets are gone, and a couple comes close to realizing this desire, for their rotunda is empty of objects, and a rap would produce a ringing sound "a ring as in the imagination the ring of bones." A verse of *Matthew* reads: "Whited sepulchres, which indeed appear beautiful outward, but are within full of dead men's bones." The sepulchre of *Imagination* resembles that of *Matthew*, but the bones are not quite dead. At the third mention of two bodies filling the rotunda, we learn that they are sweating—first evidence of life. As if seeking a return to the whiteness of nonbeing, the narrator leaves the rotunda to reenter it—"Go back out . . . go back in"—and upon reentrance, he distinguishes in the whiteness a pendulum movement of heat and light, swinging during the course of twenty seconds from black zero to white heat.

However, he cannot sustain this description that sounds like a physics text. For all the resolutely scientific approach, approximations accumulate: first there are "pauses of varying length"; then the twenty-second pendulum swing becomes less regular; variable pauses occur at the extremes or even in midswing; the full swing may not be completed before reversal. In spite of these variations, however, with their attendant vibrations, the movement is regular in the main—"world still proof against enduring tumult." After half the piece has been devoted to the problematical physics of the rotunda, the narrator leaves it and reenters to focus on the two white bodies, each inscribed in its semicircle.

"On their right sides therefore both and back to back head to arse," each of them lies in a modified fetal position in this approximate half-egg structure. Unlike a fetus, though, each body lives an independent life, without umbilical cord: "Hold a mirror to their lips, it mists." The ambiguous imperative implies movement within the rotunda, for the two heads are too far apart to mist a single mirror, which has to be moved from one head to the other. The mirror will not reflect the constellations of *Assez*, but a minimal residue of life. The couple will not stampede in the equatorial circles of *Assez*, or lie companionably enfolded in one another. Instead, they are still, inscribed in an eternal circle, back to back. After reading *Imagination*, we can appreciate the relative richness of *Assez*, with its memories of vigor and variety—more than enough. In contrast, the couple of *Imagination* touch without communicating, and indeed the two bodies are virtually indistinguishable, except that the woman has long imperfectly white hair.

"Sweat and mirror notwithstanding," declares the clinically observant narrator, the bodies might seem dead except for the stubborn blinking of their respective left eyes "at incalculable intervals." And by way of their eyes, we sense not only life but a hint of communion: "Piercing pale blue the effect is striking, in the beginning. Never the two gazes together except once, when the beginning of one overlapped the end of the other, for about ten seconds." Significantly, the narrator's first comment upon the *effect* of what is seen precedes the first and only hint of communication—a shared glance.

Shelley's many-colored life stained the white radiance of eternity; in the irregular strobe lighting of *Imagination*, the pale blue eyes may be only briefly visible, but they too stain the still whiteness of eternal nonbeing. And they inspire climactic events—"a thousand little signs" of life that crystallize into the murmur "ah" and the infinitesimal shudder spied by the "eye of prey." Does that eye belong to the narrator, the reader, or both? The narrator tries to return to the calm of the void, but the stain of life spreads over the end of *Imagination morte imaginez*: "No, life ends and no, there is nothing elsewhere, and no question of ever finding again that white speck lost in whiteness, to see if they still lie still in the stress of that storm, or of a worse storm, or in the black dark for good, or the great whiteness unchanging, and if not what they are doing." Being, vulnerably evanescent, breathes up from the negatives, the calming series of "st" sounds, the resonant series of "or" possibilities, and the black-white eternity that melts into the final diaphanous clause: "and if not what they are doing." Beckett ends on life's lyricism against the white background of nonbeing. The imagination that began by declaring: "No trace anywhere of life," ends with a trace in the implied query: "what they are doing." Only living beings *do*.

Bing

Chronologically, *Bing* follows *Assez*, but musically and methodologically, *Bing* follows *Imagination morte imaginez*, since it records further effort to find "that white speck lost in whiteness." After completing *Assez*—a kind of "with him"—Beckett moved gradually toward the third part of this new version of "how it is." Juggling large populations as in the third part of *Comment c'est*, he put the work aside as "untractable," though he subsequently salvaged *Le Dépeupleur*. Then, trying to make a fresh start with a single minimal being in the vast void, he slowly evolved the verbless incantation of *Bing*, an artifact woven of permutation, repetition, and emptiness—not unlike *Comment c'est* to the ear, but very different to the eye. Limiting himself to extremely short unpunctuated phrases, gathered into seventy sentences and printed as an unbroken block on the page, Beckett produced what is probably his most difficult work to read.

250

From his earliest fiction, Beckett has forced his readers to read every one of his words. Dictionaries and encyclopedias might supply the punch-lines of jokes in *More Pricks* and *Murphy*. In *Watt* and *Comment c'est*, Beckett challenged the reader to become a mathematician, so as to check his figures and combinations. In *Imagination morte imaginez*, Beckett defies the reader *not* to pick up a pencil and become a mathematician, so as to draw geometric figures and graph periodicities. In *Bing*, and even more in the English translation *Ping*, Beckett compels the reader to become a fellow-writer, rearranging the words on paper in order to see the significance of repetition, permutation, combination, or singularity.

In this text of 1030 words (in English), a mere 120 are permuted and combined into one of the most remarkable verbal melodies ever written. As Ludovic Janvier has noted, the piece grows from its two opening sentences, which situate an individual in his environment: "All known all white bare white body fixed one yard legs joined like sewn. Light heat white floor one square yard never seen." The compression is startling and puzzling, but it does depict the small nude body fixed in its box. The triple use of "white" is ambiguous, but it seems to point to all that is—body and object alike. The rest of the piece adds details as needed by the omniscient elliptical narrator, who describes a quasi-alternation between the body and its surroundings. And yet the opposition of "all known" and "never seen" implies that we are once again in the realm of the imagination.

In *Watt*, completed over twenty years earlier, Beckett wrote: "So [Watt] continued to think of himself as a man. . . . But for all the relief that this afforded him, he might as well have thought of himself as a box, or an urn." In *Play*, written some four years before *Bing*, Beckett immured his characters in boxes, which he then revised to urns. In *Bing*, it takes determination to distinguish body from box.

The narrator hiccups his description of a yard-long body

fixed in a box measuring two cubic yards—white contents of a white container. Sweat and mist no longer give evidence of life, but eyes and murmurs again betray the white stillness "only just almost never." In the unparagraphed prose of *Bing*, where periods are the only guides to meaning, the syllable *bing* (or *ping* in English) seems to have an elusive association with life. Onomatopoeia or command, the title orders us like a pebble into a pond, or a ball into the air, into a lyrical narration in which character, image, and murmur coalesce.

As in *Imagination* the narrator tries to describe the white figure in a white container. But in spite of steady light, perspectives are treacherous, and every item in turn is designated as invisible—the meeting planes as well as the parts and whole of the fixed bare body. Though we are thrice told of silence within the body's "haught" head, insidious murmurs arise: "perhaps not alone," "perhaps a way out," "perhaps a nature," "perhaps a meaning." As the effort at scientific precision in *Imagination* yielded to the "eye of prey," the contained phrases of *Bing* admit the several "perhaps"s and the many "bings"s, climaxed by the entrance of an eye, twice described. The black-and-white eye, owner unknown, is more suggestive of life than all the white body, and yet it is not lively. "Dim" on first appearance, the eye is finally "unlustrous," and yet on both occasions the long eyelashes implore, evoking response. (Since English *Ping* rests more heavily on its "ping"s than French *Bing* on its "bing"s, further discussion will deal with English *Ping*.)

Though the black-and-white eye intrudes only toward the end, it is obliquely prepared by the sound "ping." Of the thirty-four repetitions of "ping," nine are followed by "elsewhere"—an abrupt movement that might suggest life. Seven "ping"s are followed by "murmur" or "murmurs"—sounds that again suggest life. Four times "ping" is followed by "silence," but the silence lasts only at the fourth repetition —as the antepenultimate word of the piece. Twice "ping" is coupled with "a nature," twice with "not alone," and these four couplings are found in sentences with the word "image." Once "ping" is immediately followed by the word "image," and once by "a meaning." These last six "ping"s reënforce the insidious hints of the murmurs—that all is not quite ready for burial in the white box. Between the "ping last elsewhere" and the delayed account of it, "ping last murmur," are two iterations of "ping of old." Only after this tale of "ping"s has been fully told, is "ping [indeed] over." There has been a slow unsteady trajectory from "ping"s of physical displacement toward "ping"s of human murmur, toward a living being before all "ping"s are over.

Three "ping"s sound in the last sentence of *Ping*, which, like the last sentence of *Imagination*, contrasts with most of the remaining fabric. But in *Ping* that sentence is a repetitive echo, rather than a cumulative climax. In the sixtysecond sentence of *Ping*, the half-closed, dim black-and-white eye is rooted in an image and a memory. In the last, seventieth, sentence, when the blue eyes are finally dead white, the last murmur evokes the other eye: "Head haught eyes white fixed front old ping last murmur one second perhaps not alone eye unlustrous black and white half closed long lashes imploring ping silence ping over." "Old ping last murmur" does not qualify this final hint of life with "only just" or "almost never." Life improbably erupts, unlustrous black on shining white, lashes on smoothness. Its supplication denies the whole effort at objective narration. Like the "eye of prey" in *Imagination*, this unlustrous black eye seems to be that of the narrator, or of the reader, hunting for life in the ubiquitous white void.

Even on first reading, without resorting to pencil and paper, we are compelled to puzzle over the "ping"s, a word Beckett first used in *Dream*, for characters that would function as musical notes. And even on first reading, if we do not verify with pencil and paper that certain words are used only once, we are drawn to the human resonance of "flesh," "nails," "hair," "scars," "torn," and the imploring black-and-white eye. As in *Imagination*, we are drawn to them in part because they are so rare in the blinding whiteness. The word "white" recurs some ninety times in the English text of *Ping*, and it is sometimes in apposition to "invisible" or "infinite," but it is also attributed to the body or its parts. Being and nonbeing are now indistinguishable by color. Other colors—black, blue, and rose— are mentioned as "given." Rose is associated with flesh and nails. Blue, specifically designated as "only color," is associated with "unover" eyes (Beckett's translation of *inachevé*), and it is found in the longest phrase of the piece, "blue and white in the wind." This is all that remains of the images in the light of *Comment c'est*—"the blue there was then the white dust." Colors are the only residue of a larger world, remembered or imagined. But the third color, black (except in the imploring eye) fades to gray, which is generalized into "traces." All three colors fade to "almost white," the color of Nothing because it absorbs all colors. At last, the noncolor white combines with black to form an eye, as blue and white combined in the wind. Neither body nor world is quite coffined.

Beckett has permitted publication of nine earlier drafts of the French version of *Bing*, so that we can study its development. The first draft of the as yet untitled *Bing* resembles *Imagination* in its effort at geometry and physics, but simplification has already taken place; a cube supplants the vault, a single being supplants the couple, and sudden swift displacements supplant the irregular fluctuations of heat and light. Toward the end of this short untitled piece, these displacements are suggested onomatopoetically— "paf." Less than four hundred words in length, the piece did not satisfy Beckett, and he crossed out all but the following: "Toujours même pose. . . . Si peu de savoir. Si peu à savoir." (Always same pose. . . . So little knowledge. So little to know.—my translation.)

Bing #2 is even shorter, still written in simple jerky phrases, still situating the nude white body in a rectangular white container, but displacement is conveyed by "hop" instead of "paf." *Bing #3* adds details to both body and box. Phrases are now combined in somewhat longer groups, so that the rhythm is less choppy but more hesitant. Only in *Bing #8* will this rhythm dominate the presentation. In *Bing #3*, repetition of part of a relatively long sentence emphasizes its climactic quality: "Bref murmure de loin en loin que peut-être une issue," and "Bref murmure de loin en loin que peut-être pas seule." The brief murmur suggests a way out and a companion as parallel possibilities.

In *Bing #4*, as in the previous version, Beckett mentions alcoves and tunnels, which he was to siphon off into *Le Dépeupleur*. In *Bing #4*, we find the first "bing" for inexplicable murmurs: "Bing murmure. Bing long silence. . . . Bing murmure de loin en loin que peut-être une nature." (Bing murmur. Bing long silence. . . . Bing murmur now and then that perhaps a nature.) Within the rigorous white geometry, through "murmur" and "perhaps," *bing* may lead to "a nature" or some form of being.

Though some five hundred words longer than the final version, *Bing #5* has much of the final meaning and melody. Focus is relentless upon the six white planes enclosing a nude white body, whose life is suggested only through "hop"s, "bing"s, eyes and traces that are "unover," Beckett's subsequent arresting translation of French *inachevé*. As in the final version, it is a foreign eye that at once notices and contains life; it sees the "unover," and it implores—twice.

Bing #6 introduces scars into the description. *Bing #7* adds a mouth "like sewn" to the holes for eyes, nose, and ears. Only in *Bing #8* do the opening sentences appear in final form, and *Bing #8* also introduces an area of gray before the climactic entrance of the black-and-white eye, but this disappears in *Bing #9*, which is virtually the text as published.

In this last of Beckett's *Residua*, emotion dissolves into sudden sound or motion, onomatopoetically announced by "ping." For Sartre, man was a useless passion in a stone-cold cosmos; for Beckett's recent narrators, all passion is spent in a colorless cosmos—emptier through the French word *blanc* than English *white*. And yet, life stubbornly continues to flicker as residua in or of or through an eye. Different as the three *Residua* are—*Assez* a story with characters and scenes, *Imagination morte imaginez* a construct of considerable coherence, and *Ping* a tantalizing echolalia—they come to comparable conclusions: the androgynous narrator of *Assez* evokes life in the shape of an old hand on old breasts; the sourceless voice of *Imagination* wonders about the deeds of a barely living couple; the observant narrator of *Ping* finds an imploring eye through an almost lifeless scene.

Beckett has grouped *four* pieces as *Têtes-Mortes* in French. All four are lost faces or fragmentary remains of fiction, but *From an Abandoned Work* and *Assez*, punctuated into paragraphs, are passionate recollections of protagonist-narrators. *Imagination* and *Ping*, by contrast, are efforts at objective calm, plying neutral words in a confined timeless space. They are not texts for nothing, however, but minimal notes on being. From abandon to ping, the *Têtes-Mortes* trace the difficulty of writing fiction, which becomes synonymous with expressing Being in the void.

Le Dépeupleur

The void threatens in *Têtes-Mortes*. Its white stillness presents a temptation to the active protagonist of *From an Abandoned Work*. Stars and flowers appear mutually reflective against its immensity in *Assez*. In *Imagination* the impersonalized narrator, tempted by white stillness, tries to confine his words to a world reduced to the observable, the measurable, the describable. He fails, of course. The living being cannot retreat into a frozen world of nonbeing, however it may tempt him with its lack of suffering. *Bing* is perhaps Beckett's ultimate expression of that temptation and the impossibility of its fulfillment. In *Imagination* as in *Bing*, two very different short pieces, the perceiving eye enters

256

the image, introducing humanity into an inanimate world.

Beckett traveled from *Imagination* to *Bing* by a literally circuitous route—the cylinder of *Le Dépeupleur*. The French title is a Beckett neologism which leans on a line of verse from Lamartine's "L'Isolement": "Un seul être vous manque, et tout est dépeuplé!" (You miss a single being, and the world is depopulated.) Lamartine's isolation resulted from the death of his beloved Mme. Charles, and his poem describes the beauties of a sunset that leaves him indifferent because of his loss. In an earlier verse of the same poem, Lamartine says: "Je contemple la terre ainsi qu'un ombre errante:/ Le soleil des vivants n'échauffe plus les morts." (I view the earth like a roaming shadow: the sun of the living no longer warms the dead.) As we might expect, Beckett converts Lamartine's romantic melancholy into a version of his wasteland, in which Being is eroded by Nothingness. The French *dépeupleur* is death, but the English title shifts emphasis, for *The Lost Ones* would seem to be the dead, or those who never existed but who are deemed lost. In this "Abode where lost bodies roam each searching for its lost one" death imperceptibly claims the living: "And far from being able to imagine their last state when every body will be still and every eye vacant they will come to it unwittingly and be so unawares." As Victor Krapp remarked in *Eleuthéria*: "Liberty is seeing yourself dead." But the lost ones, like us all, are denied this liberty.

The narrator describes the abode of the lost ones as a rubberlike cylinder in which yellow light and dry heat dessicate living beings. As the seventy sentences of *Bing* alternate between a body and its surroundings, the fifteen paragraphs of *Le Dépeupleur* alternate between a population and its abode. As precisely as the narrator of *Imagination* tried to build a picture of a white dome and its two inhabitants, the narrator of *Le Dépeupleur* builds his far more complicated picture of a cylindrical city and its 205 inhabitants. Again, measurements are exact (though there are errors in the English edition), and again light and temperature fluctuate. But irregularities do not intrude into the systematized universe of *Le Dépeupleur*; or if they do, they are quickly suppressed. After the "unthinkable first day," all activities are repetitive until the "unthinkable end," which we witness.

Halfway up the cylinder wall are twenty recesses arranged in irregular quincunxes. Propped against the cylinder wall are fifteen ladders of different length, all with rungs irregularly missing. These ladders permit cylinder-dwellers to climb to the recesses, which are much coveted because the cylinder floor provides only one square meter of living space per inhabitant. Though the first sentence announces that the cylinder-dwellers are seeking their lost ones, it becomes apparent that the goal occasionally dissolves into the elaborate rules of the search.

The inhabitants may be classified by their activity: 1) the climbers who move constantly, 2) the watchers who sometimes stop, 3) the sedentary who prefer immobility, and 4) the vanquished whose immobility is accompanied by lowered head. Though these categories are not rigid, the proportions at the time of narration are neat multiples: 5 vanquished $\times$ 4 = 20 sedentary $\times$ 3 = 60 watchers $\times$ 2 = 120 climbers, or a total population of 205—200 in round numbers. Among them only the vanquished are gradually particularized: in the tenth paragraph we are introduced to a white-haired woman and her baby, seated against the cylinder wall. And in that same paragraph we learn about a vanquished man "in the arena stricken rigid in the midst of the fevering." Only in the fourteenth paragraph does the narrator describe a vanquished woman, seated against the wall, head bowed so that her heavy red hair covers her body. We never learn the identity of the fifth vanquished one.

Among the population there is widespread belief in a way out of the cylinder, but division is sharp as to the location of this exit. Some believe that a tunnel in the wall leads to the world of nature, and others believe that a chimney through the ceiling leads to the sun and the stars. At the time of narration, the ceiling-supporters are more numerous because the ceiling is invisible from the cylinder floor, and it is reachable only if several inhabitants cooperate to hold the longest ladder vertical. However, such cooperation does not occur, since the requisite "instant of fraternity" is as foreign to these people as to butterflies.

Absence of fraternity necessitates social laws: each ladder may hold only one climber at a time, with descent having priority over ascent. On the cylinder floor the ladders must be carried in one direction only, and prospective climbers must line up before each ladder unidirectionally along the cylinder wall, which also supports the sedentary and the vanquished. Searchers not yet in line for a ladder must circle "counter-carrierwise," in an inner circumference, and still other searchers may gather pell-mell in the central arena. Though passage is permitted from one of these three floor zones to another, strict rules govern such movement, and infractions are violently punished. Even light and temperature fluctuate according to given laws: "For in the cylinder alone are certitudes to be found and without nothing but mystery."

In spite of ordinances, questions arise at the end of the twelfth and longest paragraph. And instead of answering them, the narrator proceeds in the thirteenth paragraph to describe coition, "prolonged in pain and hopelessness" in this desiccated world. The paragraph ends on the lulls between fluctuations of light and temperature, followed by resumption of "the twofold storm."

Orientation is difficult in the press and gloom, but the searchers can use a vanquished woman as a north star of the cylinder. She is the red-haired woman in fetal position, whose fixity converts her into a beacon. After this fourteenth-paragraph introduction of the red-haired north, Beckett found himself unable to continue *Le Dépeupleur* in 1966. Gradually, relentlessly, stressing order and harmony, sounding Dantesque and Miltonic notes, he had built an inferno that horribly mirrors our earth. Only in 1970 did Beckett think of the "unthinkable end": universal death claims the cylinder-dwellers, as it will claim earth-dwellers. The interior of the cylinder achieves "dead still"ness— mentioned four times during the course of the narration.

In the final scene of unique, nonrepetitive movement a last searcher approaches the north of the vanquished woman. He kneels down before her, parts her heavy red hair, and raises her face. (The gesture of kneeling to search eyes with eyes repeats the Murphy-Mr. Endon scene, written over thirty years earlier.) He opens her eyes with his thumbs, and gazes into them until "these calm wastes" close his own eyes; then her eyes close, and her head falls forward again. He leaves her and assumes his own final pose as the temperature drops to zero, the light to darkness, and the insect hum to silence. As had been predicted in the second paragraph, "In cold darkness motionless flesh." *Le Dépeupleur* ends on this first searcher to look *down* before rigor mortis stills the cylinder. After deft manipulation of a whole population, Beckett ends his story on a single human being seeking what?—witness? love? death?

The narrator never intrudes into the consciousness of any of these 205 people, but his clinical descriptions reveal suffering as pervasive. With parchment-dry skin, the cylinder-dwellers are tortured by touch, and yet the lack of space forces constant contact. The cylinder's rubberlike wall discloses no hint of foot, fist, or head beaten against it. But pain is prevalent. A climber may deal a blow to a thinker on a ladder, a sedentary one may burst out furiously when stepped on, unclassified inhabitants try to brain themselves with ladder-rungs, coition is sadistically frenzied, and violence breaks out whenever rules are infringed.

As the moving picture develops, eyes become the prime instruments of torture and expressors of pain. In the central arena the watchers "devour" the climbers with their eyes. Similarly, the sedentary "devour" every passerby with their eyes. The vanquished close their eyes, but even they may experience a return of "ocular fever," replete with "ravenous eyes." As eyes move toward the blindness of defeat, "They would be seen to redden more and more in an ever widening glare and their pupils little by little to dilate till the whole orb was devoured." The effect is as horrifying as cannibalism. Differently horrifying are the eyes during the temporary lulls in fluctuation: "Stranger still at such times all the questing eyes that suddenly go still and fix their stare on the void or on some old abomination as for instance other eyes and then the long looks exchanged by those fain to look away." Before the cylinder world ends, the searchers live through endless ends in these exchanges of the eyes, which never find the lost one.

Le Dépeupleur seeks to extend the scientific objectivity of the narrator of *Imagination*, describing a world coldly conceived. But his syntax is more archaic and involved, his repetitions more insistent. He curtails his imaginative bent with eight iterations of the phrase "So much for . . ." The conceptual nature of his construction is implied in six iterations of the phrase "if that notion is maintained." The word "harmony" recurs eight times in this inferno. The one proper name in the account is that of Dante, for the vanquished sit "in the attitude which wrung from Dante one of his rare wan smiles." The posture belongs to slothful Belacqua in the Purgatorio, but the whole cylinder recalls Dante's conical Inferno, even to rumors of a way out to the stars.

Though the narrator does not name Milton, he too contributes to the infernal atmosphere, as Christopher Ricks has shown. In contrast to the English Puritan's "darkness visible," Beckett creates ubiquitous light that permits minimal visibility, for eyes approach blindness. And Milton's pandemonium is recalled but not tolerated in this ordered world.

Dantesque, Miltonic, contemporary, the world of Beckett's *Dépeupleur* blends single striking images into his

261

desiccated mannered prose: bodies that rustle like dry leaves, a substance impervious to the life it contains, fifteen ladders each with an acrobatic climber and a queue at the foot, contortions of dry coition, and two vanquished women seated like Belacqua against the cylinder wall, the one with white hair and an infant in her lap, the other with heavy red hair curtaining her body. All these cylinder images are haunting concentrates of our own round world.

Sans

Le Dépeupleur—literally, the depopulator—brings a small population into Beckett's work for the first and only time since Part 3 of *Comment c'est.* As the cycles of the earlier work blur into eternity, the movements of the later work freeze into fixity. Eternity and fixity, forms of non-being, always surround the feeble flicker of being, and *that* is the image that recurs through most of Beckett's lyrical fiction, including *Sans.*

In one of his last poems, "What would I do without the world faceless incurious," Beckett uses the word *sans* seven times in the French original. When he translated the poem, *sans* became "without" only three times, but "sans visage" became English "faceless," "sans voix" English "voiceless." The whole poem defends the persona's private world against the absurdity of life in the large world. Over twenty years later, in the 1969 *Sans*, Beckett blends experiences of being into a frail bulwark against nonbeing.

The French title *Sans* is a nasal monosyllable like *Bing*, and the fifty-two repetitions of the word *sans* in the French text seem like an extension of the nineteen *bings* of the earlier French text. As in *Bing*, short phrases are permuted in different combinations, which build unpunctuated sentences—sixty of *Sans* as opposed to the seventy of *Bing*, but those sixty sentences are then repeated in a different order. An observant third-person narrator again creates a spare world at whose center is again a small immobile upright naked male, with beating heart and blue eyes. No longer in a box, gray rather than white, this little body is again juxtaposed against its environment, but the environment is more complex in *Sans* than in *Bing*.

The similarities between *Sans* and *Bing* are as significant as the differences, and the similarities are significant in the light of the differences. In both pieces, Beckett carefully fixed the quantity of sentences at round numbers—seventy of *Bing* and one hundred twenty of *Sans*. But the one hundred twenty break down into twice sixty; that is to say, the same sixty sentences are repeated in a different order and in different paragraph lengths. For unlike the unparagraphed block of *Bing*, *Sans* is divided into twenty-four paragraphs or verses, varying in length between three and seven sentences. Though the text is almost bare of figures, it compels calculation, and the resultant numbers serve to call attention to human time. The number of sentences per paragraph stops at seven, the number of days in a week. The number of paragraphs reaches twenty-four, the number of hours in a day. The number of different sentences is sixty, the number of seconds in a minute, of minutes in an hour. But the repetition of the sixty sentences in a different order suggests the capricious arrangement of passing time.

The concentration of *Sans* lies not in its concealed numbers, however, but in its revealed words, and here as in *Bing-Ping*, the English translation so shades off from the French original (brilliantly analyzed by Edith Fournier) that I will discuss only the English. Beckett translates French *Sans* not as *Without* but as *Lessness*, which is less absolute, diminishing toward zero rather than arriving at it. The word "lessness," almost a spondee, slows down the English rhythm as French *sans* does not, and Beckett uses the heavy syllables more sparingly. Nine attributes are coupled with the fifty-two *sans* of the French text, but only two (end and change) with the twenty-six English "lessness"s and three (end, issue, and time) with the twenty-two English "less"s. By far the most frequent combination, is "endless" and "endlessness." It is against that weighty

263

synonym for infinity that verbs energize the world, creating a possibility of time, light, sound, beauty, religion, and emotion—all evocative of mortality.

Other repeated phrases abound in suggestive ambiguity: "issueless" is both without exit and without matter. "Long last" is both long-lasting and at long last. "Touch close" is both close enough to touch and touchingly close. "Blacked out" suggests fainting, erasure, or disappearance into darkness. "Rain again" and "reign again" sonically relate an improbable future. "Time out of mind" is heard against a burden of "all gone from mind"; they may be synonyms or antonyms.

Even without knowledge of the method of composition of *Sans*, we would have difficulty in discerning a narrative thread, such as is provided by the zooming eye in *Imagination* or the cumulative *pings* of *Ping*. Consistent in *Sans* is an opposition of the body's uprightness against the fallen walls and the surrounding ruins, sometimes called a refuge. Given the complexity and density of *Sans*, we may recall the verse of *Ecclesiastes*: "God hath made man upright; but they have sought out many inventions." Perhaps because of their aridity, the sentences about the endless ruins seem more numerous than those about the upright body. Contradictions pit aspects of Nothing against the little body: heart beating–not a breath; face to the open sky–no relief; he will stir–no stir; in imagination this wild laughter these cries–no sound. The major strength of the "he" is attached to past and future tenses of verbs. Wherever such verbs occur, particularly when they begin a paragraph (e.g., 3, 6, 11), the endless void is punctured by lyrical energy belonging to a world in which time has passed or is to come. Though the present "true refuge" may be a sandy infinity, past and future verb forms cast color into the narration, resisting the gray void.

Blue is the only literal color left in *Sans*, for eyes and rhyming skies, but it bears in its archaic wake the whole world of human imagination: "Never but imagined the blue

in a wild imagining the blue celeste of poesy." Even unhappiness and cursing belong to "blessed" days of vigorous
life, with their dreams, figments, and imaginings. Despite
such flights in the actual words of *Sans*, environment is more
ponderous than body through most of the paragraphs;
refuge from life is refuge from suffering, but in the climactic
last paragraph, three of the four sentences open on "little
body," thus asserting its primacy, however it may grow gray,
however it may have to face the void. And the final sentence sounds a perhaps hopeful note: "Figment dawn dis-
peller of figments and the other called dusk." This melodic
sentence resists paraphrase, but I will risk it: Dusk and
dawn (or passing time) may be illusory, but within that illusion the dawn can nevertheless dispel other illusions,
which in turn will be dispelled by dusk, and so on through
the illusion of passing time.

The power of the final paragraph seems uncanny when
we know how Beckett composed *Sans*. He wrote his sixty
different sentences in six families, each family arising from
an image: 1) the ruins as "true refuge"; 2) the endless gray
of earth and sky; 3) the little body; 4) the space "all gone
from mind"; 5) past tenses combined with "never"; 6)
future tenses of active verbs and the "figment" sentence
quoted above. Within each family Beckett composed sentences of repetitive melody. Beckett wrote each of these
sixty sentences on a separate piece of paper, mixed them
all in a container, and then drew them out in random order
twice. This became the order of the hundred twenty sentences in *Sans*. Beckett then wrote the number 3 on four
separate pieces of paper, the number 4 on six pieces of
paper, the number 5 on four pieces, the number 6 on six
pieces, and the number 7 on four pieces of paper. Again
drawing randomly, he ordered the sentences into paragraphs according to the number drawn, finally totalling one
hundred twenty.

Beckett described this process as "the only honest thing
to do," but I suppose that many readers will share my

disturbance that random distribution should organize his work. On the other hand, Beckett's work through the 1960's *does* seem to culminate in a piece in which the elements are all known but the organizing principle remains mysterious. The human being is adrift in a world that he did not make, that is indifferent to his suffering, and that leaves him vulnerable to the calm of nonbeing. Beckett has rendered this very minimal mortality in *Imagination, Le Dépeupleur*, and *Bing*, where the changeless calm void beckons. But *Sans* suggests that the endlessness is changeless, timeless, issueless, and *therefore* a true refuge. And yet the future intrudes with its chimerical life, which brings the illusion of change through the perspective of temporary rearrangements. As the two acts of *Godot* posit an endless wait; as the repetitions of *Play* posit endless recollection; the two parts of *Sans* posit an endless future intruding into the present peace of ruin without memory.

The narrator of *Assez* stated: "the art of combining is not my fault. It's a curse from above." In *Sans* Beckett lyrically combines a world with nonmemory, ruins with an immobile body, time abolished with future tenses; and he provides the curse from above.

In spite of Beckett's elaborate device of combination, he thought that the sentences could best be conveyed on radio, with each family of sentences spoken by a different voice. After broadcasts in Paris, London, and Stuttgart (in French, English, and German respectively), he rejected his own idea because he found the differences among the radio voices too marked; they should be shadings of a single voice—that of the omniscient narrator who knows so little.

Examination by families nevertheless offers insights that are obscured by the random arrangement. The initial impression of a dominant environmental void is not justified by the family proportions; two families—true refuge and gray endlessness—are given almost wholly to the encroaching void, but three families—little body, past verbs, and future verbs—announce being. Most problematical for interpretation is the family containing the phrase "all gone from mind." What is gone from the mind is the content of *Bing*—whiteness, light, head, and calm eye. We can understand the narrator's dismissing such subterfuges as white walls and light sources, but it is harder to guess at whose mind and whose calm are in question. I tend to think that the answer to both is the same: that of the narrator.

In the endless gray present, time past may be a figment, future time an improbable whistle in the dark. Even the effort at geometric concentration and dispassionate empiricism cannot be sustained against the devouring void. But in spite of endlessness, in the face of it, the upright little body will make the step of life. He will court again suffering in time, feeling pain in rain and in love. Mortality is invincible in its very vulnerability.

Beckett's lyrics of fiction are hard to read, and they seem to reflect too little of the world into which we were born, as well as too little of the personality of their author. I have tried to suggest that this is only a surface appearance: an author reflects personality through his words, and these pieces show Beckett's unparalleled control over words— their tone, rhythm, and subtleties. Not the least of his achievements is to render in words the wordless void.

The *Textes pour rien* circle around nothing, vigilant to smother each something that lifts its mortal head. But vigilance does not spell success. *From an Abandoned Work* restores the full physicality of a narrator-protagonist, seduced by the neutrality of white stillness but condemned to his moving mortal passion. *Comment c'est* is a long last lyrical effort to breathe being through words, before burial in a neutral mud. *Assez*, the last of the protagonist-narrations, derives calm from an absent patriarchal figure whose absence becomes an energetic presence. But Beckett abandons the anguish of personal narration: enough. Instead of a voice straining against or toward Nothing, Beckett tries to efface his narrator in a precise impersonal account of an inanimate world, but inevitably life stirs in that world, and Beckett's phrases stir with it. Objective observation is pierced by an observing eye in *Imagination* and *Bing*. And eyes are ravenous or devouring as they seek their lost ones in *Le Dé-peupleur*, where the nihilotropism is less rigorous than in the last of the *Residua*. Loss and less are contained in the English titles *The Lost Ones* and *Lessness*. Different in idiom and rhythm, both admit life's lyricism, *The Lost Ones* in its poignant fifteenth paragraph and *Lessness* in its evocation of a future that may be dream or figment. A still uncompleted piece of lyrical fiction, describing itself as both "image" and "anecdote," imagines a shifting human triangle in a gray dust under a gray sky—stretcher-carrying dwarfs, fallen body, and giant head.

For all its progressive concentration on the nature of the self, Beckett's fiction of the 1940's was recognizably fiction, couched in prose of syntactical order. But Beckett's pieces of the 1960's are minimally fictions that probe behind self to the being that all men share. The prose reflects Beckett's most generalized view of reality—the infinite void in which, against all probability, life briefly stirs. Beckett's unique achievement has been to create a void from repeated phrases, and to spark life from a few simple words.

Though the fiction of the 1960's is composed of phrases, condensed from piece to piece, they are the residue of Beckett's immense vocabulary and syntactical skill. A phrase like "blue celeste of poesy" expresses nostalgia for all the love and lyricism of earlier Beckett works; the archaic and ironic bareness has been earned through his mastery of language. "Wild imagining" groups the images of our world only to set them aside as "wild" in a reality where, as Democritus said, nothing is more real than nothing. Into that reality intrudes a syntax of such weakness that its strength endures through translation. Thus, as Klaus Birkenhauer points out, Beckett finally writes world literature as Joyce wrote an international language—the one inclusive of everything, the other penetrated by Nothing.

It is the invasion by Nothing that differentiates Beckett's fiction of the 1960's from that of the 1940's. The trough of the texts, the mud of *Comment c'est*, the whiteness of *From an Abandoned Work, Imagination*, and *Bing*, the grayness of *Sans* and his still unfinished work: all are metaphors for nothing, since, as Sam realized in *Watt*, "the only way one can speak of nothing is to speak of it as though it were something." In the fiction of the 1960's, however, as in the fiction of the 1940's, Beckett's central obsession remains man's mortality. The earlier work drafted conscripts in the battle of soliloquy against yawning nothing; the speaker-writer-protagonist drew upon all aspects of his and our world—love, faith, art, sensory response, conviction of self —and he was intermittently successful in staving off nothing. But from the *Textes* on, these afterimaginings are residual "images up above," no longer effective against the ubiquitous burden of the void. The fiction of the 1960's tries faithfully to render the endless void, seeking comfort in its painless calm, but life always asserts its fragile self.

Beckett's late lyrical fiction will never attract as large an audience as his novels have done, just as his novels will never attract as large an audience as does his drama. Most of us are too caught up in the somethings of this world to respond to the lure of his nothing. But as we age and fail, as we watch suffering and death, the seduction of Nothing can take on palpable reality.

AFTERWORD

By DWELLING in and on Beckett's works, I hope to induce others to seek the same lonely, companionable abode. But for me as for Watt, explanation risks exorcism, and I do not want to conjure away any of Beckett's hovering spirits. At the end of this book, then, I will avoid ordering the particulars into generalizations.

In Beckett's first extant publication, he wrote that literary criticism is not book-keeping. One technique of such book-keeping is reduction of an œuvre to a few major themes. But what have we grasped of Shakespeare when we reduce him to appearance-reality? And what of Beckett when we reduce him to life-death, self-other, silence-words, being-nothing, though these tensions are present in his work? The unaccountable wealth of his œuvre is not reducible to themes, and the whole œuvre is greater than the sum of its part. But we know the whole only through the parts, and the consistency in the parts is astonishing: the "assumption" of Beckett's first published story is sustained through *Lessness*; the "ping" of his first unpublished novel sounds through one of his last lyrics of fiction; "Cascando" is a poem in 1935, a drama in 1963; Belacqua appears from the 1932 *Dream* sporadically through the 1966 *Dépeupleur*. But consistency of focus is not necessarily a virtue unless the vision thereby acquires penetrative power. And it is deepening penetration that distinguishes work after Beckett work, accumulating into an œuvre that moves through a residue of wide range into depth.

Beckett himself occasionally speaks of his œuvre as though it has taken place in his absence; or as though he were a resonator for works that speak through rather than from him. He feels that the root of each of his works lies in a previous work, and he is sometimes puzzled by the order

270

in which the works come to him—as in the case of the *nouvelles* or the *Têtes-Mortes*. What he sketches is a variant of the artist as seer. And yet, it is not into his works but into himself that Beckett sinks in order to write—a self that cannot be divested of its experience, nor of words that, willy-nilly, recall experience.

Through the years Beckett has concentrated both experience and words to produce a pure precipitate, but the process of precipitation leaves us with a wealth of by-products. No one has explored more genres than Beckett—lyric poem, tale, novel, play, mime, radio play, film, lyric of fiction. I have tried to show that each of Beckett's genres examines the anatomy of that genre, but he does not write mere metagenre; he reveals how each genre delineates the human situation. Plots have interested Beckett less than genre, and yet he has woven arabesques upon the plots of waiting and voyaging. He has moved characters through space and time in *Murphy*, and through emotional crises in *Play*. By a few phrases, he can etch indelible characters: not only his heroes and their heroes, but such minor people as an old butler who slits his throat, an old servant sitting on her rocker, a boy in *Godot* or in *All That Fall*, an Eastern sage with fingernails growing through the palms of his hands. Beckett can draw tragic resonance from a boiled lobster, and he can make a clown-show of two dwarfs eternally carrying a stretcher. His scenes live in a timeless kind of place, so that he can shatter us with the varieties of love and death: love—the music of Celia and Murphy, Molloy and Ruth-Edith-Rose in a garbage dump, Nagg and Nell in touching ashbins, the mountaintop image of teen-age lovers, the narrator of *Assez* enfolded in his mentor, the exchange of glances in *Le Dépeupleur*; death—Cain in the moon, Belacqua on the operating table, Murphy's ashes on the barroom floor, Krapp watching the dirty brown blind go down, Malone's last broken sentence about Lemuel, the suicide of Pam Prim. And the meaningful scenes between love and death: Molloy distributing his sucking-stones,

271

Lucky spouting his wordfall, Willie crawling in his morning clothes, a motionless white couple in their igloo, a mouth palpitating in the dark.

At every level Beckett's work is haunting, but each level is composed of words. The apparent poverty of Beckett's work of the 1960's and 1970's carries the traces of thirty years of rich reference—people, things, ideas, emotions, rhetorical patterns, a cultural heritage. The traces have had to earn their right to spareness—"only just almost never." The traces are the residue of basic human experience, distilled into phrases that resist paraphrase so that we must go back to the words of Beckett.

SELECTED BIBLIOGRAPHY

Bernal, Olga, *Langage et fiction dans le roman de Beckett* (Paris, 1969)

Birkenhauer, Klaus. *Beckett* (Hamburg, 1971)

Blau, Herbert. *The Impossible Theatre* (New York, 1964)

Bray, Barbara, "The New Beckett," *The Observer* (June 16, 1963)

Canaris, Volker, ed. *Samuel Beckett Das letzte Band* (Frankfurt, 1970)

Cleveland, Louise O., "Trials in the Soundscape," *Modern Drama* (December, 1968)

Coe, Richard. *Samuel Beckett* (New York, 1964)

Cohn, Ruby, ed. Beckett Issue, *Modern Drama* (December, 1966)
——— ed. *Casebook on Waiting for Godot* (New York, 1967)
——— *Samuel Beckett: The Comic Gamut* (New Brunswick, 1962)

Coover, Robert, "The Last Quixote," *New American Review* #11 (New York, 1971)

Duckworth, Colin, ed. *En attendant Godot* (London, 1966)

Esslin, Martin. *The Theater of the Absurd* (New York, 1968)
——— ed. *Samuel Beckett* (Englewood Cliffs, 1969)

Federman, Raymond. *Journey to Chaos* (Berkeley, 1965)
——— "Samuel Beckett's Film on the Agony of Perceivedness," *Film Quarterly*, vol. 20
——— and Fletcher, John. *Samuel Beckett: His Works and His Critics* (Berkeley, 1970)

Fletcher, John. *The Novels of Samuel Beckett* (New York, 1964)
——— *Samuel Beckett's Art* (New York, 1967)

Fournier, Edith. " 'Sans:' cantate et fugue pour un refuge," *Les Lettres Nouvelles* (March/October, 1970)

Gessner, Niklaus. *Die Unzulänglichkeit der Sprache* (Zurich, 1957)

Haerdter, Michael. *Materialien zu Becketts "Endspiel"* (Frankfurt, 1968)

SELECTED BIBLIOGRAPHY

Harrison, Robert. *Samuel Beckett's Murphy* (Athens, Georgia, 1968)

Harvey, Lawrence. *Samuel Beckett: Poet and Critic* (Princeton, 1970)

Hassan, Ihab. *The Literature of Silence* (New York, 1967)

Hayman, David, ed. Beckett Issue, *James Joyce Quarterly* (Summer, 1971)

Hesla, David. *The Shape of Chaos* (Minneapolis, 1971)

Hoefer, Jacqueline, "Watt," *Perspective* (Autumn, 1959)

Janvier, Ludovic. *Pour Samuel Beckett* (Paris, 1966)
——— *Samuel Beckett par lui-même* (Paris, 1969)

Kenner, Hugh. *Samuel Beckett* (Berkeley, 1968)
——— *The Stoic Comedians* (London, 1964)

Knowlson, James, ed. *Samuel Beckett: an Exhibition* (London, 1971)

Kolve, V. A. "Religious Language in *Waiting for Godot*," *Centennial Review* (Winter, 1967)

MacWhinnie, Donald. *The Art of Radio* (London, 1959)

Mayoux, Jean-Jacques. *Über Beckett* (Frankfurt, 1966)

Mintz, Samuel, "Beckett's *Murphy*," *Perspective* (Autumn, 1959)

Mood, John, "The Personal System—Samuel Beckett's *Watt*," *Publications of the Modern Language Association* (March, 1971)

Reid, Alec. *All I Can Manage, More Than I Could* (Dublin, 1968)

Ricks, Christopher. "Beckett First and Last," *The New York Review of Books* (December 14, 1972)

Robinson, Michael. *The Long Sonata of the Dead* (New York, 1969)

Schneider, Alan, "On Directing *Film*" in *Film* (New York, 1969)

Shenker, Israel, "Moody Man of Letters," *New York Times* (May 6, 1956)

Smuda, Manfred. *Becketts Prosa als Metasprache* (Munich, 1970)

Thomas, Dylan, "*Murphy*," *New English Weekly* (March 17, 1938)

Library of Congress Cataloging in Publication Data

Cohn, Ruby.
  Back to Beckett.

  Bibliography: p.
  1. Beckett, Samuel, 1906-   I. Title.
PR6003.E282Z618   848'.9'1409   72-14024
ISBN 0-691-06256-0